FRONTIER ON THE POTOMAC

By JONATHAN DANIELS

A Southerner Discovers the South
A Southerner Discovers New England

FRONTIER ON
THE POTOMAC

by

Jonathan Daniels

New York

THE MACMILLAN COMPANY

1946

PRINTED IN THE UNITED STATES OF AMERICA

FOR

my favorite bureaucrats
ELIZABETH BRITE

and

ANNE BLAKISTONE
who worked for the United States and for me

Contents

Contents

I

Thursday Afternoon

SOMEWHERE between the human swarm and the constitutional abstraction, there is, I am convinced, a Government of the United States. I have been hired to watch it. I have been hired to work for it. It is not easily seen. It seems reasonable, nevertheless, to believe that it is there. Its capital is not merely between Maryland and Virginia, but also somewhere between American awe and American derision, between the statistics and the bewilderment, between the political scientists and the political people. It rises like a monument and a mirage on the shores of the Potomac. Every citizen either feels its hand on his shoulder or has his hand out for its favor—often both. But even Presidents keep looking over their shoulders at the country. That hot wind in Washington is the country blowing on the back of Washington's neck.

I have blown. And I have also felt it singeing the bottom of my hair. I have met people who have seen the government. I have even met clerks who were confident they were it. I have sat within the paneled elegance provided for scholarship in the gleaming white Supreme Court Building and listened while a learned Justice, speaking a vernacular which he did not take from the Constitution, expressed the considered view that some of his colleagues had only the vaguest notion as to what the government is. I suspect that the Government of the United States is both the forest and the trees, and that we are the forest. And I begin to believe that nobody, including the dullest scholars of theoretical unrealities, the doctrinaires and the disenchanted, can write about it except as an autobiographical enterprise. We have just finished dealing in our greatest war with some notions about the citizen and the State. We do not confuse them. But I am America. So is everybody else between the big Lakes and the warm Gulf. America—God bless us or help us—is what we are.

The republic of the atomic age is still the government of a very human people, and the problems of people coming together for government may still be more significant than disintegrating the atom. Uranium is very mild stuff beside Americans. We are still at least as dependent upon politicians as upon physicists. We almost forget that the atomic bomb was a political product. And I know that there was at least one moment when the whole process of its development was threatened because some business men who had not become adept bureaucrats issued orders in WPB which they had not cleared with other bureaucrats in the same agency. Guarding scarcities and unaware of atomic plans, in 1942, they sent firm orders down to Tennessee prohibiting the construction of new power plants needed to produce electricity required by the physicists in the process of smashing the atom.

I did not start out to find the Government of the United States. Nothing, indeed, could have been further from my mind. I went out to look at the country itself, late in 1940, when the defense boom was pouring a golden stream across the land. I got to Tennessee before the physicists did. And the thing that impressed me was the people. I talked to them in new-turned mud around the rising camps and the big growing dams, by the rivers and the trailers and the juke boxes, in crowded bars and overwhelmed city halls. Down in the country under the nation's planners, some of whom were in new army and navy uniforms, the people themselves were like the pioneers putting the power of America together again— pioneers at a gold rush. They took the wages, grinning about them. They would have worked for less, but if any army wanted to count every countryman a carpenter, they would not argue. They lived in the woods. They slept in the back seats of their cars, and cooked out of cans. And, among them, the big, rich confusion from Washington was an easy American joke. I think I was the man who first brought back the joke from the crowded country towns to the effect that the defense boom had brought them cooperators, coordinators and cohabitators and they did not know which did the most harm. Also, the story about the Louisiana Negro who looked at his wages, made sure that there had been no mistake, and whooped his not unpatriotic feeling:

"Thank God for Hitler!"

I guess that looking and writing about government as it hit the country ("at the local level," Washington called it) is the way I got into government and began to look at it from the inside. The inside was not quite new to me. I grew up in Washington as a Cabinet member's boy. The statesmen and the politicians, the admirals and the newspapermen, used to come for meals with the family. I remember best that most of them told good jokes. Also, I particularly remember William Jennings Bryan's eating; it was a spectacle for the admiration of a small boy whose own hungers seemed always certainly infantile afterward. I was shocked when a small Republican schoolmate suggested, as we passed the White House on the way home from Keith's Vaudeville, that even Woodrow Wilson had to go to the bathroom. It was logical, but somehow appalling.

I was smuggled into the House Chamber when Wilson asked the Congress for war in 1917. I remember war coming then, not in terms of the challenging ring of Wilson's voice, but of the beat of the hoofs of the horses, Nip and Tuck, pulling the carriage in which Father and I drove home through the dark Washington streets from the excited Capitol. My heart seemed to beat with the sound of their hoofs. Government and America seemed suddenly altogether grander than the politicians who came to our house. My own father, tired and serious in the carriage, seemed grand, too. I have not

changed that idea since. Indeed, I have had reason to extend
it to other men in a growing faith in the possibility of patriots
in places of power—and that such patriots are to be found
among Democrats and Republicans, liberals and conservatives alike.

That infantile view of the inside of government was a long
time ago. When I went to Washington, in 1942, I had watched
government from the outside for twenty years, in the basement of the City Hall in Louisville, in the Legislature at
Raleigh, in the press gallery in Washington. I had been writing in Munich when Hitler was just beginning; but, to destroy
my reputation as a political interpreter at the outset, he had
seemed to me just a little less interesting than Huey P. Long.
Then I came back and looked at business men a while instead
of politicians, as an editor of *Fortune*. Even then the similarities were more striking than the differences. I began traveling
around America seeing the American bust and then the American boom. Each seemed a phase of the tossing and turning of
Americans in the American dream.

I went into government, I think, by way of a huge hall in
Atlantic City. There, though Democrat and New Dealer, as
critical outsider I spoke of governmental confusion. Charles
P. Taft, the President's son and a good Ohio Republican but
an early and able wartime bureaucrat, spoke in its defense. I
can report now that it was much more fun on the outside
raising hell than it was on the inside trying to make sense.
Pearl Harbor blew me into Washington as a sort of professional man from the country in a capital which was more than
ever concerned about the country. Charlie Taft grinned a
little when I came in, but gently. Also, he told me a story
about government, which he had inherited from President
Taft, about an army colonel in Texas who had a thousand
men who had never seen a horse and a thousand horses who
had never seen a man—and all he had to do was to make a
cavalry regiment. It is a story that will stand even in the atomic
age.

Without the expression of undue pride, I think I can say that I participated in bureaucracy in its most difficult form in the Office of Civilian Defense. I know that other civilian veterans of the war in Washington will debate that. I still respect the idea that, through OCD, Federal, State and local governments might cooperate together from hamlet to continent in crisis. Those who designed OCD for home defense did not underestimate the patriotic energies of American volunteers. But I can testify that they minimized the violence still implicit in mobilized American individualism. I know that in the chaos which grew when no bombs fell, I was lucky to get out of OCD.

In a Washington which can be darker than most cities under its shade trees, I worked only seven months in that belabored war agency. I escaped to a room in the basement of the State Department doing a hush-hush job which, being secret, was also secure. The rats which came out of the holes with the heat pipes did not disturb me. Down the quiet hall was a room in which, I remembered, a nice old gentleman in an alpaca coat (I suppose he must have been a bureaucrat, too) had shown me when I was young the bullet the surgeons had taken from Lincoln's skull.

The room in the basement would have been a quiet place in which to spend part of a war. The quietness did not last. I became Administrative Assistant and later Press Secretary to President Roosevelt. Those jobs were not designed for serenity. But, if there was any place from which to see the government, I had it. Congress had specifically exempted my job from the Hatch Act, which prohibits the participation of government employees in politics. So, I suppose I was politician by Act of Congress. But fortunately or unfortunately, I think I was created long before a spectator by Act of God.

I not only saw the White House. I also saw government, in the agencies and departments, branches and bureaus under and around it, in a Washington in which Cabinet officers are not less human than taxi drivers. That government is a business not merely of conferences and Congress, but of cocktail parties and hotel rooms, of bishops and John L. Lewis, of little lost girls from Minnesota typing steadily all day long in huge typing pools, of bureaucrats in The Lobby and The Press as well as in the Veterans' Administration. Its powers include not merely the President and Supreme Court Justices, career ambassadors out of Groton and a Texas school for the deaf, but also such figures as old man Bernard M. Baruch sitting on a park bench playing a role originally written by Anatole France, and Tommy Corcoran playing his accordion as well as his government for his clients.

It was crowded from the slums around the Capitol to the mansions over Rock Creek. There were all sorts of people in the crowding. I doubt that any sample of America was missing. I remember the millionaires in their new navy uniforms in the big houses on Kalorama Road and down below them the old converted mansions turned into boarding houses bulging with country girls. People moved in and out of Washington like a procession.

Items of it stick in my mind: an insistent patriot with hands that tapered like those of an Assyrian rug peddler with the same combination of sensitiveness and indecency in his fingers; a pretty stepmother walking very primly through Lafayette Square with a solemn, sallow child; a young novelist awkward as a new officer; an official's discarded favorite talking like a jilted girl; Harry Hopkins looking like Death on its way to a frolic; the unwashed, unfed people disgorged from the early Pullmans to the shortage of taxicabs; Senators with their vests unbuttoned in the evening; Congressmen dancing at the Shoreham, the dipsomaniac wife of a tough official, the Assistant Secretary of State who picked his nose and rolled the result into neat little balls; Henry Wallace grinning; Harry Truman blushing and looking at the floor; Mrs. Gifford Pinchot's red hair, the perfumed pre-war smell of the women in the Mayflower, the Saturday bridge games in Eric Johnston's suite, Georgetown gardens in May, the pretty young wife of the elderly Cabinet officer; and gay Catholic Presidential Secretary Bill Hassett singing:

> Would you leave gaiety
> All to the laity,
> Father O'Flynn?

Perhaps they do not sound like the items of government. They are as much its items, nevertheless, as an income tax blank or a questionnaire. Perhaps I remember the lively items best. Some of us could be happier if the psychologists were right and there were no memory of pain. But it was not all gay. Washington is the capital not only of pride but of complaint, too. It can also be the capital of hurt feelings and hard work. It abounds in phonies. But at least as many of them are visitors from out of town as residents of its marble corridors. There are simple people there worth any man's conversation. And some are sad. There are Negro messengers, Irish politicians, Jewish lawyers, demagogues who sometimes look like statesmen, and statesmen who often act like demagogues. It is a town of people clinging in political insistence to small-town residences while they are dependent for life on room service at the Mayflower. There are pathetic rich lobbyists who had a notion, when they were young, that they wanted to be statesmen, and statesmen secretly envious when the lobbyists reach for the check. And Washington certainly has a great American corps of devoted public servants more interested in their jobs than concerned about their pay. Frustration is often normal. Ambition is standard. Envy can be malignant in a town in which everybody can know everybody else's pay.

Washington has many of the characteristics of a company town. Also, as is not generally the case in company towns, those who do business with the company, who sell to it and who hope to profit from it, live there, too, or have their representatives living there. More newspapermen than there are members of Congress are always looking at the company's books. It is a teeming place of people rubbing up against each other and energetically exercising their personalities. There is a basic similarity to Hollywood in the exhibitionism of the successful and the sycophancy of the hopeful. But most of the national indiscriminate belaboring of the bureaucrats hits the wrong people.

"I am a bureaucrat," I said when I was in Washington.

But I remember my associate, William McReynolds, laughing his low Kansas laugh which thirty-nine years in the government service had not made less Kansan.

"You're boasting," he said.

I think he is right. One of the worst troubles with bureaucracy in the expanded American Government has been the acute shortage of really first-class bureaucrats. A good many business men who came to Washington as officials began to understand that after they had tangled themselves in their own lines once or twice. Some just stayed tangled and mad about it. And some bureaucrats who stay longest remain dull as long as they stay. Unfortunately, if bureaucrats are effective, there are always places at better pay for them in the huge bureaucracy of business which grows, largely from their ranks, in the office buildings around the government ones.

I was not a bureaucrat. Bill McReynolds was right about that. I hope I am still a reporter. I had had, with other newspapermen, to listen to enough politicians and officials say that they used to be newspapermen themselves. Franklin Roosevelt never quite got over having been an editor of the *Harvard Crimson*. And Harold Ickes, now in his seventies, was still a reporter in the Chicago of the days before the story came through that somebody had shot McKinley.

"I used to be a government official myself," I can say with the proper note of patronizing reminiscence of the escaped.

But I am still a reporter. And I hope a reporter who can look not only at the stuffing in Senatorial shirts but also, beyond the preserved Constitution in the case in the Library of Congress, to the swarming government of Americans around it. I am also anxious not to write any inside story. Others will do that. What I am concerned about is the wide-open story of a government which has grown big beside us and with us and is still as bewildering as we often are ourselves. I am not a political scientist (indeed, I doubt that there is any such science). But I looked. I enjoyed the chance to see. Seen at its worst, the Government of America is worth seeing. What I report is only one man's view of a government which deserves all men's eyes.

As big as it is, that government is not easy to see all in one place at one time. But I think I saw it clearest and best for myself and for the inrushing pattern of the American future the night that Harry Truman, as the clock under the portrait of Woodrow Wilson in the Cabinet Room passed 7:09, suddenly ceased to be "Harry" and became "Mr. President." Then within the time it takes for the clicking of cameras, he was the almost superstitiously honored man-symbol of America who can still, after our pattern of reverence, be described in the native argument in the American language as one angry truck driver would describe another.

Just fifteen minutes before sunset that evening they had found him in the pleasant hide-out office of bald-headed Sam Rayburn, Speaker of the House, on one of the maze of hardly used corridors in the Capitol. The Vice-President, dry after presiding over hours of Senatorial debate on a water treaty, had come to join the Speaker and other convivial officials and friends in late afternoon relaxation. "Harry" smiled through his thick lenses as he came in eager for the Speaker's bourbon. He got the telephone call instead.

It was nearly dark when he drove into the White House grounds. And behind him, swiftly in the deepening twilight of a hot April, the Government of the United States began racing through the guarded gate. Then the people came to mass themselves against the great iron fence: A mass, that grew through the evening, of patient and pathetic people, curious citizens and spectators before history. Ed Stettinius, beau-

tiful, rich young man, ran across Executive Avenue from the
State Department where before him Cordell Hull had talked
to Jap diplomats in the language which in Cordell Hull's Tennessee youth had been reserved for United States Revenue officers. All the Cabinet came, except Postmaster General Frank
Walker, who had been caught by the news in Lynchburg,
Virginia. Sam Rayburn, his bald head gleaming above his grim
face, led Democratic Congressional leaders through the newspapermen who swarmed around the big mahogany table in
the lobby of the Executive Offices. Minority Leader Joe
Martin, a Republican partisan as implacable as any of the
Democrats, hurried across Lafayette Square from his apartment in the hotel built where that other Massachusetts man,
pessimistic old Henry Adams, had watched democracy with
an erudite fastidiousness. Senators arrived. The Chief Justice
of the United States came, and Bob Hannegan, the moon-
faced Irishman who had risen from the precincts of St. Louis
to national chairmanship of the party in power. Harry Truman walked slowly along the covered back gallery by the
rose garden from the White House residence to its offices to
meet them. In the long Cabinet Room he looked like a little
man as he sat waiting in a huge leather chair. Mrs. Truman was
late in arriving.

The government waited, for the government had come in
the personages described by the Constitution, in its human
pieces and checks and balances and powers—as human as the
men in Philadelphia who had designed their functions. They
were the men of Lincoln's central imperative preposition—
the "by" people of democracy.

Chief Justice Stone wore no robe of judicial sanctity. He
was an aging, kind-eyed man in a blue serge suit—the sort of
suit professors get chalk on and which scholars wear bright at
the elbows and the seat. Somehow, Truman waiting was still
"Harry," whose room on the seventeenth floor at the Stevens
in Chicago the summer before had been so full of sweaty
well-wishers. He wore his solemnity and his affability to-

gether. All around the room, the Congress of the United States was a collection of people, shocked, puzzled, a little wary, and as precise as well-trained children in the proprieties of the hour. The Executive Branch stood about the room or sat in the big chairs as the men most hurt and most uncertain in change. There was an uneasy feeling of an era ending and of careers interrupted. There was an eager feeling present, too, concealed but tangible. The clock under Woodrow Wilson was speaking of the future.

Here was change. No American feared any tumult such as might elsewhere attend such change. But in it men wore masks as solemn as the Constitution itself. The heartbroken were self-contained. So were those whose hearts quickened. The masks were worn—but the masks were off, too. There was time for the proprieties but not for prolonged pretenses. Men moved in unconscious nakedness which showed in the tone of voice they used in speaking to the little man who was to be Bigness so soon. A certain sleekness slipped into the words addressed to him by attendants and some statesmen. There was real grief, there was also patriotism, shrewdness, understanding of power and a wonder about its directions. There was order and dignity. Here, also, was the whole human struggle of a nation. Here were States' Rights, the division of powers, the hope and push of the Right and the Left. Here were the insistent contending American regions, the conflict of minority rights and majority rule, little ambitions and big questions, privilege and politics. Around the little man in the chair were the same forces that have been shaping America around the written document from the beginning.

Mrs. Truman came in, sad and a little frightened. The Government of the United States arrayed itself in an arc of faces across the end of the room. Before it the Chief Justice repeated the great oath. In his flat Missouri voice the President responded from a little sheet of paper. America spoke its greatest man-pledge under the glare of lights and the clicking of cameras. There were more newspapermen and photographers than officials there. They sprawled over the Cabinet table. They quarreled almost automatically among themselves. And the President took the oath a second time, not for greater certainty but for more pictures.

He was not Harry Truman any longer; he never would be again. The prison of the Presidency dropped around him. The Secret Service scurried beside him as he moved. The personages shook his hand and fell away. The President of the United States walked down the hall to the big lobby past the wide mahogany table. His car had turned into a procession which roared him out to his Connecticut Avenue apartment where he ate a roast beef sandwich in a neighbor's flat. Behind him the big reception clerk spoke an old day's-end speech above the noises of the lobby:

"The President has left his office."

He spoke transition.

It was not easy then to see what transition was. There had been no such transition in America in great crisis since Lincoln died and Andrew Johnson took the oath in the parlors of Kirkwood's Hotel. In an April, too, Johnson swore to defend the Constitution in a future which was to be filled with the furies of the American struggle through anger and aspiration, corruption and partisanship toward the American destiny. Nobody could count the similarities and differences between the futures beyond 1865 and 1945. Times, not men, had changed: Johnson was a tailor until he was thirty-four; Truman was a haberdasher when he was thirty-eight. Haberdasher and tailor together could perhaps have counted the change in costume and appearance. There was not a beard in the Cabinet Room when Truman took his oath. But the same tempestuous, teeming, determined America was around it.

It was the same oath. Chief Justice Stone repeated it in the lobby to the swarm of newspapermen.

He smiled: "It is a good one if you live up to it."

And it is a good Constitution. It is no mere document. It is certainly not the mere body of the determinations of men in the past. It is the strange informal and inflexible, solemn and irreverent, ruthless and sentimental system by which we live as a people together. We know that our politicians are the damnedest set of men on earth—and that together they make the greatest government in the world. Much of it the Founding Fathers would not recognize. Some citizens and foreign visitors do not like it—and may get a false notion that many of us don't like it either. We ourselves cuss it, cherish it, cheat it, and argue about it. We shall probably do so eternally and certainly as long as we do we shall be what men have always meant when—hesitating, in observation, between dismay and admiration—they have called us Americans.

The people standing quiet in the street before the White House that April night understood that. The President was dead, and they stood in sorrow; the President drove past them into the night, and they saluted him in loyalty. They waited in grief, without fear. There was nothing strange about the future; they had faced it before. It would be America; they are it.

II

Office by the Garden

THERE were people still standing in the street and in the park beyond the gate when Harry Truman came down at eight o'clock the next morning to be President. The Hudson River prints still hung on the walls of the oval room but the toys and bric-à-brac which had littered the desk the day before were gone. The sun came in the south windows and touched Truman's thick glasses. His eyes were magnified behind them. But papers were there for him to sign. Transition is routine. He read and signed. And he swung around in the President's chair, as if he were testing it.

He was an institution as well as a man. And becoming an institution is not quite so routine a business as transition even in an orderly democracy. Impertinently perhaps, I was a little sorry for him. I took my papers out, thinking about the man in the chair and the man who had been there before him. Men have a lot to learn in that room. They need a lot of help. I remembered a student of government with whom I had talked not long before about Presidents and the Presidency, power and democracy. I was not sure he could have helped Truman. I suppose the people teach the Presidents as the Presidents teach the people, roughly sometimes, with flattery often, honoring and cheapening, and in the terms of both pressure and history. It is a relationship which is somehow not only constitutional but mystic when you think about it, and sometimes almost comic when you see it—never quite.

My scholarly friend is no dull theorist about it. He is a delicately made little man with a precise mind, elegant before the background of his paneled office and obviously intellectual against the rows of his books in it. He has a scholar's pride that he understands life as well as scholarship.

"I found out," he said smiling, "that to understand Washington you only have to read the society pages of the newspapers and the list of the President's engagements."

Beyond such reading, he suggested, the whole pattern of power in Washington emerged. You could shape the cliques and the bodies of great American contentions from their dinner partners. And from the list of those who saw the President, a scholar could put together all the pieces of power. My friend is wiser than I am. I respect his thesis. But I know that some important men, dog-tired in democracy, stay at home in the evenings. Also I know that there are two doors to the office of the President, and that even if a man knew everybody who went in and out of each door, he might be surprised at the matters and the men which loom largest in Presidential concern.

The people are always outside the gate, but it is not easy always to shape either America or the Presidency from the persons who come inside it. I remember the recurrent coming and going before that time of James B. Conant and Vannevar Bush and other scientific gentlemen. They had not looked like the planners of the atomic bomb. They were college professors in a Washington in which college professors have often been made to seem much more comic than Congressmen. The Senators who went in after them seemed much more impressive: I only happened to find out later that one wanted a job for a constituent and the other hoped to save the face of a constituent's son. The meaning of the obviously important personages is not always easy to evaluate. The leader of a great pressure group may be more concerned about impressing his pressure group with the ease of his access to the Presidency than impressing the President with the importance of his pressures. An official may even get the President to work out a little assignment that will quiet a restless wife. Going to see the President is like going to Mecca. The pilgrim may be helped. His neighbors will certainly be impressed. And, as for Presidents, they must be often bored, but they are seldom allowed to seem so. Boredom is a part of the job.

The visitor is not bored. I remember myself as a visitor early in 1942. Stepping on the grounds was an American adventure. I still have that day's vivid memory of the big elms and the uneven paving of the Pennsylvania Avenue sidewalk, which was shut off from ordinary passers-by in those early days of the war. Soldiers stood at regular intervals and others sat, half-concealed, in armored cars ready to roll. The policeman, who afterward I discovered was a gay, red-haired ex-hack inspector, seemed very formidable at the wide iron gate. He let me through, down the drive to the Executive Offices and into the quiet lobby which later I was to see so turbulent. I remember the tall, balding usher who could be by turns pleasant and pompous, the gracious brown servants, the vast gleaming table and the big shut doors.

All the diversity of people, waiting in the big leather chairs, seemed somehow both elated and subdued. Beyond, behind doors, which had to be opened by concealed buttons as well as knobs, was the intimate anteroom, tiny beside the temples outside the doors of Cabinet officers or even bureau chiefs. There were water colors on the walls. The windows opened on the wide green grounds. The receptionist, a blue-eyed woman with graying gold hair, looked like a lady beside a garden. The center of the world seemed pleasantly withdrawn from the world. The General swung open the door to let an ambassador out. He gave him a hearty good-by, in an Alabama accent.

"My God!" he said, "they're trying to kill him today. The man can't see everybody in the world. You can finish up in five minutes, can't you, Jonathan? Old man Hull's on his way over, and what's the name of that damned fellow from California, Roberta?"

He swung open the door, and there beyond was the round room under the round plaster Seal of the United States, a room lined with prints of ships and of the Hudson Valley, and in it, behind a desk covered with gadgets, a big, laughing man. He had the air of a gentleman with all the time in the world.

What a little time ago it was. The General and the man he guarded died within two months of each other of the same sickness that strikes down quickly men who live under strain. A young Irishman guards the door now. But the same ceremony around the same pressure of a whole nation on a single man remains. And Roberta Barrows, who came in under Hoover, answers in the same soft voice the people, who querulously, confidently, desperately or pathetically must see the President, when they telephone. The room is very quiet except when a crowd of the more confident gather in it with jokes and gossip and legs thrown over the arms of chairs. Other men sit in the chairs thinking what they are going to say. And outside the window the garden is as quiet as one back of a country house in the Hudson Valley or in Jackson County, Missouri.

There is a country quality about any President of the United States. He is not only world chief, but in the White House still the kind of big citizen to whom all sorts of people tell their troubles in country towns. Of course, he is a politician. He also has jobs to give. Sometimes he seems to be engaged in almost every aspect of human assistance except the small-loan business. I take that back. He is, as President, in that business, too, and the big-loan business, also. Sometimes, indeed, he seems a world leader whose time is chiefly consumed in concerns which might bore the secretary to a Congressman, but each of which is dramatically important to the caller and as such may become important, politically or otherwise, to the President himself.

Sometimes it seemed to me that saving faces consumed more time than most of the matters which get into the papers. Roosevelt was perhaps sometimes too kind. But all Presidents must reduce to a minimum the internal frictions which grow from internal incompetence. Few people are fired, under any executive, in the upper ranks of either government or industry, or the elaborate feudalism of labor. The management of industry knows the problems of old directors, and directors understand the difficulties of removing inept managers. Some labor unions seem almost designed to perpetuate old men on the payroll. But in government the process is made more difficult by the public exposure of the ejected and is apt to be made acute in such a case by the screams of the ejected and their friends. Also, a man who fails in government may have a claim to gratitude in politics, and friends in the Senate who remember it. The result is that a vast amount of time and labor is spent by Presidents and for them in working out face-saving devices for those who must be kicked out. The mission to England was one wartime device. The British Isles got to be known as Siberia. President Truman has found others. And ingenious Presidential assistants will probably be engaged down the corridors of the future planning others.

Civil Service on the inside and full employment on the outside in recent years have protected the President from the worst aspects of his role as employer-in-chief. Presidents still have to devote long hours over the business of jobs and job hunters. Those who would be judges and ambassadors can be more imperative than those who merely want jobs for living. Senators and Congressmen become engaged, and the pressures can grow greater in proportion to the job involved.

The mass of trivia which cannot be treated as trivial is almost overwhelming. Every national organization seems to require a Presidential greeting at its annual conventions. Such details can be handled for the President in most cases, but not even his assistants can save him from some consideration of the trivia. He is the desired center for every publicity campaign for every good cause. At least half of a President's time is devoted not to the great responsibilities which he has been given by all the people but to the vanities of the great and small individuals who want something not for the country but for themselves, or their friends. But the patriots and the predatory talk the same language and wear the same clothes.

The faithful must be honored. Recommendations must be heard. Pressure groups must be seen. Not all cranks can be stopped at the gate by Secret Service. Indeed, cranks sometimes must be most quickly seen. The biggest job of the President of the United States is listening; and considering some of the conversation a President gets, it never seemed to me strange—though some of his listeners with much to say squirmed—that sometimes Franklin Roosevelt did most of the talking himself. The President's job is long talk and long listening. And inevitably in the case of any President everything is politics—even freedom from politics, which can sometimes be the most effective politics of all.

The institution of the Presidency is best seen in relation to the variety of people who come through the President's door. They feel the power as they come and depart, but sometimes both the Presidency and the President's powers seem more myth than reality. The President remains a man. And the man never quite possesses the power which he has. It is too big to wield. There are more checks in the balanced pressures around him than there are in the Constitution. Also, theoretically (except in those duties of ceremony in which he must appear in person and those responsibilities to public opinion in which his voice must be heard) he can delegate every duty and leave himself free to the pleasures of the palace. He does delegate practically every power he possesses, but he does not escape any responsibility he has assumed. Some of the delegated powers stay delegated, but many of them come roaring back through the anteroom to the President's desk. Generally there is more pressure than pleasure in the palace where he sits.

But the whole process is quiet, decorous, often informal. The familiar use the phones on Roberta's desk as they wait. "I just called up Norman Davis. He says he's got a hundred cases of good liquor and he thinks they'll last as long as he does."

They did.

The sun pours in the south windows. The President sits in his round office with his back toward them, but all Presidents are conscious that the country is out there over their shoulders, even if they are not always so sure that the procession coming to their desks is the country. Woodrow Wilson rejoiced because the view from the south windows contained no sight of Washington but, across green parks and the hills of Virginia, the United States of America.

And the United States and the world in important matters and trivial matters, international and personal affairs, sit in the south sunlight waiting. I used to watch them. I know the same people—or people like them—are coming still.

Lord Halifax sat and waited, a thin, tired man who had seemed to me when he first came as Ambassador too much the epitome of a British past overbred to delicacy and arrogance. But waiting in that room, he talked directly and quietly of those days in England when the chief of British air forces dropped on his knees when France fell and thanked God for it because his last few planes were saved to fight with a chance, if not much chance. Halifax was matter-of-fact about it. He remembered how Britain, unarmed, waited for discarded American rifles. Britons lived in a strange reversal. Home help was in the New World, where so few centuries before the wilderness had been. But Britain seemed, in 1940, a sort of pioneer outpost counting time, waiting for aid in a sudden wilderness of its own. And the savages were not far off. In the quiet room, as Halifax talked, you could see on the charts the ships which they watched coming, full speed but slow in the eyes of those who waited. They could feel the victorious German push across the Channel. Halifax was very simple about it. But even in peace there are charts like that in the heads of Presidents as well as Prime Ministers. While people talk, time is moving.

Jimmie Noe, of Louisiana, Democratic National Committeeman, waited with at least the confidence of an ambassador. He was so fat that he looked as if a pin properly applied might explode him over the room. He had come to tell the President what was what.

I remember a fat Dutch admiral. He looked less like a driven exile still courageously keeping a little of Holland on the sea, than a man from a land of sausages and cheese, rich watered farms and good Dutch guilders out of Java. Neither history nor war ever casts all its players in perfection.

The Tennessee hills seemed a long way behind Cordell Hull. Maybe he carried, as some of his subordinates said, a long knife. He looked fragile rather than tough. He and Halifax seemed like men of the same breed.

Senator Bilbo of Mississippi came, and Walter White of the National Association for the Advancement of Colored People (though never together). Not even the color-sensitive Bilbo would recognize the pink-cheeked Walter White as the Negro he so insistently is. But beside Walter White, Mary McLeod Bethune, walking with a cane like a staff, seemed almost Africa itself or a queen just come from the Congo.

You got a sense of Israel still sonorously homesick in Rabbi Stephen Wise. He seemed as much a man out of the Old Testament as Isaiah in striped pants. Francis Joseph Spellman was a very modern archbishop (cardinal now), pausing on his travels, for his country and Peter's Church, to the ends of the world.

A group of heroes, come to receive their medals from their commander, were still scared schoolboys about to go into the office of the principal.

Anna Rosenberg swept through, laughing from the doorway, with a new pert hat on her head. She stopped to let Roberta Barrows admire it. Tough old Admiral Leahy stood waiting to go in with dispatches. Harold Smith of the Bureau of the Budget had papers, too.

Ed Flynn of the Bronx: He is probably the quietest of the

politicians, reticent and shy, a man born to security who did not have to fight his way up from the precincts, yet he looks almost as if he had chosen his clothes to make himself look like a ward heeler who could at last afford the snappiest haberdashery. Old man Bernard M. Baruch looked almost baggy beside him. But both wore carnations. (In Washington clothes do not make the man, but they can destroy him.)

It is a procession which never ends. The Ambassadors, the Senators, the party leaders, labor leaders, the soldiers, the administrators pass through the door. The newspapermen come in, and the letters. (Yes, if it seems significant, the President may get the letter from the old lady in Dubuque.) The memoranda and the documents pile up in his basket. Today even a Prime Minister may be on the telephone—or in town. And the President may have to drive to the station to meet the Regent of Iraq because he is, like the President, a Chief of State. The Princess Juliana of Holland comes for dinner, and even a President may be amused by the indiscretion of the blond wife of the Dutch Ambassador in being so much prettier than the Princess.

A President needs to laugh. Despite his great power the Secret Service can tell him what to do, the State Department Division of Protocol can also, and sometimes the Congress. Everybody else in a nice, deferential way tries to tell him. Strangely, the chief of protocol's powers in America are easiest to understand. He is not an official imported from monarchial courts. In the same clothes, he is in Washington blood brother to the town undertaker who makes similar arrangements on other ceremonial occasions. And like some other such men of ceremony in the United States, George Thomas Summerlin, of Rayville, Louisiana (population 2,076), chief of protocol in recent years, was a gay man, tiny, baldheaded, and not made solemn by his craft.

I suppose it is necessary that history be solemn. Presidents might be expected to be. Inescapably under the Constitution the President performs his duties as ceremonial chief of state, executive officer of the nation, chief of foreign affairs, and commander-in-chief of the army and navy. But Jefferson and Jackson added greater jobs than any of these when, without any constitutional amendments, they made the President the leader of the party and of the people as the only Federal official, except the Vice-President, chosen by the vote of all the people and responsible to them.

Those who most strenuously urge delegation of power are often the first to demand Presidential intervention in details. The jobs Mr. Jefferson and Mr. Jackson provided are non-transferable. And they make also non-transferable all his other duties as well. They do not make his leadership absolute, however. Party leadership is not merely a matter of holding the loyalty of the rank and file of the party as Roosevelt did for a longer term than any other American, but also of pleasing those who wear its label in the Congress and are its subordinate captains in the States. In our times neither of the two great political parties can elect or re-elect a President with its own members alone. A President has to lead the people, as both President and politician, or he and his party will be out of power. Behind Roosevelt his party remained in power in the Congress throughout his Presidency, but it did not always follow him as a national party. He could count on the West for support for domestic reforms which the South opposed. The South supported him as he moved toward preparation for war, from which the West held back. He had to deal with both.

It was a magnificent show. I hope I was helpful in a little way to him and to history. I was happy toward the last, when he took me out of anonymity in his service, and I came over as his Secretary to succeed Steve Early, who was leaving the government after twelve years to make some money before old age and the horse races finally overtook him.

We went up in the mornings to the small bedroom Roosevelt occupied on the south side of the White House. He sat in bed in his pajamas and a loose bed cape. I remember that he had a cigarette hole burned in his blue pajamas below the second button and I was impressed, *in re* the majesty of the Presidency, to observe that he wore the same pajamas four days running. The laundry situation was bad in Washington that year. But he was back from Yalta, where as American Chief of State he had presided at the conference of the Big Three. Our foreign relations had never been better. At home the greatest domestic problem was the grumbling about food at a time when America was better fed than all its people had ever been before. The Commander-in-Chief of the Army and Navy knew better than any of us how near we were to victory. The strange plants down in the Tennessee Valley had not only broken the atom but, long before, the bottlenecks in WPB.

There was a characteristic detail he wanted arranged. His old friend and schoolmate, Mackenzie King, Prime Minister of Canada, was coming visiting and he wanted to arrange a little publicity for him. King had an election coming up.

And Bill Hassett recited a newspaperman's poem about a previous King visit:

> William Lyon Mackenzie King,
> He never gives us a God damn thing.

The President laughed. And Fala barked at him from across the room. None of us there, I think, had any sense that history was waiting just down the wide hall for a not far distant Thursday afternoon.

And on Friday, Harry Truman came down at eight o'clock to be President. He came in with friends and to find friends who had arrived by train and plane. Missouri, the Senate, the 129th Field Artillery, a new diversity of Democrats, old acquaintances, those who did not want to lose by change and those who had nothing to lose by change swept around him among the pushing, the patriotic and the energetically disinterested who had merely come to wish him and America well. Men stood mob-thick in the big lobby of the Executive Offices. He was the oldest man to become President since Buchanan. He was also the inheritor of more power than any President ever possessed on entering the White House. And the inheritor, also, of all the strange complexities, divisions, diversity and contention around the power. He moved with an easy Missouri stride. But I remember him sitting in the big chair and swinging it around.

History was hurrying about him, too. It came across the days in false starts and false stories, but it came. I remember that first day of May when the news ticked in that Hitler was dead. I ran into the President's office with the yellow sheet. The room that now stayed so full was almost startingly empty. Mr. Truman had gone out to the swimming pool, and I went through his open doors, across the terrace, by the rose garden, to the pool. I heard men laughing in a little room beside it, and went in. He had finished his swim and lay stripped to his shorts on the rubbing table.

A lieutenant-commander in his undershirt, who had learned his business of caring for Presidents as a pharmacist's mate under Admiral Cary Grayson, was giving the President a vigorous rubdown. Vice-Admiral Ross T. McIntire, Surgeon General of the Navy, stood solicitously beside the table as he had in the years past. And around the table were new and old aides and politicians. The President, lying there, did not look sixty-one years old. He was fit and pink, joking and happy. The Presidency had not marked him. He was as unpretentious as a county official in Missouri getting a Turkish bath in the Kansas City Club. He read the message, and the comment went around the table. The words were the comments of men in a bathhouse, but the tones were those of men standing close to power and pleasing it, hoping somehow to shape it, too. They clothed him with deference, but somehow the deference also left him naked and alone.

III

Time Becomes Visible

THEY roll up to the White House for their meeting in long cars, each marked with the painted seal of his department, in a procession to the weekly solution of all America's problems. Across the street a few tourists stand and watch. It is not always easy to remember that tourists, like bureaucrats, are the people. They watch a spectacle.

"Big shots," said a passing marine.

An old lady was trying to get a child to look at the Cabinet instead of a pigeon. An old gentleman stopped and looked at an old show.

"I feel sorry for those fellows," he said. "When there's a war behind them even little men make big shadows." He shook his head. "Not afterward, never afterward."

But inside the White House, peace or war, Republicans or Democrats, they are impressive always. A President does not need to seem lonely with his Cabinet about him.

"Mr. Secretary—Mr. Secretary," the doorkeepers say with an intonation only less reverent than that reserved for "Mr. President."

I watched them move by the doorkeepers, past the gleaming mahogany Aguinaldo table on which newspapermen pile their coats and hats. Before he marched out of the Cabinet, Harold Ickes came with short-legged precision. Fred Vinson ambled like a man on the way to a Kentucky courthouse. Henry Wallace moved like a tennis player in his fifties, an athlete who when he sits down looks laggard and inert. There was a cat quality like a fighter's in the way Jimmie Forrestal moved which matches the prizefighter look of his broad nose. Tom Clark was a slow Texan. Patterson moved headlong like his mind. Bob Hannegan was slightly slue-footed, like a cop moving on his beat. He always gives me the impression that he needs a billy to swing. And Jimmie Byrnes of South Carolina can, upon occasion, such as coming back in hope of being Secretary of State, seem to move fastest of all.

The Truman Cabinet, as the new President first shaped it, in 1945—and more rapidly than any succeeding Vice-President had ever shaped one before—met all the specifications political Cabinet-makers have long prescribed. Geographically, its members came from coast to coast, and from Texas to Chicago. A President who came up through Congress had four members of his Cabinet who had come up the same way. (Incidentally, before Truman, Presidents with Congressional experience had occupied the White House less than four years in this century.) But none of them, including the President, had had large administrative experience before taking the jobs that brought them into the room. Seven of the ten were lawyers. There was an investment banker, an insurance man, an editor. The ten men came from nine States; in a moving America, only three of them came from other States than those in which they were born. In terms of political unity, all the new members were Democrats, though Robert Porter Patterson had not dropped his Republican designation from *Who's Who* until after 1940. Both Ickes and Wallace had begun as Republicans. Ickes said, as he left in 1946, that he had never become a Democrat. (He was, however, a Democratic delegate from Illinois to the Democratic National Convention in 1944.) The average age of the ten men was fifty-five, running from Hannegan to Ickes. And when Ickes staged his exit in an auditorium and young Julius (Cap) Albert Krug succeeded him the average age came down to fifty-two.

(Incidentally, the last Republican Cabinet came from nine States, too, from New York to California, as far north as

Minnesota, south only to Virginia. It had exactly the same Missouri content as Truman's. None of its members were as old as Ickes or as young as Hannegan. Only one of its members had had Congressional experience. One had been the Governor of a State. Of the ten, seven were lawyers, one was a professor of medicine who had become a college president, one was an automobile manufacturer, and one was a labor leader who had begun his career in Rural Retreat, Virginia.)

They go every Friday into the big, long room beside the rose garden. They sit in chairs marked with their titles around a long, black, coffin-shaped table. Mr. Truman has provided the innovation of an agenda for its sessions. He has brought in, as a sort of Cabinet secretary, one of his own Secretaries, Matt Connelly, who sits at one side taking notes. But what they say and do is a secret preserved for a Cabinet member's memoirs or for leaks to Cabinet members' favorite newspapermen. Sometimes laughter sounds through the shut doors. A President's jokes are always funny, even to his Cabinet. Occasionally, voices are raised in sharp disagreement. The Executive is gathered from the country and from its departments. And long before he became a member of the Cabinet, Secretary of Agriculture Clinton Presba Anderson described what happens there.

"Time becomes visible," he said.

He was not speaking then of time in a world which had had war and wanted peace. He was not then concerned with the hungers of both farmers and consumers. He did not then sit in the Cabinet of a nation which had had to wait for a war to get rich and did not picture peace merely as a time in which to get poor. When Secretary Anderson spoke of time, he had just come, as exactly the sort of prosperous, inspirational executive a president of Rotary International would have to be, to Congress from New Mexico. He was talking about the rush and the lag of time and of history in America in terms of New Mexico, where tourists go by plane to find the sun, where Indians still dance for rain, and where sometimes you can still hear the tom-toms in the same deserts the government used to test the devastation wrought by nuclear power.

"Time becomes visible" was still a pertinent remark in Washington in 1945 and 1946. Above Anderson's head, the clock that had timed the entry of Harry Truman into the Presidency still sat under the portrait of Woodrow Wilson. Cabinet members at the north end of the table could hear it ticking behind their backs. Others, including the President, could watch its hands. They moved.

The importance of time in statesmanship seems to have grown in our days. Literary men and prime ministers began long ago to make metaphors around the clock and the calendar. It was later than we thought. There was too little until almost too late. And the atomic bomb did not blow up the clock; it seemed even to have speeded its hands. Politicians were aware of time even before the physicists; the days move toward the elections. People spoke of Roosevelt's genius for "timing." That meant measuring the mood of the people and the time it takes in leadership to help make their mood. It meant understanding politics in awareness of history. Sometimes, of course, timing can be a politician's trick. It is always also the statesman's task. A President works between the eagerness of Negroes and the stubbornness of Senators. Filibustering Southern Senators and organized strikers are equally ready to stop the machinery. Stopping in America or in the Senate may both mean accelerating the pace of problem to Presidential decison.

"Time is running out," Harry Truman said to the country, in 1946. In less literary language, it is safe to assume he had said the same thing to his Cabinet before. He may have looked for the meaning of time in some Cabinet members' faces. They watch time with him as it sometimes becomes almost terrifyingly tangible. And sometimes with them under the clock he is very much alone.

No institution is more a body of one man's men than the American President's Cabinet. Though they may be picked to make an effective design in American geography or politics or power, they remain his creatures. They constitute no ministry. The President who has all the power and all the responsibility meets with the men who administer it for him. He can hire them or fire them at will. Theoretically, they are his men or nothing. Actually, they may represent forces that he cannot disregard or debts that he has to pay. Certainly, they are apt to be—or to become—prominent personages with ideas and ambitions of their own. And inevitably in the complex democracy of this strange republic each in his department becomes the representative—or the combatant—of forces which already move with determined ideas of their own in the field assigned to him.

Not only are the Secretaries of War and Navy apt to become the men of the admirals and the generals and the professional patriots arrayed behind both. The career men in the State Department were there before the Secretary of State, and will probably be there long after him. Not all those who are glad to lead a new Secretary by the hand or push him hard from behind are the subordinates he finds waiting for him. The divided forces of labor unions have an expectant and possessive interest in the Department of Labor. The organized farmers in the Farm Bureau and the Grange and the Farmers' Union are concerned with the control of the directions of the Department of Agriculture. Oil men and water men, conservationists and friends of the Indians and of electric power have their own possessive notions about the Department of the Interior.

I remember looking at the assembling Cabinet with a long, middle-aged expert in public administration whose job it has been to work with Cabinet members for the Bureau of the Budget. He is still there. He might not be if I used his name.

"They're all pretty good fellows," he said, "and some of them are damn able men." He laughed. "But they act like commanders in the field and not like staff officers helping the President plan his strategy."

Certainly it is generally a body of individualists each intent upon his own job first and the unified strategy afterward. That may be inevitable in the dimensions of their individual commands. It certainly seems inevitable in the type of men who come generally as individualists intent upon the destinies of their own persons or programs to Cabinet positions. The dramatic ones are more easily seen. When I first saw Lewis B. Schwellenbach on his way from the security of the Federal judiciary into the Cabinet he seemed less dramatic than reluctant. Also, he seemed slouching and grinning, somehow like the Scarecrow of Oz. There was some of the same look of befuddled good will about him.

Some of those who are not official members of the official Cabinet of ten, but as heads of agencies sit with it, may be more—or less—egocentric than the others. John Snyder, when he was director of War Mobilization and Reconversion, seemed in appearance still more suited to the anonymity of a St. Louis bank vice-presidency than to the exhibitionism which seems almost inherent in Cabinet status. But I remember a labor chieftain defending him from a sneering charge of insignificance.

"Don't be fooled," he said. "He's not just a dumb friend from Missouri. He's a smart, conniving son-of-a-gun."

None of them are insignificant. Their jobs are news; also, all of them maintain information men to keep them in the news. But individual eagerness for individual purposes is not always easy to discover from appearances. Even the gentle, grinning Henry Wallace, as he indicated in the historic Jones-Wallace fight over the economics of warfare, is ready, if it seems necessary to him, to throw everything in the arsenal at an antagonist who sits beside him at the table.

Jesse Jones, in trying to get his way, was as ready to describe himself as a poor old man as he was to cut a competitive Cabinet throat. Also, Mr. Jones was one of those who in dealing with a President developed forgetfulness as a fine art. Half of a President's suggestions, which theoretically carry the weight of orders, can be safely forgotten by a Cabinet member. And if the President asks about a suggestion a second time, he can be told that it is being investigated. If he asks a third time, a wise Cabinet officer will give him at least part of what he suggests. But only occasionally, except about the most important matters, do Presidents ever get around to asking three times.

Even the most combative seem more cooperative than contentious about the table. Harold Ickes, who, as a highly articulate Cabinet officer, described himself as a curmudgeon and whose own assistants spoke of his "kleptomania" in seeking new pieces of government for his capacious Department of the Interior, can look not only like a belligerent sourpuss but also like a shy child ready to blush. Long before the curmudgeon left, or Truman came, he sometimes seemed in the Cabinet the embodiment of contention. With him it was an art and an avocation; it was sometimes hard to tell the difference between his public vigilance and his private vindictiveness. Some good men as well as some bad ones wear his scars. I remember how his name came naturally into talk of Cabinet quarreling long before he retired at seventy-two in such a way as to rebuke both Truman and old age at the same time.

"They won't work together," said my friend, the public administration expert. "There never was an interdepartmental committee of Cabinet officers that would work. They get jealous before they get started."

It was a generalization too wide to be just. I said so.

"Of course," he said, "jealousy isn't all. The situation almost shapes up to make them fight. Take old Ickes. He's too good a fellow to be lined up with old Senator 'Kay Dee' McKellar of Tennessee to destroy David Lilienthal of the Tennessee Valley Authority. But to tell you the truth, I have more sympathy with McKellar than I have with Ickes. McKellar thinks Dave's a carpetbagger and, of course, he is. You need more such carpetbaggers in the South."

Cabinet officers do not work in a simple government. Once,

perhaps, all government was neatly contained under the Cabinet. Now there are not only other agency chiefs, directly responsible to the President, but a diversity of theories about the whole plan of the relationship of the government to the governed. The Ickes-McKellar-Lilienthal contention involved not only men but philosophies. Ickes and Senator McKellar seemed unlikely allies. David Lilienthal, indeed, seemed a little David beside them. But the three of them put together the picture of an inescapable contention.

Lilienthal's strength and his sin is that he has developed an idea. The TVA is not a departmental approach to the government of America, neatly placed in the governmental hierarchy under a Cabinet member who sits at the Cabinet table. Outside of any department, it was set up, not to deal departmentally with a part of America's problems; it was set up in a region and a river valley to deal with all the problems of the river's development. It does not work out of Washington. All the powers of big government are locally administered by it as one operation where the people of its valley are and where they can understand, seeing its failure or success.

Senator McKellar's objection to Lilienthal was not really against Lilienthal but against the law Lilienthal administered and developed. That law contained a proviso that TVA was to be free from politics. That meant that in Tennessee, even the United States Senator could not make patronage of its jobs. It meant that dams were to be placed where the engineers decided and not where the politicans proposed. It was a plan for administration at the grass roots which rejected the fact that McKellar, even though aided by Boss Crump, of Memphis, and the poll tax of Tennessee, was the representative of the grass roots. Local administration of big government seemed to mean getting government closer to the people but further away from the politicians. It is not necessary to like McKellar to expect McKellar to like that.

Mr. Ickes's position was not merely "kleptomania." Even the most disinterested students of big government generally urge the greatest possible simplicity in its huge design. Efficiency and neatness both suggest to them that all government functions—or nearly all of them—should be departmentalized under the Cabinet of the President. Ickes's Department of the Interior had responsibility for most of the government's operations in the public power field. Ickes could—and did—make out a case for the absorption of TVA by his department. But Lilienthal had made TVA an exciting symbol of something new and effective in a working democracy. Big government and the grass roots, the near and the far, the nation and the people seemed somehow brought together. And Ickes seemed only to be grabbing.

"You've got to remember, though," my friend said, "that even McKellar's got a little nail to hang his grudge on in democratic tradition, and that Ickes grew up in the Puritan Progressive movement of old Theodore Roosevelt. In conservation, the Progressives felt that America had to be protected from the Americans. The old fellow—Ickes—knew the rapacious forces at the grass roots. From his office in Washington, he was ready to protect America, and also, in terms of 'good administration,' as he saw it, to consolidate the government's whole power program in himself. I'm not sure that's selfishness; he just didn't know anybody else he was willing to trust except Harold Ickes. It takes a good man to really grab. The crooks will bargain."

Maybe Truman ended that fight when he reappointed Lilienthal. Ickes, I think, dramatized both conservation and dangers to it when he resigned from the Cabinet. That fight is never won unless it is always watched. I know that other fights continue in the Cabinet. The contending ghosts of Mr. Jefferson and Mr. Hamilton have remained at every Cabinet table since George Washington called both of them to his. New grudges grow with the generations. And new problems: The Secretaries of War and Navy began to fight at home, immediately after victory in the world, in the contest over the unification of the armed forces. And besides such open warfare, undercover warfare at or close to the Cabinet level goes on all the time. Perhaps the reason is that the members of the Cabinet in dependence upon their continuing staffs become captives, too, in old governmental quarrels. These quarrels run back into the country where interest groups and bureaucratic groups are partners in pushing. There are not many American problems that are the problems of single departments any more. The country, perhaps unfortunately, is not neatly departmentalized. Also, sometimes Presidents may permit fights in the family, watching to see which side to take themselves, after the public has taken one side or the other.

But personal vanity is not to be minimized in Cabinet contentiousness. Every Cabinet officer knows that, of the four hundred Cabinet officers in our history, seven have become Presidents. A good many more have hoped to be. At seventy-two, perhaps Mr. Ickes found it easier to leave the Cabinet because of the knowledge that he had outstayed every Cabinet officer in history except one—James "Tama Jim" Wilson who stuck, as Secretary of Agriculture, sixteen years, from McKinley through Taft. James Francis Byrnes knows that five Secretaries of State became President. He also feels that twice he was cheated out of the Vice-Presidency, once when Truman was nominated.

"He thinks he's running a race with John C. Calhoun," a South Carolinian told me. "He can't win, and it's about to kill him."

I remembered that first Friday when Byrnes had come back by plane to put himself at Truman's side. Time was hurrying for him then. His thin gray hair was an ineffectual fringe brushed across his pink skull. His eyebrows were dark and bushy, with a certain swing to them above his bright eyes. In his florid face his nose ran long to his whimsical mouth. I noticed that his hands were both delicately made and covered with dark hair. In them he held papers which needed the new President's immediate attention. They were about

Russia. And he was the man who could help the President with them.

"The State Department," he said, and I remember the contemptuous twist of his mouth and the neat movement of his shoulders. But he looked transparently hungry for the State Department, too.

"Ed Stettinius," said a newspaperman who stopped by my desk, "may be going out to San Francisco to shape the world's security, but I wouldn't give a dime for Ed's."

It is not necessary to be ambitious or contentious to be in the Cabinet. It is possible for a man to be both the administrator of a great department, which by its very nature almost puts him at the head of great forces which may run headlong into other forces, and also be a thoughtful, cooperating member of a staff which puts departmental decisions together as overall policy. It is a divided task requiring more than rigid minds and headlong ambitions. Truman's Cabinet, indeed, seems better qualified for the general strategy than for the great individual jobs of administration. Four of the men Truman pulled about him had had experience in Congressional give and take. None of them, before they entered the Cabinet, except Bob Hannegan briefly, had been administrators of large organizations.

"The truth is," my government expert said, "that most of the confusion in government begins at the top. They all come in as amateurs at big administration. And they try to do too much. They get caught in details and they bring their details—which they only begin to understand—together. No wonder they get snarled up. What we need is some sort of system of permanent undersecretaries who know and handle the details. The Cabinet members as amateurs try to do too much, and get tangled up in doing anything at all."

I am not sure about that. The average Cabinet officer, of course, must be an amateur when he comes. And on the American average, not many of them stay long enough to become professionals at their jobs. When Mr. Byrnes became

the fifty-first American Secretary of State, the average service in that office had been three years, though Cordell Hull
served more than eleven. Eleven others had served less than a
year each. The permanent officials remained, but the State
Department did not for that reason seem necessarily superior.
Neither the amateurs nor the professionals have always been
either excellent or inept. There is no school in which men
can be trained to be both technical experts of government
and the planners with the President of the policies of politics,
which is the basic business of overall government in the United
States.

There are such men all the same. Sometimes they come
from unlikely places. I think President Truman had one in
Fred Vinson, as Secretary of the Treasury before Truman
made him Chief Justice of the United States. He comes from
the almost professionally poor and backward country of the
Kentucky Hills. I think he is even more conscious than Clinton
Anderson that around a government time becomes visible.
But he keeps, also, a sense of the American continuity in
time, which is sometimes better preserved in the hills than in
Rotary Clubs.

Vinson keeps his hill look. He is tall and long-spoken, with
a mountain twang in his drawl.

"I'll tell you what we're going to do," he said to me. "We've
just gotten Henry Morgenthau's picture holes puttied up
down in the Secretary's dining room, and we'll go down there
and eat."

We ate well. And Vinson talked well while we ate; about
politics in Kentucky and the problems of Cabinet government and party government in Washington. He was not dismayed about the difficulties of men working together in
government. He had come up through Congress and a judge-
ship and a series of bigger and bigger jobs both Roosevelt and
Truman had given him, without losing touch with the people
and the hills or faith in them either. It seemed strange under
his native talk to notice suddenly, by the salad and the coffee

and the pie, silver plates fixed to the table in commemoration of settlements made about it of the debts to America of various countries after the First World War. The debts seemed a long way behind, but good Civil Service servants had kept the plates shining. They seemed, however, less substantial than the pie.

We got up. There were only a few pictures on the newly plastered walls, but Vinson flung a long hand in the direction of some correspondence behind glass in a black frame.

"There it is," he said, as if it were the whole future.

I stood before the framed letter and read. There was a declaration of faith in the American future signed by representatives of labor and farmers, business, industry and the public— men who were almost the captains of the American pressures. And beside it was the answer Roosevelt had written just five days before he died:

". . . Victory, without the use for abundance of the powers we have developed for production in war, would be, indeed, a hollow victory. We must plan security and abundance together. . . . Abundance at home depends upon organization for order and security in the world. . . ."

The statement hangs in the Treasury, but I had a feeling that it ought to hang in the Cabinet Room itself. Certainly, it seemed to me, it should hang somewhere else than beside the table with the neat plates to commemorate futility. Not any one Cabinet officer could deal with those imperatives in the frame. There seemed to be, as time passed through Truman's dark first winter after his first bright summer, some question as to whether all of the men who sit about the President could deal adequately with them together. Or whether America around them could shape the answers to the inherited imperatives.

"Time becomes visible," Clinton Anderson had said, and even his old associates in Congress were keeping time on him. Ickes had rung an alarm on the clock. Sometimes in the State Department world peace must have seemed to Secretary

Byrnes to come more slowly than he had come in eagerness to the job of shaping it. Time and taxes went together in Fred Vinson's office. Soldiers counted time impatiently in Bob Patterson's army. They—and the others—brought all their pieces of delegated power to the Cabinet. They might help Harry Truman put them together again. But somehow, the Cabinet is often less impressive in what it produces than in how it appears. And in this impressiveness perhaps quarrel is implicit, as in the Congress, and beyond Congress.

I went back on Friday to watch them depart. I wondered what they had talked about around the coffin-shaped table. I stood looking from the excellent vantage of the sidewalk before the old, and somehow decrepit-looking, building of the Carnegie Endowment for International Peace. It sits cater-cornered from the White House where Jackson Place runs into Pennsylvania Avenue. Old Andrew Carnegie had been dead a long time and peace was still only a prospect in the world. Mr. Carnegie would have been interested in knowing that around the corner now the United Steel Workers of America (CIO) has a building, too. The problems of peace seemed closer together if not nearer solution.

I walked across the street toward the White House gate as the last of the big cars moved out beside the saluting police-men. Fred Vinson waved as he drove back toward his office, the framed letters, and the silver plates. Clinton Anderson was the last man and he looked, I remember, a little harassed.

"Time becomes visible," I said to the back of his car.

But I did not laugh.

IV

The Palace Guard

THE news of the world comes in on tickers which, both in the old Executive Offices and in the new East Wing, are located in toilets. Hitler's death ticked in on the yellow paper beside the wash basin and the stool. Pretty girl secretaries, when the bell rings on the ticker, go through the office of the Press Secretary to his lavatory to clip off the news flashes with long scissors.

The White House is like that—outside as formal as the architects could make it, but inside as informal, often, as a residence in which even the clerks are members of the family about the President. It is an informality which is often irritating to Cabinet members, who resent the notion that any people are closer to power than they are. It is an informality, also, which has sometimes shocked the sense of neatness of experts in administrative management, who would like the White House to seem at least as well organized as police departments under efficient city managers.

I doubt that it ever will seem well organized to experts who judge efficiency of organization by the neatness of an administrative chart. They like precise boxes with clear lines. But recent Presidents have not seemed so neat. Too many agency heads throw lines up straight to the President. In the judgment of the experts, too many members of his own staff sit around him with no other boss except himself. Sometimes, undoubtedly, it results in confusion. Mr. John Snyder's office may clear an administration program with the President without bothering to mention it to the Budget Bureau. General Harry Vaughan, the military aide, may give news to the press without mentioning it to Charles Ross, the Press Secretary. Confusion may begin in government good-naturedly and in intimacy at the top.

Government always needs to be reorganized. It often is. The experts propose. The President considers and requests. The Congress gives him, if he is lucky, part of what he asks. It still looks, and will still look in the White House, administratively fuzzy at the edges. I think it always must be. Nobody will understand Presidential powers, Presidential checks on the exercise of powers delegated by him to his impressive-looking Cabinet, or the needs of a President, who does not realize that the staff of his office as executive must include both intimates and experts.

The experts have a science, but a President understands that, within government as outside it, the intimacy which is essential to a great lonely man is an art. Nobody yet has made a good administrative management chart of personal loyalty. They will not soon. A President's faith and dependence move around. Some of his aides go out. There are always the kiss-and-tell boys. Some are dropped. But in the art of intimacy and loyalty upon which a President above all other men must depend, no President likes to hostage himself to one man. A President may lose faith in competence without wanting to fire a friend. More than most men, he is utterly dependent upon personal loyalty. But he understands—or he fails as President—the necessity of protecting himself from friends. He almost inevitably becomes skilled in the art of great candor in little pieces. His whole mind belongs to him alone because of the fractional dispersal of his confidences. No sensible President gives his whole faith to any one man. Some who did have been badly hurt.

I thought about that when I listened to the old Presidential Secretary talking. He sat in his big chair with his thin knees pulled against his chest like a cowboy squatting by a corral and talked about his colleagues. He was actually very fond of them but they irritated him sometimes, as I know that sometimes, too, he irritated them.

"That's the way it is. When the President leaves town, they all hit out and leave this whole place to me."

He shook his long head.

"He's got sense enough to do what he's doing," he said of a colleague, "but actually he's just a half-wit."

I listened. I had heard his colleague say, "Christ, here I am doing nine men's work for a measly $10,000 a year."

Then the old Secretary put it together in judgment. "If the next President of the United States ever asks my advice, I'm going to tell him to have just one Secretary."

He grinned. "Boy, could I handle that job!"

I smiled. There would be others who would like the chance. But I doubted then, as I do now, that any one man could handle it. I looked out the window across West Executive Avenue to the State Department, where the lights in the afternoon were beginning to come on. There were not only diplomats behind those windows, but experts in administrative management watching the budgets and the proposals of every department and agency for the President. On the other side of the building, I knew, there were Administrative Assistants doing the President's chores and running his errands. There was a President's admiral and his military and naval aides. There were special assistants, a statistician, personal secretaries, other associates with offices in the White House or near by. There were men in various departments who by the nature of their work were special assistants, too, though not listed as such. There were friends outside who served as advisors. A President's staff can be as wide as a President's need and concern.

The full personal staff of the President is not often seen. A good many of its members, indeed, never see the President. And the staff that is seen alters and changes. Its members appear on the long sofa, in the big chairs, perched on the edge of the table, at the President's press conferences. As an ex-

and an out, from the press side of the President's desk, I looked at them late in 1945. Samuel Rosenman, still the President's counsel then, sat big and squat, blinking through blond eyelashes like a mole or a man who keeps himself shut up with Presidential papers. Bill Hassett's bland solemnity hid his scholarly and sometimes scandalous sense of humor. Brigadier General Harry Vaughan, the President's military aide, looked less like a soldier than like the crosstie creosoter he had been in civilian life. Young, hard-working Matt Connelly, a handsome gum-chewing Irishman, who handled the President's appointments, ran his hand across his smooth black hair with new streaks of gray in it. Dave Niles, pale and thin-haired, sat with his long thin fingers across his increasing middle. Charles G. Ross, watching the conference as part of his job as Press Secretary, seemed tired and a little older than he had been in May. George Allen, who seemed fat in the role more leanly played in the past by Harry Hopkins and Colonel House, gossiped laughingly with a gentleman I had never seen before.

Not all the intimates who work beside the experts in the tight core around the President were there. But they were important among the men who stay when the Cabinet goes. Also, they stay behind, I know, in informality and immediate loyalty around the President's desk. And around it, they can make a face at the mention of a man. They can laugh at somebody's proposed policy. They have the power of contact which is sometimes difficult to maintain in big government. They work with the force of friendship which presumably has no other concern. And sometimes because of it they can, if they wish, play little Presidents themselves outside the room. Indeed, sometimes even a White House usher may set himself up as a Presidential agent with the innocent—and in old cynical Washington the innocent abound. Also, often, the greatest show of power with the President may be made by those who know, in a sickening secrecy, that they have less place in his planning than before.

Not only do some of the great questions of government

come with them around the President's desk, but gossip and jokes, also. Indeed, in George Allen (who amused even Republican Senators when they considered his qualifications to become a Director of the Reconstruction Finance Corporation) the President has one of the best-known clowns of the capital, but no fool: Allen has the confidence of both the fire insurance industry and the President of the United States whom he served at the same time. He is a Washington success story. In twelve years he came up from hotel manager to approximately the position of a manager of the government. And sometimes, even in 1946, he could still get a friend of the President's a room or even an apartment in Washington. He has good jokes:

"I was talking to Eisenhower back before the invasion in Europe. I had a lot of good ideas and I was laying 'em out. He listened, then he stopped me. 'Thanks, George,' he said, 'there are two fields in which everybody agrees that the amateur has it all over the professional: one is military strategy and the other is prostitution.' "

The laughter rises to the ceiling all around the frescoed Great Seal of the United States, and nobody laughs louder than George. And beyond the laughter the telephone may ring and Attlee, in London, may be waiting to talk to Truman. Certainly not everything is laughter or foreign affairs or even politics. And though no fixed formal training is provided in the circle of intimacy for the assistants of the President, not all of them are amateurs. There is no more respected newspaperman in Washington than Charles Ross. Bill Hassett is an American artist at correspondence. It is always almost pathetically essential that the President's intimates on the payroll be men with some sense of the art of government as well as the art of friendship. Splashing with him in the swimming pool may not suffice either for assistance or for friendship. Indeed, sometimes friendship when its public display is too convivial may bring letters in a President's mail that not even a President can answer. And some of President Truman's

friends did come into the White House as if they were on
their way to the room where the boys were singing at an
American Legion convention.

The experts are as essential as the intimates, even if often
they get less space in the papers. I went across Executive
Avenue, which serves as a sort of private White House parking lot, to the State Department to see them. Some of the
intimates are housed there, too. Once—perhaps still—the
row of offices, where the Secretary of War used to work
long before he got the Pentagon, seemed the barracks of the
so-called Palace Guard—the Secret Six—the Presidential assistants romantically described as men of "high competence,
great physical vigor and a passion for anonymity." Sometimes
columnists made them seem a sort of Presidential gestapo.
I can report, as a veteran of the service, that neither the men
nor their tasks were often so romantic as they sounded. But up
the corridor, beyond the Palace Guard's sinister doors are
the experts who sometimes seem not sinister but too persistent
and too powerful to those Cabinet members who resent the
administrative controls Presidents keep on them still.

Harold Smith,* Director of the Bureau of the Budget, is
not a politician. He did not know Roosevelt until he came to
take his job. Truman had been only one of ninety-six Senators
to him. But as Director of the Budget in the Executive Office
of the President, he has the job not merely of preparing the
budget proposed by the President to Congress for the executive branch as a whole, but of approving for the President
every proposal of every Cabinet officer and agency head for
money, for legislation, and for employees. He has a staff of
government professionals who sometimes seem a sort of central spy system to administrators. Policy is, in general, outside his province. But in a government in which everything
depends upon money and legislation, he sits directly under the
President, and, as the President's man, undertakes to shape an
order out of what might otherwise be the greater chaos of

* Recently named vice-president of the International Bank.

agency heads and administrators operating in exuberant independence all over the governmental map. He is the captain of the President's experts, and to him government is a science and not an art to be exercised in intimacy.

He was sitting that day when I came in, like a guest in his own big outer office, talking in relaxation to his own secretary. He looked tired. If he is not, God knows why not. He arrived in 1939, when the Reorganization Act permitted the transfer to the President's own office of the tiny budget staff which had been in existence since 1921. He began to expand his staff to ride herd on the agencies when the agencies began roaring in preparation for war. He sliced billions from what they were permitted to request of Congress. And he held the power to cut afterward even what they received. Sometimes, he pushed them as well as cut them. Under the President, he worked on their quarrels with him and with each other. No wonder he was tired. At his desk, he grinned and showed me a collection of pills the doctors had given him to take. Fortunately, he has a sense of humor as well as a stomach.

Out in Michigan, where he was Budget Director before he came to Washington, one of the governmental traditions he tried to buck was a costly vanity maintained for citizens which permitted them to get special license plates with their initials on them. He got nowhere for a while. Then he wrote the Governor:

"I am a founding member of the Society of Budgeters. I, therefore, ask that a tag be issued to me bearing this inscription: S.O.B. No. 1."

And maybe that is the best description of his job in Washington. He does not look it. He is, despite his drive, fat and forty-seven. He grins in friendliness, but when a proposal comes to him that seems strange, his face drops into an expression of shock as well as surprise. He can look very glum, indeed. His patience seems to be protected by the easy show of irritation. I think he is an emotional man, but the essence of his appearance is of deliberation and weary relaxation. He likes to talk. He understands the conflict between the individual eagerness of administrators and the necessity for overall governmental order over which he presides.

"The dilemma is this: How to accord the head of an agency sufficient freedom of action so that he can get his job done and be held properly responsible for results, while at the same time limiting his administrative authority by reasonable and adequate standards safeguarding the use of public funds and personnel."

The dilemma remains. He does not, I think, expect it ever to be neatly solved. But against Cabinet members and agency heads who can roar, he does not present any brittle notion that anything as complex as government can always be precise in its certainties.

"A certain amount of waste and inefficiency is the price of the democratic process."

He is philosophic as well as firm. He does not speak the jargon of the scholars in administrative management whose leader he is. He certainly does not mean to be caught behind any barbed-wire fence of terminology while talking to politicians. He understands them. It is his job to deal with them. And in the Secretariat of the President—as he essentially is— he has very individual notions of secretarial assistance for himself.

"I always made it a rule," he said, "never to take anybody with me to a new job. When I came down here I took the secretary that was here and came on in by myself. I knew that if I brought anybody in I'd be turning too quickly to him for help and that the other people in the organization would feel it. I think it is always better to come in alone."

No President in his right mind could quite do that. Some of those students who always look at the very different British Government before making suggestions for America have been envious of Britain's permanent Cabinet Secretariat. But, by the very nature of the American President's job, he has to have men around him upon whom he personally can depend.

Also, he needs men, such as Harold Smith, who are experts rather than intimates. The important thing every President must hope for is a combination of intimates who have also the intellectual capacity of the experts, and if possible some of their "know how" in government; and experts who bring to the science of government some of the human qualities of loyalty and ease of human relations which politicians possess.

Lucky Presidents do find the combination. Most Presidents also find both experts and intimates who fail them. And sometimes, men who are essential to Presidents and who seem to possess only one of the necessary qualities have them both. The White House is always so surrounded by quarrel and gossip that both the Presidents and the people around them emerge from it in a distorted picture.

Certainly, sometimes the human qualities which a President requires in men close to him can seem all too human. The other side of loyalty can be, even in big strapping men, an almost feminine jealousy. Being loyal to the President can develop into a contest.

"What you trying to do, be Teacher's pet?" one associate may demand of another.

I remember one Secretary who grew a little pompous in his confidence and who sent a pre-emptory message to another by an assistant. The receiving Secretary listened. I can see his big jaws setting now.

"You tell him," he said, "to put it in writing so I can laugh at it."

The contentions can seem like confusion. Occasionally they are. One of President Truman's assistants, before he changed his mind, announced that he "wouldn't run in this 'rat race' for a thousand dollars a week." And after he changed his mind, the President had to change it again for him. Apparently, he actually believed it was a rat race, and was running that way. Presidential assistants must be expendable. In the White House they have no purpose except to protect the President. But Presidents are notoriously reluctant about dismissing old friends. Sometimes it is easier to leave them in office divested of faith. And by the very nature of the great powers he would have to assume—even to watch as a technician all Presidential business—one Secretary as a sort of Presidential first assistant would be hazardously located both for himself and for the President.

Though the phrase has been flung about, "an assistant President" is an institutional impossibility. What Presidents need is hard-working men—several of them—upon whom they can depend, men who are able enough to do their complex chores, and who have common sense enough not to take themselves too seriously. The last may be more important than anything else.

I remember old Rudolph Forster, Executive Clerk of the White House, who had served under a whole succession of Presidents as one of the excellent career staff which keeps the continuity from day to day and from President to President. He was a fragile little man (tiny beside the equally able Maurice Latta who succeeded him) who immortalized the too much neglected tradition of service to Presidents without either sycophancy or self-seeking. I think he immortalized it once in a dry sentence in the midst of hot current concerns.

"You would be terrified," he said, "if you knew how little I care."

But the Presidential papers moved. The staff worked. The details were remembered. The imagination and the ambition, the push and the politics were to him only parts of a succession from McKinley which may have changed the world but did not interrupt the processes of the continuing, small, unpublicized bureaucracy upon which all Presidents depend.

Other selfless men come in. I remember one. I have seen him making the ultimate sacrifice in a secretariat of seeming to be stupid for his boss. All Secretaries are willing to do hard work. Most of them will readily take the licks and the blame off Presidential backs. There may even be candidates for the dramatic sacrifice. But the man who is willing to seem in an atmosphere of reflected brilliance not quite bright if such stupid seeming will serve his Boss is a jewel Presidents often seek. There is no apparent trouble about finding a fool who is one. But the man who will sacrifice even his own show of superiority in a craft in which all must combine toughness with courtliness, is still a rare man rarely found. I remember talking about such a man with an observant official in Washington who had known several Presidents and many Secretaries.

"He was a kind of test for me of the understanding of people," he said. "As you well know, there were those who thought he was merely an elevated court jester—a good spinner of yarns and a good deflector from the affairs of state. How wrong they were! Behind that relaxed Newfoundland dog kind of detachment there lay great shrewdness and wisdom."

Washington and sometimes the White House are crowded with self-confident wise men. But in America, there is no surplus of men able to take Presidents more seriously than themselves.

V

The Bridge

He did not look like a policeman. He was lank and gray, and he stood in a big recessed window with his elbows resting behind him on the wide sill. He seemed almost country-polite in the Capitol, and completely at ease. I looked at his badge. We can call his number 31.

"I don't understand it," he said. "In this building if you tell people how to go, they always go right ahead and turn the wrong way. Look at that woman. She's going right past where I told her to turn."

Undisturbed, he watched her confusion as if it were perversity. But I could sympathize with the lady. As man and messenger, newspaperman and government official, I have been moving through the corridors of the Capitol for nearly twenty years. I still get confused. It does not depress me. I like to remember that neither the sitting Congress nor the current President invented confusion in Washington. The Capitol is its monument. It was designed by an amateur and an eccentric who was educated to be a doctor but became instead a painter, a poet, a horse-racer, an inventor, the promoter of a gold mine, and was withal a poor man who was happy to become a bureaucrat. This gentleman, Mr. William Thornton, quarreled with the builders and other architects and involved Presidents in his quarreling. His Capitol wears its second dome. The statue of Freedom above it was redesigned by Jefferson Davis so that its cap would not resemble that one worn as a symbol by liberated slaves. It took sixty years to finish it. And though George Washington was there in a mason's apron at its beginning, it was not completed until after the present chairman (1946) of the House Ways and Means Committee was born.

"Well, she made it," said Policeman No. 31, as if the movements of citizens following his directions were a matter in which he took a gambler's as well as a philosopher's interest.

Somehow I was glad I did not have to ask him my way. It is easy to find the House Chamber with its casual-seeming congregation of statesmen under the galleries against its gray walls decorated with American shields. Most of the Congressmen look as if they had just happened to be going by and had stopped in because they had nothing better to do. Outside, and off the big corridors, the Capitol's passages run to the offices of those Congressional elders who, by seniority, have offices in the Capitol itself. Seniority not only emphasizes their eminence, it saves them steps.

Somewhere a bell rang and tourists and Congressmen began pouring into the halls. It was hard to tell them apart, except that those who looked as if they might know where they were going might be Congressmen.

"See that boy?" said No. 31. He jerked his thumb toward a blue-suited youth. "Son of a Congressman." He named him. "He's a page, his wife's his secretary. He's got others on the payroll, too."

I looked at No. 31 with more interest. As protector of Congressmen and a guardian of the Capitol, he seemed just a little garrulous. I presume somebody had got him his job. Somehow he did not look like a career man as a cop, but he was clearly a career conversationalist, even in blue clothes.

"A good many do it," I suggested casually, even a little apologetically, though nobody had hired me to protect this Congressman or any other.

"It ain't right, though," he said. "It ain't right."

He sounded more like the critical American from the back country than any of the tourists he directed. He had no idea who I was. If Congressmen have numerous relatives on the payroll I might conceivably have been one. Another lady stopped and asked her way.

"Turn at that next door—right where that man's going."

He watched her as if her turning were no better than an even bet. But she made it, and I followed her. I was going in the same general direction, though I had to turn sharp left just beyond Statuary Hall through a narrow corridor into a big one to get to the offices of Speaker of the House Sam Rayburn of Texas. I had come up to talk to him about the regular weekly meetings of the Democratic leaders in the Congress with the Democratic President of the United States. It is the nearest thing we possess to a parliamentary ministry in our government. It is not very near.

I had watched the leaders gather at the White House and depart: Rayburn; lank John McCormack, Massachusetts Irishman who is House majority leader; old, florid, dank-haired Senator Kenneth D. McKellar of Tennessee, president pro tem of the Senate; and aging Alben Barkley of Kentucky, the majority leader of the Senate. They looked like no such ministry as a casting director would assemble. But they made all other government in Washington seem somehow transitory. Presidents come—and, as Franklin Roosevelt proved, they may stay a long time. But Congress is nothing if not continuity. The four men, when I watched them, averaged sixty-five years of age. They had served an average of twenty-eight years each in the Congress. All but one of them were Southerners, though dependence of their party, under Roosevelt, had passed from the South. Its hope of continuance in power under Truman remained outside the South. Since no party can elect a President by its own votes, they met with a President, who as a politician as well as a statesman, must look beyond party. But they came under a constitutional system which required all of them, both as statesmen and as politicians, to look short of national party to their separate constituencies in the States. They do not work for the President as the Cabinet does. As party men, they work with him. He does not control them, and they do not control in the Congress the parties they lead.

I went first to Sam Rayburn's office as Speaker just off the floor of the House. It is a dark room. I have a sense of old plush about it and a remembrance of the big old chandeliers and the overstuffed leather furniture which seems to be requisite in all Congressional interior decoration. The room seemed less the room of a man than of a tradition. You get a feeling there that Congress does not change very much. But the dark, pretty, Texas girl at the desk was young. She showed me the way to the Speaker's other office. (Actually he also has a third, where party fellowship can be served in the nation's service. Harry Truman was there that Thursday afternoon when he got the news that brought him hurrying to the White House.)

I could understand No. 31's troubles with those he directed when I went to Rayburn's office, although, when you reach it, it is simply placed on the west front of the Capitol. Across the peaceful corridor is the office of Republican leader Joe Martin, who would be Speaker if his party had the votes, but must lead a much more pleasant life with no President to pester him and only the duties of opposition on his mind. (Sometimes, I knew, he seemed to more ardent young Republicans a little less energetic in leadership than the job required.) But Rayburn's office is pleasant, too. It seemed less ornate than his other one, more the office of a man than of a Speaker.

It was very quiet there. I was early, and before he came in, as he always does like a little man full of energy, I looked at the room. There were five photographs of Robert E. Lee on the walls, grouped in a sort of garland of devotion. But Ulysses S. Grant was up there, too, because a sentimental Texan remembers graciousness and generosity to his Lee. There were Woodrow Wilson and Franklin Roosevelt. Rayburn had been in Congress long enough to work with both of them. And Lincoln's picture. I mentioned Grant and Lincoln when he came in.

"I realized I was a national officer and had to have some Republican pictures."

He laughed and I knew Joe Martin across the hall would have laughed with him, and would himself probably, if he moved into the office, hang up Jefferson's picture out of a past far enough back to be politically undisturbing. The national quality of the Speaker's office sits in a grand sweep outside his windows. Just below is old John Marshall sitting in eternal thoughtfulness in a bronze chair, and beyond is Grant riding west on a great black horse on the long grassy way to the white memorial to Lincoln. Lee's house is across the river on the green hill. It was hard from that window, as it sometimes is in Washington, to remember that The Hill of the Capitol is only eighty-eight feet high, no mountain in Washington, and a stumpy little knoll in the United States.

Sam Rayburn does not look like a figure in history. He is a stout little man, firm on his feet. His face is almost explosively expressive. After thirty-two years in Washington, he still looks like a country Congressman from Texas, and he seems country-wise, too, in the crowded city of politicians, promoters and insistent national patriots. His feet are still firmly fixed on the earth in little Bonham, in Fannin County. He likes to get back to his farm in even smaller Ivanhoe, where the sandy land is better for cattle than the Blacklands which grows cotton across most of his district. He thinks of the nation in the specific images of people, many of them in Bonham and the country around it, and not in terms of any abstract nationalism of statistical norms.

He stands in Texas, but he is not lost there. He had a local fight for his life, in 1944, because he was a national leader when the anti-Roosevelt folks down there, flush with money as Texans can be, undertook to beat the Speaker of the United States House of Representatives in the Fourth District of Texas. They didn't. On the other hand, some Liberals, outside of Texas, feel that his national liberalism falls short of the need of the Democratic Party in America. If they tried, as those

Texans did, they could not beat him either. He leads a party in Congress which can be hell-bent both ways, and often is. It is his job to lead it as Speaker. Behind his leadership, it can look more divided than disciplined. But he leads both John Rankin, of Tupelo, Mississippi, and Adam Clayton Powell, Jr., of Harlem, New York City, whose similarities in venomous opposition are seldom noted. And all the human Democratic variety between them.

I mentioned the old days when Congressmen had chafed under Roosevelt's Presidential leadership. I had seen Sam Rayburn petulant himself. Then Mr. Truman had undertaken to create party effectiveness in Congress by Presidential good-fellowship with his old associates. That did not work to perfection either.

"Um-huh," said the Speaker, nodding as if the obvious had been disclosed.

He spoke for Congress.

"A Congressman hasn't got a chance," he declared. He pulled open the top drawer of his desk and fumbled for a paper. "I guess I haven't got it here. Nick Longworth wrote it. Anyhow, if a Congressman follows the President, he's a rubber stamp and if he doesn't he's a traitor to his party and probably to his country as well."

At the other end of town, I knew, a President always seemed to be either a dictator or a dope in an America which seldom speaks about Presidents except in extremes.

The Speaker spat over his cigarette, sharply and accurately at his cuspidor.

"The truth is—they'll always deny it—but the people like something like a dictator. They always like a President who pushes Congress hard."

A Speaker of the House in his capacity as national leader sits between. So do the other leaders who go with him to those meetings at the White House. There is no set pattern for Congressional leadership. There is the tradition of tyranny which, along with bawdy humor in politics, was dramatized under old Joe Cannon. Sam Rayburn's predecessor, John Nance Garner, left a tradition of toughness behind him, too. Indeed, some of Rayburn's friends think that Rayburn failed to be elected Speaker earlier only because Democrats who wore Garner's scars took it out on another Texan.

"I can't be tough," Sam Rayburn said.

I doubt that. He can look like a small Texas bull with his feet set for charge. Undoubtedly, however, he has based much of his effectiveness in Congress upon the affection which most Left-wing and Right-wing Democrats feel for him as a man. Becoming Speaker of the House is something more than a popularity contest. Seniority enters into it (only two members of Congress have served longer than Rayburn, but one is seventy-nine and the other eighty-two; eight Republicans have served longer than Joe Martin). But a Speaker's leadership of a Congress can depend upon affection as well as force. Members can occasionally be disciplined in one way or another. But discipline does not close big divisions. And often, when headlong prejudices or principles or the direct interests of their districts are not involved, men who might otherwise slip away in the voting will follow the Speaker.

His rug is a parade ground for the distressed. And some of the distressed had a seniority scarcely less than his. They controlled committees.

"Hell, Sam, if it wasn't for you there are about fifty of us from the South who'd walk right out on him."

And there are men on the other side of the philosophic aisle on the Democratic side who can get angry, too.

Old fellows in Congress, secure in seniority, can get their feelings hurt very easily. An elderly politician with tears in his eyes does not seem a conventional Congressional picture. He occurs. And the young, too. Sometimes a Speaker has to deal very gently with their bright ideas. Indeed, since J. William Fulbright, as a freshman Congressman, got national publicity with a resolution about preserving world peace (for which, incidentally, even Ham Fish and other isolationists voted) the young have been even more eager—and sometimes hard to hold.

Some of them have been concerned with the problem of relations between the Capitol and the White House. As if it were a new idea, they brought the proposal that Cabinet members be permitted to speak on the floor of the House to present and defend their programs. Rayburn remembered that the idea was about when he came to Congress more than thirty years ago. Under his leadership the old and the young collided over plans for reorganizing the committe system of Congress.

And all are Congressmen together. They develop quickly the quickly disturbed pride in institution.

"Did the President speak to you about that before he sent it up, Sam?"

It makes a lot of difference, regardless of the merit of the matter, if he can say yes.

And sometimes he does have to be not only father confessor but the stern old man. They gathered around his desk. Half a dozen of them had plans for trips with the army and the navy to the ends of the earth. Two of them had already made such trips. And now all of them said that, if he would just say that it was all right to the army and navy, they could be flying.

"What in the hell do you think your people sent you up here for?" And just for extra, he added, "Hell fire."

Tough or not, he looks physically tough even if the hair has all disappeared from his small round skull in the thirty-two years he has been working between Bonham and Washington. But he moves as if his short legs were pistons (strangely Joe Martin moves more slowly, like the Southerner he is not). He is Speaker of the House, but he is Democrat all over town. He knows better than anybody else that there are more links between the Capitol and the White House than that provided by the weekly expedition upon which he sets out with Barkley and McCormack and McKellar. The separation of powers so neatly provided in the Constitution may sometimes become terrifically and formally important to members of Congress and to Presidents. But informally, what is supposed to be separation can actually be a swarming of legislators in the executive departments and of administrative officials in the Capitol.

It may be true that today all legislative desires of the executive must be cleared through the Budget Bureau for the President before they go to The Hill. There is still no greater lobby —and not always in support of Presidential plans—than the people who work in the departments. And Congressmen, even if they wished it, would not be permitted by their constituents to stay out of the departments and the agencies. Socially, and sometimes effectively, the branches of government come together at such a pleasant place as Rayburn's own bachelor apartment in the Anchorage near Dupont Circle. Certainly the country, which ought to know all about separation of powers, complacently and completely disregards it. It wants the government to work and is not much interested (except in editorials and oratory) in notions of separation or balances or checks (except those on the Treasury). Its orders and notions, desires and directions come by telegraph, by mail and in person.

"My God," says the Speaker, "I'd hate to represent a district with towns in it big enough to have chambers of commerce. Once they get a secretary of a chamber of commerce who has to make a show about his job, a Congressman's life can be hell."

I laughed. We got up and I looked again out of his window at the long view. I was glad Rayburn was at this end of the scene below us. I did not mistake him for history, but he did not seem confused in the Capitol or the capital or the country. He may represent the triumph of Congressman over the Capitol.

The waiting room outside was crowded. There was a Texas look about it. Dean Acheson, Undersecretary of State, was there waiting to come in. I had seen him that morning in the State Department. As always, he was the immaculate, well-dressed gentleman with neatly trimmed mustache. He looked like Groton and Yale and Harvard and the State Department walking. But he was, I thought, one working man in government going in to see another. In their persons Groton and Bonham did not seem far apart.

He laughed. "Jonathan, are you following me?"

"No," I said, "but we are both working on a crowded road."

The tourists were still wandering about in Statuary Hall. There is a dank, medieval quality about it. And somehow, America there looked a little callow contemplating it. The country that comes to look seems to leave behind it, as government sometimes does, the liveliness and strength of the country itself. Indeed, the country carrying a camera can look as empty-faced as a bureaucrat watching the country's clock. But two men came through, striding and talking. They were not tourists. They did not glance at a statue. I did not recognize either of them as a Congressman, but they knew where they were going and they did not look as if they would easily be stopped or lost in the corridors of old William Thornton's Capitol. But plenty of others were not so sure, and down the corridor old Policeman No. 31 was still giving Americans directions and, I presume, a little gossip on the side. He seemed to be enjoying his work.

VI

Over the Dashboard

HE WAS having some people, Senators and others, out to dinner and he asked me to come.

"Just a few," he said on the phone.

"I'll be delighted."

"All right, old fellow," he said. "Keep your tail over the dashboard!"

In Washington, the injunction was the private, almost patented injunction of encouragement of Senator Lister Hill, of Alabama, majority whip of the Senate. Sometimes it is needed in Washington, but that evening among the Senators, we seemed only people serene in the suburbs. Forty-ninth Street in Spring Valley runs up a little hill. Trees are planted on the sidewalk. The grass is green. And the street might be in Montgomery or Raleigh or Seattle or any of those streets in America where the architects or realtors have managed to produce a similarity in pleasantness for the mortgagees whether they be Senators or editors or salesmen.

We sat on a porch, which might have been an Alabama piazza, above a back lawn across one end of which ran one of those gardens which in wartime even Senators were encouraged to plant. The Hill garden was green but not calculated to provide any substantial competition to the truck growers of Alabama. But Senator Hill's colleagues contemplated his vegetables with derisive incredulity. The judgment of the Senators there assembled was that he must have been overworking his wife in the sun.

Henrietta Hill laughed, not looking overworked. I am not sure Lister Hill looks like a Senator. I am not sure any Senator looks like one. But Henrietta Hill, I am sure, represents Alabama as it would romantically like to appear. And she possesses, as some Senators do not, a sense of humor which is not intimidated by anybody's sense of self-importance. I had a feeling on that porch that she does not take Senators quite as seriously as the country sometimes does and as Senators almost always do. But she fed them well. Washington seemed not only over the hill but a long way off. Even constituents seemed safe in the great distances. After dinner, Senator Alben Barkley, of Kentucky, sang *Wagon Wheels* in a baritone which was only beginning to crack. Also, I remember, that after much insistence, he told again his old story about the long and carefully tended constituent who had decided, on top of all the favors he had received, not to vote for the Senator again.

"Well," he explained in response to the Senator's recital of favors and expression of surprise, "you ain't done nothin' for me lately."

And all the Senators laughed. Their delight in it is durable. More than any other, maybe, it is the story of the Senate. Senators remember home. They look like home. They hope to be remembered there. In Washington, they are just a little lower than the President. They not only have the biggest votes in connection with the legislation that he needs, but they also share his executive function in approving his appointments and his foreign agreements—or not approving them. They no longer seem in their suburban houses or their hotel rooms the members of the Rich Man's Club they were supposed to be when Lord Bryce said that some were Senators because they were rich and some were rich because they were Senators. Neither do they any longer seem merely bigger Congressmen (in the 79th Congress only twenty-two Senators had come up through Congress). But such is their power that only a few among them feel any necessity to strut with it. They keep the historical tradition of their collective self-esteem. But most of them can laugh—even at themselves.

I was a little surprised when on the porch one Senator broke the laughing with solemnity.

"I don't know whether it's worth it," he said.

There was a moon over Senator Hill's vegetables. The party was breaking up. Lister Hill himself had had to slip away to drive an elderly Senator home to bed. Alben Barkley's song and joke were gone. But the Senator who did not know whether it was worth it hung behind. So did I. The porch was quiet.

"Why?" I asked.

He sprawled on a porch swing, dangling a foot.

"I'll tell you the truth about this Senate business," he said. He looked around at the few of us who remained.

"Hell," he said, "people keep saying stuff about Senators being national statesmen. They don't give us time. I'm going to tell you about my day and I'm going to name the names, but if you ever say I said so, I haven't seen you."

He told me. His supporters had been in town or on the phone. He named them and what they had done for him. He recited what they wanted him to do. Their desires included everything from railroad reservations home to complex operations before the departments. One man wanted a special favor for his son in the navy.

"I called up Admiral Soandso and he couldn't do it. But the old man won't believe me. He thinks I could get it if I wanted to. And, between ourselves, maybe if I called up the Secretary and put it to him just like it is, he might do it. But I know that the next time he wanted something, it would be just like that back to me. I don't want to get in that fix."

He flung out his hands.

"They don't give you time to be a Senator. You don't even have time to read the bills. That's the way it is, ain't it, Josh?"

Josh Lee, who had been elected and also defeated as Senator

from Oklahoma, and so was qualified, spoke out of the darkness in a flat voice.

" 'Bout right," he said.

Even in a time when oratory has been rare in the Senate, his voice sounded strangely undramatic for a gentleman who had made his living as a professor of public speaking before he began to be a public official.

" 'Bout right," he said. Then he added: "Of course, you can institutionalize your support."

The phrase sounded like the sort of trade jargon which professors and plumbers—as well as Senators—use. He told about a Senator who had everything arranged in his State, so that local bodies of organized pressure groups carried his strength.

"Like the Baptist Church and the Coca Cola Company and the utilities?"

"Well, yes, groups like that."

"Doesn't he sometimes run into pressures in different directions?"

"Oh, yeah, of course, he may. But he's been lucky so far."

"That's easier for a conservative than a Liberal. A whole lot easier."

"Well, there's the CIO and its PAC."

"Lord have mercy," said another Senator. "In my State I'd rather have the smallpox."

But the first Senator was insistent.

"I don't care who your supporters are, they'll come here and worry you to death. They don't give you time to be national. That's the whole truth."

"Is it tougher," I asked, "on Senators from nearby States than from States far away?"

"Well, there's debate about that, too."

He shook his head and looked sadly at the dark garden.

"There isn't time to be a national statesman," he said.

He sounded almost comically sad. Senators did seem a little pathetic, self-described as institutionalized messenger boys instead of national statesmen. But not many Senators, I know, share the feeling expressed by old John Sharp Williams at the last that he would rather be a hound dog baying at the moon from his Mississippi plantation than a member of the United States Senate. No people are more insistent upon their localism than Senators themselves, nevertheless. They are not only the proud representatives of the States; even those who become most accustomed to the comforts of the capital describe themselves as residents of inconsiderable villages.

Senator Walter George, of Georgia, who handles the taxation of the greatest businesses, comes from little Vienna (pronounced Vy-enna), in Dooly County, where before World War II began less than one person in five hundred filed an income tax return. Tom Connally, chairman of the Foreign Relations Committee, comes from Marlin, Texas. (Population, 1940, 6,542.) Senator Kenneth Wherry, of Nebraska, the Republican whip, not only keeps his residence in a village but maintains in person the familiar small-town tradition of providing from one establishment furniture for the living and funerals for the dead ("licensed embalmer and funeral director for past twenty years in Nebraska, Kansas, Iowa and Missouri"). It is hard to think of anything more country, sweet and sad together, than his country funerals. But in a national Senate which must approve all our international agreements, young J. William Fulbright seems to have set the pattern better than his elders. He came to the Senate on a platform of world peace, but his official autobiography as Senator reports that "he has been engaged in farming most of his life." However, the rest of that autobiography suggests that, if its cultivation had waited for his presence, the grass roots would have been thick in his cotton.

Obviously, somewhere between national and international statesmanship and insistent localism, the Senators come together as people. They do not meet only in the Senate Chamber, where they seem most impressive; they meet, too, at good dinners, like that one at Lister Hill's. Within their occupational fellowship, they divide not only into parties but into congenial groups as well. There was one coterie of such statesmen in Washington during the war which seemed to take its solidarity from the appreciation of its members for jokes which went back to the livery stables if not the grass roots. There were more serious groups brought together by joint interests in great questions. But the whole Senate seems to become inevitably not merely our Great Council but also a club.

In terms of entrance requirements, it is no longer the rich man's club it once seemed to be, though there are rich men in it. (Homer Capehart, of Indiana, president of the Packard Corporation, gives his leading occupation as "farmer.") There are poor men in it, too. Harry Truman had to put his wife on the payroll in order to pay mounting war taxes. Senator Kenneth D. McKellar, its president pro tem, had his relatives on the payroll both before taxes went up and after. Though free debate remains, the Senate is no longer the great organization of orators. Even reporters who cover it scratch their heads in seeking the memory of a great modern oration in it.

That does not necessarily mean that its quality has declined. It may mean that we are inclined to romanticize the past. There are able men at its desks now, or gossiping in its cloak-rooms. Of course, there are arrogant stuffed shirts, too. And men who mistake their own vanities for institutional pride. By and large, it is about as able as a body representative of America and the forces running loose in America could be expected to be. Some of its members may seem great men someday. Someday, a good many of them, as always, will just be little men dead and forgotten.

It is a club still, and in important aspects, is run like one. Tourists are familiar with its excellent bean soup and also the dining rooms marked "For Senators Only." Citizens can read in the *Senate Manual:* "The barber shop, and bathrooms connected therewith, shall be reserved exclusively for the use of Senators." Sometimes, in protecting each other's patronage the lines in the Constitution about its "advice and consent" in approving Presidential appointments seem club rules, too. But the most exclusive aspects of the club are maintained in rooms euphemistically described as the office of the Secretary of the Senate, and which Senators themselves call Biffle's Tavern after the Secretary of the Senate, the Honorable Leslie Biffle, of Piggott, Arkansas.

Mr. Biffle maintains the country tradition of the Senate. Piggott, Arkansas, is about as far into the country as you can get. Indeed, Piggott is the eastern county seat of Clay County, which has two county seats because the citizens couldn't get across the Black River bottoms from one side of the county to the other. However, close as Piggott may remain to his heart, Mr. Biffle, as Senators hope to be, has been a Congressional employee for nearly forty years. He is secretary not only of the Senate but of the club.

I remember attending, as an outsider may, one of its luncheon meetings when Mr. Biffle's predecessor (who had been a Senate employee then for forty-five years) presided. Harry Truman sat at the table in those days and he, as he indicated in his plans for effective conviviality as Vice-President, appreciated the club. It was to it he came the first day he was President in his determination that an old Senator and continuing Senators should get along.

It is not so far from the floor. Senators go in past clerks and ledgers. There always seem a large number of elderly gentlemen on the Senate's clerical staff. Beyond them are a small room and a long one. I remember that the smaller room has windows in a southwest corner which look across to Lee's house and Lincoln's memorial. Also, I remember that there was good whisky on the table. And that it was a place where good fellows get together—but not merely for pleasure. At that time, the chief topic for discussion was some officials, who under the banner of "No Politics" were letting Republican Governors suggest Federal personnel in their States instead of Democratic Senators. But the political atmosphere was not as savage as some of the political conversation. Indeed, sometimes even Senators can take their troubles lightly, or at least humorously.

The thing I remember in that room is not the complaint but

the companionship. We laughed around the table in the anteroom. Senator Joe O'Mahoney, of Wyoming, was telling a
funny story about one of the camps in which Japs had been
interned and to which a man—maybe a Senator—had gone to
inspect it. They showed him one tiny Jap boy. The visitor
asked his name.

"Tojo," said the child.

And the visitor said in the automatic amiability which comes
naturally into political mouths, "That's a nice name."

"You think so?" asked the little boy. "That's the name of
the son-of-a-bitch that started all this."

We laughed before we went in to eat lunch and gnaw on
public officials who misunderstood the rights and needs of
Senators in their States.

The Senate changes. One of the Senators who was there
that day is no longer a member of the Senate; he is President
of the United States. One man who was there is dead. The
process goes on. When I went back to Washington as wartime bureaucrat, in 1942, there were only twenty men in the
Senate who were there when I looked down on it as correspondent, in 1925. When I left, in 1945, twelve of those had
disappeared by death or rejection, and one of those who remained had been in his bed for two years. Old Senators notice
the change amid the confident laughing of the young ones. I
remember that, in 1942, the President wanted George Norris
to run for re-election from Nebraska. He was eighty-one years
old. He had been in Congress since 1903. He hesitated in reluctance.

"I'm lonely up here," the old man said. He looked across his
desk as if he were looking at the Senate. "All my friends are
dead."

He ran, but Kenneth Wherry, the Pawnee City undertaker,
beat him and left the undertaking business to come to Washington. It is difficult to think of Wherry, who looks so alive
now at fifty-four after having buried so many people in Nebraska, Kansas, Iowa and Missouri, as moving on the same

road. As a body, the Senate does not look old and tired. Under the Constitution, they are qualified to go to work at thirty. But fourteen new Senators who came at the beginning of the 79th Congress averaged fifty-five years old. One freshman was sixty-seven. They are men of the same varying age a town's substantial citizenship has. Indeed, viewed anywhere else except against the historic background of its chamber, the Senate would look about like the membership of a Rotary Club in an American town. In such terms, the House would be more like a Lions Club, livelier but less obviously conscious of its civic dignity.

In the Senate, everything changes except the club and its basic localism. Maybe the American problem around it does not basically change. People are still hoping for liberty and security where they are, even if the threats to it may come from greater forces and greater distances. The depression hit everybody. The war reached into the little towns. Maybe there is virtue in the fact that we make our solutions, even in world problems, on the basis of insistent parochialism. Perhaps the Senate learns. When it acted on the charter of the United Nations Organization at least it did not make 1919's mistake, even if there was a certain feeling among Senators and citizens that if we avoid a mistake a quarter of a century old we avoid all other mistakes, too. I suspect that even Senators begin to understand that world security does not mean merely security for Washington and Moscow and London. It means security for Vienna, Georgia, as well as tragic Vienna far away. Nationalism is a concept. Organized security is still half hope and half phrase.

Looking down on the heads of the Senators from the Press Gallery, I smiled to myself. I doubted that politics had changed. A Senator was talking about the atomic bomb in the chamber in which elaborate steel scaffolding had been erected to protect Senators from the danger of the collapse of the old roof of their chamber. Even gravity could kill. In all dangers, old and new, Senators are not alone in dealing with a nation and a world in terms of its parts. Log-rolling may mean a division all around of Congressional swag. The country and its problems have to be put together from the little pieces and peaces, too. I remembered the history of the laughter that had greeted old Winfield Scott Hancock in American politics, when, a long time ago, he had said that the tariff was a local issue. World security is a local issue, too.

World security was down there on the floor while I watched, in the hands of men who may be national statesmen or not, but who are certainly the men of Putney, Vermont; and Wheatland, North Dakota; Havana, Illinois; Medicine Park, Oklahoma; Angola, Indiana; Beaver, Utah; and Pawnee City, Nebraska; and other towns like New York and Chicago. It will take them all, and strange local places far away whose names we cannot pronounce, to make the world—or any of them in it—secure.

I saw Lister Hill leave the chamber, and went down to catch him. He strode ahead of me with his long coat swinging, but I reached him as he was about to take an elevator marked "Senators Only," and got in with him. I beat him to his phrase.

"Keep your tail over the dashboard," I said.

He grinned.

"Well, old fellow," he said, "you ought to get it all."

He gave it to me:

"Keep your head up, your tail over the dashboard, and your face to the rising sun, and the shadows will fall behind."

"That's good Alabama doctrine?"

"Why, suh," he drew himself up. He put one hand on my shoulder and extended the other. "That's good doctrine for the world, The World, THE WORLD!"

I hope he is right.

VII

With Admiration and Affection

HE WAS hid up under the eaves of the big building. The ceilings were lower than in the rooms along the vast marble halls on the lower floors of the House Office Building, but he had more, if less ostentatious, space. The windows circling the huge court in descending rows gave me, as always, the notion that when the architects designed the building for rows of offices they somehow remembered still the huge hotels they had built for better-heeled tourists in the first opulent beginnings of Florida in the 1890's. They had designed another background for the American politician in the Buffalo Exposition at which McKinley was shot. Also, they had built great houses for the rich in those days when rich men could put their money into stone palaces instead of income taxes for Congressmen to appropriate. Inside the court there was no sense of the columned grandeur they had erected around Congressmen. But quietness was caught in the court. In the late afternoon there were no bells to ring for quorum calls, like school bells in the midst of dignity. No constituents tramped the halls. Most Congressmen and even Congressional secretaries were going home.

It was cozy in the room up under the eaves. Outside in the late afternoon, the lights were on and the walls of the court were an unevenly spotted darkness. Some Congressmen, I knew, would be bright-lit hours longer signing their mail and reading, down through the last personal and the ultimate obituary, the local papers. A woman's white arm pulled down

71

a curtain at a window. I turned into the room. There was a green burlap-and-wood screen around the basin where one of the prettiest blonde secretaries I ever saw was in the secretarial process of making us coffee.

Around this slim gold head from Texas the room came together in perfect Congressional color: the secretary's red dress, the darker red filing cases, the green figured carpet, a black leather couch with a red satin pillow on it, a green steel wastepaper basket and gray monk's-cloth curtains at the windows and on the bookcases. I could see above the books and behind the curtains a bottle of Scotch and some soda. I almost changed my mind; but the secretary had the coffee done. It smelled good. There were the signed pictures of other politicians thick on the walls. There was a comic statuette of a fighting Irishman labeled "I'm Dimocrat." And on his red desk were the Congressman's feet. They were big, and his shoes were brightly shined.

Congressman Lyndon Johnson sat—or extended—in his chair, almost parallel with the green carpet. As far as he was concerned the day was done except for conversation, which can be a very important part of a Congressman's business. Johnson is a rangy Texan who moves with a stride or subsides into a relaxation which is apparently complete. But his dark bright eyes do not rest. He looks, slim and curly-haired, joking and laughing, reporting and remembering, less like the conventional portrait of a Congressman than the conventional picture of a movie actor who sometimes comes from a small Texas town, too.

Like a lot of others, he had been not so much elected by the chance of political forces as he was the product of his own predetermined intention to make Congress a career. He had taught school in first young uncertainty as to his destination after he graduated from Southwest State Teachers College at San Marcos. But he actually began his Congressional apprenticeship when he became, at twenty-four, secretary to a Congressman. Also, as numbers of other Congressmen have done, while he secretaried he studied law at Georgetown University (where career diplomats also learn their lessons). When he was twenty-seven, he went back to be the young Texas Director of the National Youth Administration. And, in 1937, when an old Congressman died (as old Congressmen occasionally do) the young man came to Washington from the Tenth District of Texas.

There is something still of the campus politician about young Congressmen. And Johnson easily extended the campus to the District of Columbia. Judged by the inconsiderable village in which he was born and the one in which he lives, he was a countryman. He was a countryman in a national sense in Washington, in which most of the parochial yokels are sent down from Manhattan by Tammany. He worked. He has a pretty bright-eyed wife—with the good Texas name of Lady Bird—who helps him entertain. He exchanged his blue double-breasted clothes for a naval officer's blue, and went to the Pacific. He just missed defeating "Pass the Biscuits Pappy" O'Daniel for the Senate. (And some Texans insisted that the missing was in the counting.) He knows everybody worth knowing in Washington and many of them come to his house. He has, in Congress, a sense of values and a sense of humor.

I like him as man, but I am interested in him as portrait. I believe he looks more like a Congressman than many of those better-known gentlemen who have lost their hair and expanded their paunches in the service of their country. Also, he points out the fact that Congressmen, when they write their own official biographies, all reduce themselves to the stereotyped image of the national politician and hide the diversity of the American geography they represent. Johnson represented a Texas district which straddled, like a Congressman on horseback, the West and the South and which runs from plantations to ranches and from Negroes to Mexicans. It includes the capital of imperial Texas and sleepy-seeming tiny Texas towns. His blue double-breasted suit probably came from Manhattan; it could have come from Minneapolis. But

there was a gray sombrero on the hat stand. He never seemed
to make the mistake of confusing himself with The People.
He was in Washington, but he knew they were out there in
Texas still and maybe shrewdly watching him.

He ran his fingers through his dark hair, grinning.

"He may be smart," he said, "but he's a fool, too."

He was talking as Congressmen often do about the faults
of officials in the executive branch of government, as they
are seen not from Washington but out where the people see
them and report them quickly. Beside Johnson's bright shoes,
I found room for mine on the red desk, too. They were just
as big as Lyndon's but not quite so brightly shined. Then I
took them down, a little awkwardly and in an entirely un-
expected gallantry, when the lovely secretary brought my
cup of coffee. Lyndon reached for his cup with a long arm,
but he went on talking.

"He went down there to fix this mess up. He fixed it up
all right! Now every Congressman from Texas is scared to
go home."

But he laughed. Down in Dallas—or Fort Worth—there
was a gentleman who made a Texas gesture and a Texas
avocation of giving distinguished visitors big sombreros.

"Like that one over on the stand."

Also, the same gentleman, in a Texas where even reformers
can be as grandiose as grenadiers, was an officer of the Anti-
Saloon League. He made his presentation speech about the
ten-gallon sombrero. And the Washington official in genial
ignorance had suggested that if he wanted to be really useful
he might add ten gallons of liquor to fill it up.

Lyndon made a gesture of ducking defensively behind his
long arms. I laughed, not very happily. Then the pretty secretary let in two more Congressmen and a newspaperman. She
made them coffee, too.

"Joe's just come back from his State," one of the Representatives said of the other, "with an interesting story. Tell
'em, Joe."

The Honorable Joe shook his head, but he told the story, too. Nobody knew what had happened to the plane. It was all right just a few minutes before it cracked up because the pilot had talked to the ground. But anyhow, they'd hardly found it before the Governor rolled up in a long limousine with a whole squad of State Police. They went right in and found the brief case of the Lieutenant Governor who had been on the plane. The Governor took it and rode off. But when they took the Lieutenant Governor's body to the under-taker's—he paused for effect, "they found $3,600 in cash on it."

He paused significantly again.

"In small bills," he said.

He spread his hands.

"That's all."

"Has it been in the papers?"

The Congressmen laughed.

"I bet a buck," the newspaperman said, "that the under-taker won't talk. Hell, I'll bet fifty dollars that if you went back on that story, it would all be blank except that maybe the Governor went out there to be sure he saved some sort of papers that were essential to the safety of the State."

"I was telling Jonathan the story about the sombrero."

"Ouch," said a Congressman.

"I don't care how smart he is, he hasn't got any sense."

And the nodding heads all agreed. Smartness is not essen-tial in Congress, but sense, as they meant it, is more essential than seniority. Indeed, without it, there is not much hope of seniority even—or perhaps especially—in the one party South. A Congressman has it; he learns it early or he does not stay long. There is no occupation in which the hazards are so great and so regularly recurrent.

Johnson swung his long legs down from his desk.

"I've got to go," he said. "I promised to go out to Bill Douglas's for dinner." He looked at his watch. "And I'm going to be late. You all stick around."

But I went, instead, with one of the Congressmen around a corner and down a flight to another office on the court. He reached back of a bookcase and got out a bottle. Outside his window more lights had gone out on the court, but above it the sky seemed almost bright-packed with stars.

"If you're ever writing anything about me," he said, "just leave out the bourbon. This town seems to be getting full of damn fools who forget that the churches are still open in the little towns."

I am putting in the bourbon, which seems to me an essential item of legislation in America, and leaving out his name. We got our feet settled at the approved elevation.

"Here's to Congress," he said. "It could be better and it might be worse."

We talked about it. Something like a seventh of the members in every new Congress are new men. That means that one out of seven old men gets licked every two years. (Few die and fewer resign.) The hazard does not necessarily diminish with service, as even Sam Rayburn discovered. And a Congressman does not begin to mean anything even in Congress until he has won two or three times in a row. If he loses and comes back, he comes back at the bottom of the list. The old men rule as seniority prevails. Indeed, at the beginning of the 79th Congress the average age of the chairmen of all the committees, which initially handle all legislation and can generally kill it or give it a chance of life, was about fifty-eight. However, the chairmen of eleven of the most important House committees were all over seventy. The chairman of the two most important committees—Rules, and Ways and Means—were seventy-nine and eighty-two years old. Adolph Joachim Sabath, as dean of the House and chairman of the Rules Committee, seems less an elder statesman, who has served with and outlasted seven Presidents and eight Speakers of the House, than a little round man who might still be a kindly, shrewd Chicago lawyer and real estate dealer. Even older, R. L. Doughton, chairman of Ways and

Means, is as insistently countrified as Adolph Sabath is of the city. With his hat squashed down on top of his old head, Doughton looks as he marches through the Capitol at eighty-two like an indestructible Carolina cattle farmer striding up to an auction pen.

It seems positively ungallant to remember that Mary Norton, chairman of the Committee on Labor, is over seventy. It may seem even sadder to remember that Clare Luce, who became a glamorous Congressional freshman at forty, would have to wait until eleven Republicans die or disappear to get to the top on the Republican side of the Military Affairs Committee. If she should continue as a Congresswoman, she might make it when she is still a glamorous fifty-two. In important ways the elders each hold more power than whole batches of young Congressmen however glamorous they may be.

Sometimes such "elders" do not always have to be so very old to have remarkable power. In 1946, President Truman complained that some committee chairmen used their powers over legislation referred to their committees to delay or to prevent even a Congressional vote on Presidential proposals. One of the men he referred to was forty-four-year-old Representative Carter Manasco of Jasper, Alabama. He had served in Congress then for less than five years. His strategic place was as chairman of the generally unimportant Committee on Expenditures in the Executive Departments. As such, he had more power apparently than the President in the shaping —or not shaping—of Full Employment Legislation; so much more that the President of the United States appealed to the people about it.

Not many of the young get a chance to exercise such power. Manasco, though a newcomer, had been secretary to a Speaker long before he was a Congressman himself, and he knew his way around before he took his seat. But the young still come eagerly to Congress, and generally hope to stay long. There are all kinds of them. They come from all sorts of backgrounds. Most of them are lawyers, but one of my personal favorites began as a snuff salesman and became a Congressional secretary before he became a Congressman. (Incidentally, even Charles Dickens could walk through the Capitol now without fearing the slime of tobacco spitting which impressed him more than anything else about the Congress of the Republic a hundred years ago. The cuspidors remain. But there are few plugs in Congressional cheeks.) Some of the young manage very well for themselves. Mike Monroney, of Oklahoma, (whose entire name is Almer Still-well Mike M.) has stirred interest even in Congress in the reorganization of Congress for greater legislative effectiveness. He was a Phi Beta Kappa man who spent ten years between newspaper work and Congress as president of the Doc and Bill Furniture Company of Oklahoma City. (In his biography in the *Congressional Directory* he seems willing to forget the Doc and Bill years.) Estes Kefauver, of Tennessee, who took his law at Yale, has worked to revive the old idea that the legislative and executive branches might be brought closer together if Cabinet members could speak on the floor. Such relatively young men are gentlemen who, if they were not in Congress, might possibly be Brain Trusters in the executive branch or even State Department foreign service officers.

Indeed, their Republican contemporary, Christian Archibald Herter, was a foreign service officer after he graduated *cum laude* from Harvard. He was also educated outside the Congressional tradition, in Paris where he was born, at the Ecole Alsatienne. (He leaves that out of his Congressional biography, just as Monroney leaves out Doc and Bill.) Herter is also a member of Boston's exclusive Somerset Club; he was once a secretary to Hoover. He has been a Boston gentleman devoted to good charities. He is an overseer of Harvard University. He was editor of a fashionable magazine called *The Sportsman*. And he has the right to wear (which he also leaves out of his Congressional biography) the Order of the

Crown of Belgium and of the Polonia Restituta of Poland. However, that representative of the other half of Boston whose district joins Herter's and who was elected to Congress in the same election, the Honorable James Michael Curley (again elected Mayor of Boston; and now also convicted of mail frauds) is a decorated gentleman, too. He still has, though he may hide it, the Order of the Rising Sun of Japan.

Outside of Boston, most Congressmen prefer more native and practical decorations; the Masons and the Knights of Columbus have more voting members in American Congressional Districts. There are plenty of Congressmen who belong to the Odd Fellows, the Knights of Pythias, Knights Templar, Elks and Rotary and Lions. Fred A. Hartley, Jr., Republican of New Jersey, who came to Congress young and remains young though high in seniority, is the "only living person after whom an aerie of the Fraternal Order of Eagles has been named." Frank Sundstrom, who comes as good Republican, too, from the district adjoining Hartley's, lacks an aerie but was an all-American tackle at Cornell. Stigler, of Oklahoma, though he attended Grenoble University in France, is "a duly enrolled member of the Choctaw Tribe of Indians."

It takes all kinds of people to make a House of Representatives. But though many may list the loyal order of this and that, hardly any of them ever put down the things they represent, for they are not only Congressmen from Texas and Georgia and Maine, but even more pertinently, Congressmen from cows and cotton and potatoes. Some of them represent (and in no improper sense) tobacco and oil, sugar and plate glass, wheat and hogs, silver and citrus fruits. They are also the representatives of big groups and big prejudices.

Sometimes those who seem only the most noisy are—though hard to bear—very useful, too. As a matter of fact, American violence wanes in the Congress. On the floor, the House is generally decorous to dullness. No English visitor today would hear there such oaths as the "beggars in their drink reject," or open threats to cut a colleague's throat from ear to ear. The same sentiments may remain in occasional shouting. Occasionally puffy men come to puny blows. But the language is cleaner, as the floors are about the spittoons. The strange thing is that such violent opposites as remain may be in contention almost identical men.

I suspect, though I am sure neither of them suspects it, that there are perhaps no two men in the House more alike than John Elliott Rankin, of Tupelo, Mississippi, and Adam Clayton Powell, Jr., of Harlem, New York City. They do not look it. Powell is long and black; Rankin is short and white. They seem the shouters of the opposite invectives. But they are both Democrats. Both are oratorically violent. And each took, to list his accomplishments for a world which might admire, more space in the *Congressional Directory* than the amount required by any two average Congressmen. They seem almost designed as two individual and opposite symbols of a race riot. But unconsciously in Congress, they seem almost a team dramatizing at the same time the poor ignorance of Mississippi and the baffled, crowded escape of New York. Congress and America can afford to have both men working at that job. It will take some time to cure the American conditions of poverty and prejudice from which Rankin and Powell together arise.

Time, indeed, is the first requirement in Congress. And the one thing most forgotten about all of the members, who are serious in their jobs, is that Congressmen deliberately choose Congress as a career. Nobody speaks of Congressmen as career men, but in Congress under seniority rules it is career or nothing.

When Joseph C. Grew left the foreign service of the State Department, in 1945, after forty-one years' service, he had a slight edge on Adolph Sabath, of Chicago, who had been in Congress only thirty-nine years. Both Grews and Sabaths are uniquely durable in the government. Grew was a rich young man of twenty-four when he began his career as a clerk under the United States Consul in Cairo, in 1904. When

Sabath was elected to Congress, in 1906, he had already been an immigrant, a real estate dealer, a municipal judge and a police magistrate in Chicago. Career men in the State Department begin piling up seniority when they are clerks. Congressmen start only when the long apprenticeship is done. Only the few and the lucky, like Lyndon Johnson and Fred Hartley, who has the aerie of Eagles named after him, come in young. Old Sabath was forty when he arrived to begin the forty years of service to which he has been elected. Doughton was director of the North Carolina State Prison when, at forty-eight, he came to help direct the United States.

My friend, the Congressman, put down his glass and reached for the *Congressional Directory* to check the seniority of his elders. He did not seem depressed by the processes of progression in which he had to hope for his career. All Congressmen, indeed, generally seem a good deal less frustrated than ambassadors as seen in Washington. Ambassadors are important only when they are a long way from home. My friend spread the book on his desk and ran down the list of the committee chairmen.

"They're tough old birds, most of them; some of them are pretty wise—also, of course, some of them are pretty old."

He closed the book. "Good or bad, I'm not looking for it to change. I've been waiting for my chance, and I expect to get it."

"If you live and get elected," I said.

He grinned.

"Hell, of course, seniority can be a bad system. We've all seen old bumbling boys messing things up, but if we put in any other system of selecting chairmen, you'd have us politicians in the damnedest most constant political mess among ourselves you ever saw."

He winked a solemn eye. "And another thing. Never forget that a lot of times when a committee chairman seems to be indulging his own power in delaying or destroying legislation, there's actually a big secret body of support behind him in the House, the members of which hope the legislation will be killed but definitely do not want to participate publicly in the murder."

He shook his head and drank from his glass.

"One of the worst things now," he said, "is that we don't ever get home any more. Our real claim, of course, is that coming up for re-election every two years we're always the nearest thing there is to the representation of popular opinion. Maybe we are. But with these longer and longer sessions, it's hard to keep in touch, and it doesn't make it any easier getting elected."

He offered me another drink, but the bourbon had already come down several inches. I shook my head and he pushed in the cork hard and hid the bottle.

I glanced out of the window again. It was going to be a beautiful night outside, if the stars above the court meant anything.

"All set?" he asked.

We started out. The corridors seemed deserted. Far down the hall a man and a woman were coming out of an office together. There were some women with machines washing the endless marble of the halls.

"They must get dirt," I remarked, "from the shoes of constituents from all over the country."

"Plenty of it," the Congressman said.

Then, across the corridor the door opened and a man came out. He tested the lock behind him. My friend greeted him in a voice that sounded almost too gay in the empty hall.

"Hi, Jim."

The man looked tired. He was the young secretary of a Congressman, the sort of young man who might hope some-day to be a Congressman himself.

"They're trying to make it tough for Jim's boss in the primary. How's it going, Jim?"

And suddenly I saw that Jim looked as if he were almost ready to cry.

"They've got us licked," he said.

"Oh, no!"

"Yes," he said. "Bert knows it."

"Gosh, I'm sorry. Why, hell, he's made 'em a damn good Congressman. If he stays here, with his seniority—"

"Sure, sure," said Jim. "I know. We've said all that, but they've got Bert this time."

He hesitated.

"Course, I'm just saying this to you, but he wrote me. The only thing that's troubling him is his wife. She hasn't got any notion. She's just been appointed chairman of some kind of committee up at the Congressional Club. She likes Washington. She doesn't have any idea, and Bert's scared to tell her. He thinks it'll about kill her. She can't go back and hold up her head. She—"

"Oh, hell," said my Congressman not sympathetically.

The secretary was apologetic.

"You know how women—"

"Oh, for Christ' sake," the Congressman said. "Oh, for Christ' sake."

He shook his head.

"Well, give my love to Bert. I hope you're wrong."

We watched him go with a batch of campaign letters which he no longer believed would do any good.

"All Congressmen are fools," my friend said, "and their wives are worse. Nobody but a fool—" But he interrupted himself. "Come back in here, I've got something for you. Been wanting to give it to you for a long time."

We went in his office again and he pulled out a whole pack of photographs. Across one he scrawled my name and "With admiration and affection." I was a little surprised but grateful. But I would have been a little more grateful if he had not taken it out of the pile of nearly a hundred prints which I understood would be going to others for whom, I suspected, he would have equal affection and admiration.

The sad young secretary had disappeared when we went back into the hall, and only two drab women were working with their washing machines on the long dirty white floors. We went out beyond the policemen into the dark. Around the Capitol the night was as beautiful as its promise above the court.

VIII

Justice on First Street

I REMEMBERED the swarm around him.

"It is a good one if you live up to it," he said of the oath he had just administered to Harry Truman.

He was not robed as Chief Justice of the United States. He looked as if he had been working, when he was called, in the dark suit he wore. He was a big man, aging, and somehow he looked like a small-town family physician after a delivery. But he looked also as an American, I think, wants his Chief Justice, as the chief non-democratic official in the Republic, to seem—not too tidy, but human, intelligent and strong, with a tough dignity which can completely dispense with the necessity for pretension.

In the midst of politicians thinking fast in transition he seemed to embody the legend that our great judges are freed from the pressures which steadily surround politicians. The Court is quietest seeming when the nation is most noisy in contention. But the quietness may have violence in it and a robed contentiousness of its own which can be both funny and sad, too. Ambitions are not quite ended by eminence and security for life. At the final place of American decision differences may be more deeply felt even than in elections. And when a judge dies the Constitution itself may be altered as the alignments are altered in the nine who say what it is. So the perpetual quality of transition in American government was re-emphasized when Stone, who had presided over transition in April 1945, slipped into incoherence on the bench in April 1946. It was Easter Monday. The same malady of mental strain, a massive cerebral hemorrhage, had made American transition again.

I never saw Chief Justice Stone in his chambers. While he lived and presided, I never went up and watched the ritual of the judges coming to their great bench, as Stone himself is reported to have said, with a human understanding of the meaning of both grandeur and time, like nine black beetles in the Temple of Karnak. It is a good phrase, often quoted, but I had to follow the Chief Justice into the encyclopedia to understand that that temple was the one upon which the Egyptians outdid themselves in grandeur. And the Supreme Court Building, which Cass Gilbert designed for William Howard Taft, is even among the temples in Washington the one which seems shaped to a pretentiousness less like the glory of the Republic than like the stupendous, shining sort of theater the Publix-Paramount people might build if Congress gave them $9,000,000.

"It's the sort of grandeur," said a lawyer in the striped pants he had worn before the robed Judges, "that a king might want who was afraid he didn't look like a king at all unless he had on a crown."

Nothing in Washington quite equals it. The White House offices seem simple beside it. Even the Capitol, closely scrutinized, looks in comparison a little frayed and old-fashioned in its impressiveness. The very stone from which the Supreme Court Building is constructed has a glare about it like a dowager's diamonds. The lily is not only gilded but also set with jewels. And somehow it makes justice in the United States look like the sort of American lawyer who has made money so fast that he displays it in diamond rings on well manicured hands.

It would be difficult to think of a stranger, simpler looking group of men than those who work in its elegant paneled offices. Only one of the Justices of Stone's Court was born in a city—and that one in old, far-off, power-plagued Vienna;

the rest all first saw the light of day on an American farm or in a small town. Four of them had been, when younger, politicians who had run for office and got elected. Four of them had taught in law schools. Only one of them had been promoted from lower courts of the Federal judiciary. Their average age at the beginning of 1946 was fifty-eight; ten years before the average age was seventy-one. The Court is older than the Cabinet, but younger than chairman of the chief Congressional committees.

So far as I could see, Stone, before he died, looked only more elderly than he did at the bottom of the amphitheater full of freshmen in the Columbia Law School where among a couple of hundred others he tried unsuccessfully to teach me Real Property. I understand that Thomas E. Dewey, who was in that class, actually learned about Real Property as well as Criminal Law. I was more interested in the theater downtown than in the amphitheater on 116th Street. But then, as later, Chief Justice Stone was properly cast for a combination of good sense and simplicity.

It is probably impertinent to repeat the opinion of one critic that Stanley Reed is as exciting as his rimless pince-nez and black alpaca coat would indicate. He and his wife together probably belong to more ancestral societies than any other prominent couple in Washington. Those societies must have been more impressive back in Maysville, Kentucky, than in Washington, where more people are interested in the future than in the past. Certainly his colleague, Wiley Rutledge, who was also born on the Kentucky bank of the Ohio, is a plain seeming citizen. His wife was a schoolteacher in a mountain college where most of the students were both ignorant of and eager for the life ahead. I have seen Frank Murphy strolling bareheaded through Dupont Circle swinging hands with a pretty child. Sometimes Bill Douglas seemed to allow himself to be made unduly naïve by the bright boys who were always running him for President. Harold H. Burton somehow still seems Senatorial. Before Robert Jackson went off to prose-

cute war criminals (with the disapproval of at least one of
his colleagues) he had a bright eye and a gay manner off the
bench.

He was not always gay. It was he who loosed summer thun-
der above the storm in the Court, in 1946. But the deeper conflict seemed to me to dramatize two other able men. In 1937,
the conflict seemed quite clearly between the President and
the Court. In the 1940's, the fight was within the Court itself.
And under the Chief Justice, who was no mere umpire,
Frankfurter and Black personalized the question as to whether
the Court was commissioned to protect some of the people
from the aberrations of democracy or whether the Court
should, in the absence of the clearest violation of constitutional
liberties, trust the people themselves to move toward tolerance
and wisdom under their own steam. Of course, the question
is never quite that simple. Black was often as articulately
opposed to legislation by judges as Frankfurter was. But it was
a nice question—and an ancient one. In the one non-democratic branch of the American Government, Black and
Frankfurter each seemed entirely unlikely in the role he
played.

There are few, if any, abler men in Washington than Frankfurter and Black. I used to enjoy looking at Hugo Black. He
seems perfectly placed in the old house he owns overlooking
the Potomac in Alexandria where the South was sedately
settled before Washington was begun. In his garden there,
among intent Southerners and sympathetic strangers talking
of a South free of poll taxes and prejudices, he looks like the
romantic Southerner in person. He has the deceptively quiet
manner of a man who can be dangerous, which I have seen
in a good many Southern courthouses. There is an air of
indolence about him in spite of his hair-trigger mind.

Beside him, Felix Frankfurter is the man who once seemed
almost the symbol of intellectual leadership toward American
tolerance. He had been long before in Massachusetts the
scholar concerned in action for Vanzetti, the fish peddler,

and Sacco, the shoe edger, when cops and courts, Thayers and Lowells, seemed intent upon confusing admission of radicalism with proof of murder. He is a small man, perfectly dressed, who moves about restlessly in his chambers. His mind seems both emotional and precise. He can be persuasively logical and occasionally impatient. He always gives me the impression that he wants a world that is free and decorously orderly, too.

From their backgrounds a layman would have expected them to play reversed roles. Frankfurter, who was made to seem almost the protector of intolerance on the Court, had arrived in the United States, in 1894, as a little Jewish boy of twelve. By coincidence, in the same year, false anti-Semitic testimony convicted Dreyfus of treason in France. Black, the judicial foe of intolerance, had been willing when he was forty years old to accept membership in the Ku Klux Klan. It hardly seemed to make sense that it was Frankfurter who upheld the right of a determinedly intolerant little Pennsylvania town to require the children of members of the sect of Jehovah's Witnesses to salute the American flag. It seemed even stranger that it was Black, two years later, who was the leader of the "Liberal" revolt which anticipated the reversal of the decision and made Frankfurter look even more like a strange black reactionary on a new Rooseveltian Court.

The principal case decided then came from Black's own State of Alabama and the little town of Opelika, not far from Clay County where he was born. It is also not far from Phenix City where broad small-town moral notions permitted a wide-open red light district which threatened the venereal rate of American soldiers at Fort Benning just across the Chattahoochee River in Georgia. In the same area the same folk, who had permitted prostitution, wanted to eliminate proselyting by taxing tract-selling Jehovah's Witnesses.

Black said they couldn't.

Frankfurter said they could.

Back in 1940, when Frankfurter had upheld the right of a

town to require the children of Jehovah's Witnesses to salute the flag, the whole Court had been with him except Justice Stone. But in 1943, in a West Virginia case, foreshadowed by the Black revolt, the majority of the Court had swung the other way. Frankfurter stood his ground in eloquent re-emphasis of his conviction that the non-democratic Supreme Court should only with the greatest reluctance correct the follies of a people democratically made. Eloquent as he was, however, he did not state his philosophy as eloquently as West Virginians themselves had done long before. At the close of the American Revolution the rude frontiersmen of what is now West Virginia had put it in a petition asking for State-hood separate from the Old Dominion.

"Some of our fellow citizens may think," those old fellows wrote, "that we are not yet able to conduct our affairs, and consult our interest; but if our society is rude, much wisdom is not necessary to supply our wants, and a fool can sometimes put on his clothes better than a wise man can do it for him."

Mr. Justice Frankfurter followed those frontiersmen in his belief that liberty was more secure, left to the people, than it ever would be protected from Washington by a court.

"You've got to remember," said my lawyer in the striped pants, "that there is only one basic legal question. It's the old puzzle of minority rights and majority rule. It gets tied up like the old business of the chicken and the egg. I don't think we ever really want to decide it. Most of us—even legal scholars—take our sides depending upon the result we want at the particular time. We want both our democracy and our liberties, and sometimes they run bam into each other."

Justice Stone was the last of the famous nine old men of the old Court. His new Liberalism seemed at least as dramatic as Frankfurter's seeming new reaction. Old Senator George Norris, who had opposed Stone's nomination as Justice by Coolidge as the addition of another representative of corporate wealth, had recanted in admiration of Stone's comparative liberalism when Roosevelt made him Chief Justice. But those

Nine Old Men had, by their lights, been protecting liberty, too, with what seemed a quick emphasis on the rights of property. They had sometimes protected civil liberties besides corporate ones, and under the same philosophy.

Its critics—including Justice Stone himself—charged that it was making law instead of interpreting it, and doing that within the security of a Court on which Judges are responsible, beyond appointment, to nobody but themselves. They did not need to look over their shoulders at the people as Presidents and Congressmen did. They do not now. They continue while Congress changes. Justices may not serve quite so long now with the new retirement privileges which almost alone resulted from Roosevelt's fight in 1937. In history, Justices have served for average periods of sixteen years.

Judges, being human and appointed by human Presidents, may decide the law of the future in terms of the convictions of the past. Sometimes, of course, as the wits have suggested, the Judges may follow the election returns in their decisions. They do not have to do so. At any time the Constitution may be, as Chief Justice Hughes once said, what the Judges say it is. And in a moving democracy, the Judges are always the men of yesterday's selection. They can make law in a proper freedom from pressure. They can also make it without any responsibility to the people who are governed by their interpretations of the law.

"The big question does not change," my lawyer said.

The old Ku Kluxer held the Constitution up as shield between the minority group and the intolerant majority of a town.

The Jew, who was one of the first to see the hideous threat to democracy in the bloody march of Hitler, believed that the fight for tolerance should be made at the elections and in the legislatures, not in the necessarily secure but essentially non-democratic Court.

It is not a new question, or a single case. Frankfurter brought his attitude out of the past when he was one of those radicals of the law, nurtured like a serpent, some said, at the bosom of American conservatism in the Harvard Law School. As a matter of fact, it was when he was in the middle of the fight to save Sacco and Vanzetti from a Massachusetts intolerance which seemed to him determined to use the electric chair as a weapon with which to attack freedom, that he first wrote the essence of the opinion which made him appear a strange new reactionary himself twenty years later.

He distrusted even then a Court which invoked the Constitution to protect the people from themselves. He doubted that a Court which would declare unconstitutional a Nebraska law which forbade the teaching of German in Nebraska would hesitate to outlaw other laws in terms of the Judges' own notions of the propriety of legislation but under the name of constitutionality.

"The real battles of Liberalism are not won in the Supreme Court," he said.

And he added: "Only a persistent, positive translation of the liberal faith into the thoughts and acts of the community is the real reliance against the unabated temptation to straitjacket the human mind."

There is nothing in the Constitution which prohibits the people from indulging in folly by legislative act. Even unintelligent intolerance may not be against the law. Frankfurter should not be alone in remembering that liberty's name has been invoked by men who sit where he sits now to deny minimum wage legislation and other laws now accepted as neither unconstitutional nor strange to our system. It was a philosophic lady on the way to the guillotine a good many years ago in France who commented on the fact that crimes can be committed in liberty's name. And the price to democracy can be high. This young Court may seem old again to America, as it has already seemed quarrelsome. Even the old Court was young once. Only democracy stays the age of the people.

The Court is not strange in Washington. The temptation

to take a parental attitude toward the people is often most clearly seen in the executive departments. Both Supreme Court Justices and Cabinet officers can with all nobility and patriotism adopt an attitude toward the democracy of the United States best described by the American phrase "papa knows best." And often that attitude is not eliminated by the fact that its exercise is hidden in the jargon of departmental orders and the elaborate legal logic of Supreme Court decisions.

Life in a democracy is a good deal more complex than logic in a court. Not even the great contentions are always the simple ones. The simply stated dilemma of majority rule and minority rights is a greater puzzle even than it seems. The Supreme Court itself has been a tiny minority effective against the President and the Congress. Other minorities have been effective, too. And sometimes majorities have been actually fictitious, for all their countable numbers. The majority of the people, who fought a victorious war about it, their Presidents, Congresses and Courts have never been willing to safeguard the rights of the Negroes which they wrote into the Constitution. Maybe this Court begins that process. But the failure has been not so much the accomplishment of the minority in the white South as the agreement of the secretly willing majority in the white North. There are other cases. (Actually, the minorities in the Jehovah's Witnesses cases were the misguided lawmakers in the little towns and the States which made the repressive laws. In America, under the Court, a majority of the people who were aware of the matter were almost certainly opposed to the intolerant regulations.)

What rules in America even in the decisions of the Court is militancy not majority. And militant Liberals are as willing that the interpretation of the Constitution serve ends that they believe to be good as militant reactionaries were before them. As the American operates in the Town Hall or the United States Supreme Court, the Constitution—even democracy—may seem beside the point.

I remember walking down the almost endless white steps of the huge building to First Street which runs between the Court and the Capitol. Looking back at its almost gawdy, obese grandeur it was amusing to remember that old man Taft, who accomplished the erection of the temple, had said, "I love judges and I love courts. They are my ideals on earth of what we shall meet afterward in Heaven under a just God." Somehow Heaven has always been represented on this earth in over-elegant terms. Maybe it will be as glittering as the best Mr. Taft could do on earth with Cass Gilbert's help. Both Mr. Taft and his architect are in Heaven now, but their elegant ideal remains. It still seems to me more pretentious than judicial.

I walked toward the House Office Building, only one long block away. It is as democratic as the insistent constituents from the contentious diversity of the continent who fill its corridors. But on the way I stopped at the Library of Congress, where, not the robed Justices, but one of my oldest friends keeps the Constitution. He is one of those rare things, a Washingtonian (though, just to make it hard, he lives now across the line in Chevy Chase, Maryland). Years ago when I was in the press gallery I used to join him at the Library and we would walk to the Methodist Building for lunch across the place where the Supreme Court Building has risen since. The Methodists, then, were fighting a losing fight to keep prohibition in the Constitution, but they served good food. And even in those days, David Mearns was a fixed bureaucrat, though he is only forty-five now. And one of his jobs through the years has been to help keep, now as Director of the Reference Department, the sacred parchment body of the Constitution of the United States.

He and some other bureaucrats of erudition, when there seemed danger of bombing, took the Constitution off and hid it. It seemed a little materialistic to me that they hid the document, whose meaning bombs could not destroy, beside America's gold hoard in the United States Bullion Depository in Kentucky. Other revered papers of our tradition were hidden in other safe interior places. One of them, I know, was Lexington, Virginia. I am glad some of our rich past was hidden there, too, as a military secret. Robert E. Lee taught there after participating in the process of trying to interpret the Constitution by force of arms. General George Marshall, who led our military forces in our last war in defense of democracy, went to school there. It is an old town and green, with a smooth college campus running up a swift hill to the square white columns behind which Lee taught.

All the old documents are back in the Library now. The Constitution lies faded but safe in its special case. But I know that in the hiding places the Constitution and the other precious pieces of our law and our tradition were at least as secure as they ever are in the bright-to-blinding elegance of the Supreme Court.

IX

Comet in a Vault

Not all the constituents of a republic are people. Indeed, as the Supreme Court has discovered, the force of an idea may be more important than the determinations of the majority. Even Congressmen sometimes have to face facts as well as voters. And, however immune to enlightenment it sometimes may seem to be, no government in the world has so armed itself with knowledge as the Government of the United States in its gray-massed, over-ornamented Library of Congress. Built after the pattern of a great foreign opera house and decorated in accordance with the taste that prevailed in the interior decorating department of John Wanamaker's department store in the 1890's, the Library is the temple of knowledge in a technical age which can be political still. All the learning of man is there, and the only problem for both politicians and people, scholars and scientists, is getting it out.

Indeed, behind bronze turtles and bronze mermaids, the Library of Congress seems almost designed for defense. It has pneumatic tubes for carrying to Senators legislative material and detective stories. But more policemen, with sharper eyes, scrutinize ordinary visitors than watched them in the Pentagon during the war. Of course, somebody might carry off the Constitution or a much demanded copy of *Forever Amber*. But the building itself seems designed not merely as a tower of ivory turned gray but as a sort of citadel and not merely a dispensary of knowledge. Long before the Constitution and the Gutenberg Bible were carried into hiding from possible

96

war bombs, the office of the Librarian was hidden deep within the interior of the Library without a single window looking out on Washington or America.

"A painted vault," Archibald MacLeish, as Librarian, called his office before he escaped to what momentarily must have seemed the fresher air of the State Department.

"I had until a few days ago," his successor, Luther Evans, said, "an office on the west front looking out on the Capitol. Now I have moved to an office in the interior of the building, resplendently designed by a nineteenth century architect as the office of the Librarian of Congress."

Such seclusion does not insure serenity. More than any other in America the office carries with it the responsibility for the application of learning to action in the government of America. Supreme Court Justices may guard the determinations of the past. The Librarian of Congress is not only the custodian of the American record but the collector of the materials from which presumably America can intelligently shape its directions. In so important a purpose, he is protected, as Supreme Court Justices are, with life tenure. Within his vault, from which he cannot see a constituent or a reader, or even a politician walking on First Street, he can remain as long as he lives or pleases to serve in the direction of the availability of knowledge to a government in an age in which monographs on physics may turn out to be more controlling than either elections or Supreme Court decisions. And yet, I think, Librarians of Congress, like Supreme Court Justices sometimes, even Congressmen occasionally, can seem frustrated when they are most eager. The vault can sometimes seem like a cell. Sometimes even six million books can seem a dull mass like the granite Library which contains them.

The Librarian needs help, and he has it. His seclusion is sometimes a good deal less than absolute. After all, the Library belongs to the Congress; and the Congress, in steady theory, belongs to the people. The Library is the standing exhibit in refutation of the endless charge that Congressmen are insistent ignoramuses. It was also, until recently, in the pay of its staff an institution in proof of the fact that Congress is often stingier with its own agencies than with those of the executive branch of government. Some of its more important services are supported still by private endowments and not by appropriations. But Congressional pride and power in possession remain.

The chairman of the House Committee on Library is relatively young Donald L. O'Toole of Brooklyn, who had enough knowledge to be re-elected as Democrat over the opposition of the Brooklyn Democratic organization. The senior Republican member of the House Committee, C. W. Bishop of Cartersville, Illinois, puts in the *Congressional Directory* that his nickname is "Runt" and that he has been a tailor, a coal miner, a telephone lineman and a professional football and baseball player.

On the Senate committee, the Librarian has the supervision and assistance of such scholars as Kenneth McKellar of Tennessee and Theodore Gilmore Bilbo of Mississippi. With the assistance of the Library of Congress (which any member of Congress can have) Senator McKellar has written a book, *Tennessee Senators As Seen by One of Their Successors.* (Incidentally, his boss and Tennessee's boss, E. H. Crump of Memphis, still rejoices biographically in the fact that as Congressman he was a regent of the Government's scientific Smithsonian Institution.) And Senator Bilbo, presumably without the assistance of the Library of Congress, was the author of the widely and critically noticed "Dear Dago," "Dear Kike" and "Dear Nigger" letters.

One of the purposes of the Library of Congress, Luther Evans wrote of world affairs from his painted vault, is participation in the eternal opposition of enlightenment to "suspicion, ignorance and parochialism" wherever they appear. One of its needs, suggested Dr. Vannevar Bush, who, as Director of the Office of Scientific Research and Development, directed the application of knowledge to warfare in an age of fission and physics, is technical devices to make it possible for scientists (and presumably also statesmen) to find for use the knowledge which the Library possesses. I think Luther Evans may need a vault, painted or not, in the job of collecting the world's knowledge for American enlightenment which lies not only beside the Capitol and the Supreme Court, not only between Pennsylvania Avenue and East Capitol Street, but between Bush and Bilbo in the American mind and the American spirit.

I like Luther Evans. Somehow he does not look like a librarian. I say that without derogation. Nobody in America has been better served by librarians than I have. In Washington I found no agency more amiable and intelligent at the same time in doing its job. I am sure I plagued the Library's people. I am also sure that they produced quickly the facts that I wanted. There is a man named Robert C. Gooch, chief of the General Reference and Bibliography Division, who found quickly for me such diverse pieces of intelligence as the correct spelling of the name of One-eye Connelly and the exact year in which Andrew Johnson put down his scissors and took up statesmanship. (Even Gooch could not make certainty in America where certainty does not exist: no decision about spelling ever seems to have been made by the DuPonts or duPonts of Delaware for a member of which Dupont Circle in Washington is named.)

Nevertheless, even as friend and debtor of librarians, I know that the legend still persists that librarians are people somehow less lusty than politicians and even less imaginative than professors. The notion still lingers, in Washington and outside it, that librarians are gray creatures who catalogue other people's books for other people's reading. As a class in the catalogue of American condescension they are often regarded as people with a predilection for acne in adult life, with complexions which acquire the grayness of scurrying gray bookbugs. Male and female, they are remembered as sour virgins beyond the period when virginity might be something precious to be possessed and has become rather something preserved by bad embalming. In the stereotype, bibliography and biliousness seem always to go together. It is strange to remember that in Washington some Senators do look like that, and that some librarians seem as hearty as all politicians are supposed to be.

Luther Evans is the son of a railroad section foreman who was ready to match his muscles with the biggest blacks among his laborers in Texas. I doubt that Luther now could pick up a crosstie and carry it. To be honest, there seems to be a good deal of pudginess in his two hundred pounds. His hands are more accustomed to the handling of incunabula than crossties. But before he came to the Library of Congress he had not only worked his way through several colleges, beginning with the University of Texas, which was fortunately located in the next county to that Bastrop County in which he was born.

As a young man he had also (I hope Senator Bilbo will not mind) accepted an entirely rhetorical invitation for somebody to speak against the Ku Klux Klan at a Ku Klux meeting in Woolridge Park in Austin, Texas. He survived. He does not take full credit for the fact that the Klan did not. Also, between studies for his doctorate, he worked his way across the Atlantic a couple of times. He made, as Southerner and scholar, a study of America's black colony in the Virgin Islands. And he was a professor at Princeton when Harry Hopkins found him and made him a WPA worker. There were no shovels to lean on in his WPA job. He was the head of an undertaking called the Historical Records Survey which went into all the courthouses and most of the cubbyholes of America to find the forgotten, neglected and often precious pieces of the American record. Archibald MacLeish found him in that job. He came to the Library only a short while after MacLeish did, in 1939. He succeeded MacLeish in 1945.

The meaning of the Library in America seems to me clearer in its men than in its books. The books are important—and "books" includes not only books but papers and maps, pictures, photographs, manuscripts, music, monographs, documents and records, all the works of the learned and a great many of the works of the merely literate. It is the largest library in the world which MacLeish, before he departed, hoped might be also the best. Its shelves are 414 miles long, more than twice the distance from the Boston Athenaeum to the New York Public Library. And even when its most precious possessions were hidden from bombs in the United States Bullion Depository at Fort Knox, in Kentucky, and in college libraries, in Virginia and Ohio, the proposal merely to count the items that remained was postponed in wartime because such a census would require 10,926 man-days. In terms of its collected items America's knowledge has multiplied at least twenty times as fast as Americans have multiplied themselves.

The problem of knowledge in government is human still. And the meaning of the knowledge collected by America can be more clearly seen in the living men who have occupied the painted vault than in the books which they possess. Luther Evans was not even born when old Dr. Herbert Putnam, the present Librarian Emeritus, came to the Library in 1899. Old man Putnam was young man Putnam then, not quite thirty-eight, younger on his arrival than either MacLeish or Evans was when those gentlemen followed him to the same job. He may have seemed very young then to old men about the Library. And relatively, even today, the Library of Congress itself is young still. Its age can be counted in a swift succession. Putnam's father was the publisher of Washington Irving, and Irving received the personal blessing of George Washington himself on George Washington's first Inauguration Day. That was eleven years before there was any beginning of a Library of Congress—which was to be burned by the British and begun again by the replenishing purchase of Thomas Jefferson's library in 1815. (Items: 1. There were Congressmen then, not so much eager for knowledge as afraid of it, who opposed the purchase of the Jefferson library not merely as extravagance but because of supposedly irreligious volumes it contained. 2. Congress paid Jefferson $23,950 for 6,487 books, a smaller average price than the Library now spends each year in caring for its rare and precious books.)

Putnam stayed in the vault for forty years. From a distance, but with no sense of complete detachment, he has, I gather, watched it since, and not always with approval. He collected. Also he presided over a great period of expanding knowledge and of the multiplying production of the world's presses. Before he retired in 1939, his Library (which was also Congress's) had more than five million books and pamphlets, well over a million maps and views, more than a million pieces and volumes of music, a hundred thousand volumes of newspapers. An intellectual aristocrat like Mr. Putnam had a right to be proud of the collection he passed on to his successor.

There was just one little detail the arriving MacLeish discovered which, I suspect, dismayed him more than the critical disappointment of the organized American librarians who felt that a professional librarian should have been named instead of MacLeish. Dr. Putnam had been a great librarian. He was, as MacLeish recorded, a "well-loved, strong-minded, charming and particular" gentleman. He had "remarkable qualities" as the American collector of knowledge for Congress and America. While he was Librarian decisions on all details had to be made in the painted vault. And the Librarian handled all the details without even a full-time secretary of his own. But the detail which impressed the arriving MacLeish was that more than a million and a half volumes in the Library (about a fourth of the total) had not been catalogued so that any reader could find them.

Luther Evans, who participated in it, has described MacLeish's "quinquennium" as the "brush of the comet." I expect it was nothing less than that. Hardly anybody ever came to Washington with so many gifts as MacLeish possessed. I am not sure his departure was so much his own light going out in a progressive reduction of illumination as a part of the general twilight which followed the war. In his own generation he was as much the aristocrat as Putnam was in his. He had made the Yale football squad, and Phi Beta Kappa. The year he graduated he led his class at the Harvard Law School. (At a Senate committee hearing he had to tell ex-Senator Bennett Champ Clark that you do not go to the Harvard Law School not to work.) He had war service as a soldier, which he could only minimize by the heroic death of his brother as a flyer. He gave up success at the law in a Boston law firm with a resounding name, to go write poetry on the Rue du Bac. And even as poet he won the Pulitzer Prize.

He is good-looking in a long-faced half-Harvard, half-Lincolnesque way. His father, he says, was a "cold, tall, rigorous man of very beautiful speech." His mother came from "very passionate people with many mad among them." He is their son. He is disdainful of mediocrity in its presence and passionately democratic in his oratory and his poetry. In Washington he sometimes seemed arrogant to ordinary democratic people, and at the same time a dangerous leveling radical to some conservative Senators who, like Bennett Clark, had difficulty understanding his books. Some of those books are not simple. Neither is MacLeish. But when he came to the Library of Congress a comet seemed to be required.

With Evans beside him and with the advice of professional librarians, even if he was not one himself, MacLeish undertook to make it possible for people to find the books and not merely for the government to collect them. Undoubtedly, at the beginning some of the poet's metaphors as to what the new Librarian wanted the Library to be sounded a good deal more poetic than practical. But if he sought to make the Library "a city of the mind" (with life in its streets), he also sought more administrative order. He consulted with the staff he had inherited.

"They were not, I should note, the most successful meetings I can recall," MacLeish said later. "One or two of the more articulate of my older colleagues approached the discussion in the spirit of the senior benches at a faculty meeting: change was undesirable, and any discussion that might lead to change was in doubtful taste. The Library of Congress was too big and too old—above all, too old—to ask itself what it was doing and why and for what purpose."

Those were the days when the brush of the comet was a broom. But brilliant as their lights may be, I doubt that for the long term comets make good administrators. MacLeish brought passion and disdain and purpose to perhaps the most charming and erudite bureaucracy in Washington. But it must never be forgotten that he became Librarian one month to the day after Hitler marched into Poland. It must not be forgotten either that MacLeish was a voice before he became a librarian. It was hardly to be expected that the reform of the Library would alone satisfy such a man when other people were about the business of profoundly altering the world.

He was, as Luther Evans says, Librarian for a "quinquennium"; but the five years were shared by the Library with other agencies and efforts not merely to collect knowledge and make it available (take it or leave it) to people but to use facts and words as weapons in a cause. I think that at last he found the "painted vault" in "the city of the mind" a sort of prison. It was such a prison that even the State Department seemed escape from it. (Congressmen and Senators whom he often puzzled must have been puzzled most of all when he gave up a $10,000-a-year lifetime job.) But collected knowledge must have seemed a very petty thing beside a chance to work as a man for the collective security of the world. But somehow— perhaps not for the world, but for MacLeish—in the State Department that failed, too. So far as government was concerned, he was gone. In those last days I recall seeing him in his big office in the State Department, and in some uncataloguable way he seemed very much alone.

"It is obviously too soon," Luther Evans said, "to form a final judgment of his achievement."

I remember talking to Evans, a long way from the painted vault, in the men's bar of the Hotel Roosevelt in New York. I had tracked him down at the hotel on a tip from his full-time secretary. He did not look like the captive of the vault. His place between Bush and Bilbo did not make him look harassed. He looked like a well-fed professor but one who could laugh. Looking at him, I was critical only of the fact that he preferred rye to bourbon.

"Certainly," Luther said, "the Library was a great institution when he first came to it. It is quite as certain that it was even greater when he left."

He counted MacLeish's qualities and the things he had done.

"The outstanding characteristic of that brilliant episode," he said, "is not the fact that so much was consummated in so short a time, but rather that there is so little to repent."

The comet had passed. The brilliant episode was over. The processes of better administration and faster cataloguing which MacLeish and Evans had begun together went on. But I wondered if even the acceleration of 1939 might not seem slow once more beside growing collections and greater demands for even greater speed still in the pace of knowledge to the people who wanted it. Long before he published it in the *Atlantic*, the *Atlantic's* editor, Edward Weeks, had told me about the thinking Vannevar Bush had been doing about devices which might make it possible for scientists to secure quickly from the Library not merely a book but a fact. An essential piece of research might be lost in a book. If men were ever hurrying desperately for knowledge again as they had been during the war, it might take too long to find the essential facts on one page buried in a volume. And even in the war rush Bush had suggested machines which indicated needs which might grow as knowledge expanded. By more careful cataloguing, coding and photography, he suggested that a scientist might get from machinery in a Library not whole books but photographs of the printed paragraphs he sought. It was conceivable that beside such machines, the new Library of 1946 might seem as laggard as the so recently so old-seeming Library of 1939.

Luther Evans does not look old-fashioned. There is, of course, no law against his getting old, and no law that he must leave the Library even if he does get old. But even in a technical age his faith is not merely that the Library must be for people but that more and more its dependence must be upon people, too.

"If the Library of Congress," he said, "is to be a hand to lead in knowledge, rather than frantic fingers to clutch at it, there must be a human development concurrent with the development of material—more sorters and searchers and accessioners, more cataloguers and classifiers and shelf-listers, more bibliographers and subject specialists and regionalists."

It sounded as if the technical age needed more drawers of water than ever. But the well is deeper. Maybe the thirst grows.

"Until Dr. Bush's 'memex' or other 'cheap complex devices of great reliability' come on the market," Luther said, "we must look to persons for the governance of these vast accumulations. So far, the genius of invention has been more completely successful in proliferating records than in creating automata for identifying, digesting and interpreting them."

The records had been proliferated certainly. The Congress itself produces more printed pages in a year than the whole Library of Congress contained when the British burned it. Even Senator Bilbo, by merely taking the books to which he is entitled from the Government Printing Office, may quickly acquire a bigger library than Jefferson had to sell. I thought of the millions of books old man Putnam had collected and the whole new annex, bigger than the ornate gray Library, which he had built to hold them. It was not difficult to understand the piles of uncatalogued books MacLeish had found. And I knew that in wartime our own safer spies of the Office of Strategic Services, who worked in offices provided for them in the Library, had not found its collection of books and maps adequate to their need. Dr. Bush's scientists had found it hard to find all the facts they needed even when, sometimes, the books they needed were there.

It was still a lot of books for Congressmen to have collected in the Library which always first belongs to them. And some of them use it. The biographers of both Andrew Johnson, the tailor, and Harry Truman, the haberdasher, make much of the time each spent as member of Congress among the Library's books. But the Library is not crowded by members of Congress. They can stay in their own offices and read. Indeed, at one time at least, the seldom-used, gold-ceiled, special reading room for Senators was, with no intentional significance, turned over to those working in connection with the Library's services to the blind.

That day in New York, Luther Evans turned to less profound aspects of his duties. I remember that he laughed at himself over his rye. He had come to New York to speak to the Librarians Club. His amusement was a milestone. Times in the Library of Congress had certainly changed since Dr. Putnam personally directed the handling of five million books without even a full-time sceretary in his office. Luther has one. She is one of those well trained Washington secretaries, and knows better than to place any confidence in her boss when he goes out of town. She had written down every train Luther had to take and every detail to which he had to attend. It was all neatly catalogued so that even he as mere boss could not fail to follow her directions. But Luther laughed, a short characteristic professorial laugh.

"She forgot," he said, "to ask whether it was formal or not. It is. And I've got to go over to Lexington Avenue to rent a dress suit."

I walked over that way with him. I think he said it was going to cost him five dollars with a clean shirt and a necktie thrown in. It seemed cheap at the price. Also, it indicated that all cataloguing, maybe all knowledge even, is subject to human fault even in the painted vault of the Librarian of Congress.

But I had a hunch that somehow old Dr. Putnam would have arrived with his dress suit without secretarial assistance. And that MacLeish probably, under the circumstances, would not have worn one. He would, however, have made a stirring speech on the dignity of mankind—and would have given his secretary disdainful hell when he got back to Washington. Luther is Librarian at a time when few faiths or fashions are fixed and a man who means to serve must meet change without rigidity.

Knowledge is certainly power. We must have it where we can reach it. But not only Librarians of Congress but all of us in America are somewhere in the vast knowledge of an age of presses and research still somehow caught between Bush and Bilbo. The knowledge is there for the people and the politicians as well as the scholars and scientists. But sometimes Dr. Bush cannot get to it quickly enough, and often, Bilbo on the Library's committee does not seem to be aware of its existence at all.

I hope Luther's suit was a good fit.

X

The Dull and the Departing

HE KNEW the problems of bureaucracy, young Henry Kruger said. He told a story about them once which I repeated after dinner that night among bureaucrats at Lauchlin Currie's house, which sat on the high banks of the Potomac west of Washington. Young Kruger, when he told it, was assistant to the permanent secretary-general of the International Association of Lions Clubs. But he had been an F.B.I. agent and, some years before, he had been playing around in the Middle West with some local police.

One of the policemen, he said, was an expert at shooting a pistol with cardboard over the sights. But the practice was interrupted by a call from a filling station. A car had just been there with a machine gun on the back seat. They found the car at a restaurant. Kruger stood at one side by some store windows while two policemen engaged the driver in talk. The driver began to resist, and one of the policemen knocked him down. The man grabbed for his gun and Kruger, from where he stood, let him have it, shooting from the wrist.

"Did you hit him?" a Washington Lion asked.

"I blew half his head off," Kruger said casually. "He lived a little while calling for his girl, and we got one of the nurses to pretend she was his girl."

He had been a man named Greene, somehow related to the Dillinger group of gangsters. But that was not the point of the story. The point was that when Kruger drove the gangster's car to a near-by town, he couldn't collect $2.40 for the gasoline he put in it because he had forgotten to secure a signed receipt.

The bureaucrats at Currie's house, which was decorated to recall the time when he had been a Presidential emissary to the Chinese, laughed at that one. But it was not so very silly. Randolph Paul, who was then the tax expert of the Treasury, told some strange bureaucratic items from the center of the fiscal life of the Republic. And Currie that day, as Assistant Director of the Foreign Economic Administration, had had to restrain a bureaucratic assistant who wanted to fight out once and for all a quarrel over handling foreign directives with the State Department. It was a serious question, undoubtedly, but it had risen in this case over the failure of the State Department to put Ex-Lax on a list of exportable commodities. Important as the matter was to Ex-Lax, and indignant as Currie's subordinate was over the highhandedness of the State Department, Currie felt that somehow the interdepartmental issue ought not to be fought out over a laxative.

But a good many such fights do come at the insistence of business. There are also a good many citizens who come to government with a vocabulary as restricted as that of the Central American general mentioned that night by Lieutenant Colonel Corrin Strong of Lend-Lease's bureaucracy in uniform. The Central American's full English vocabulary was, "I want." It sufficed. There were then—as now—plenty of strange people around bureaucracy and plenty of strange people in it. Indeed, it took all kinds of people to make the number of civilian government employees when the number in Washington rose to 284,000, and the number in the country, including workers in arms factories and navy yards as well as clerks, reached three million. Not only have Lions Clubs been hearing speeches about that. Some Senators have been screaming about it, too. It will remain a problem in a government which hoped to cut a million employees off the rolls in the year after victory and still expected to have a million more than it had before war in Europe began.

Since that night Currie and I have left the government. And that may have been good riddance for the Republic. But America needs to be at least as concerned about some of the others who have left as it is about the mass which remains. Bureaucracy can be not merely costly; it can be costly and well worth the price. Little government is not the solution of increasing problems. But big government can—indeed, sometimes now it seems almost designed to—become a sort of Indian reservation for the dull and the insecure. As citizen and taxpayer, I went back to Washington to look at the pattern of bureaucracy which remains.

"Sometimes ideas, like people, get decrepit," my friend, who is still a bureaucrat, said when he drove me down to the building of the Civil Service Commission.

And it was strange, looking at the old Doric building, to remember that when Theodore Roosevelt as a young fellow in the Eighties marched in its direction—ready to show his big teeth, not smiling, to politicians—it had seemed young, too, like TVA in our times. It seems now more statistical than stirring. The crusade has ended up in the filing cases. Old political patronage, with a cigar in its mouth and the smell of rye whisky on its breath, may be gone forever. But the Civil Service Commission itself smells like old people now. It is less like the symbol of an efficient America operating on merit than like aging and protected mediocrity in the mass.

That is not quite true. Some of the mediocrity is young. And a good deal of the mass is not mediocre. The need for men of merit was never greater in the history of the merit system. But somehow the drama of merit seems to have disappeared. The old building emphasizes it. A plaque on one of the fat columns, holding weight which in technical times is left to steel, said that it had been begun under Andrew Jackson, whose outmoded and barbaric notion had been that the jobs should go to the swarming lusty fellows who followed his political fortunes to Washington. The plaque also said that Mr. Lincoln's second inaugural ball had been held in the building. That must have been an evening of ladies and music a little more than a month before Lincoln was shot in a theater. (Maybe even then preoccupied officials at the ball were thinking of reconversion in the prospect of peace.) But no signs of drama or history, dancing or ceremony stays in the halls. History has grown old. The old vital reform of Civil Service is a fixed system, and its triumph looks merely dull.

On the walls upstairs, the portrait of Theodore Roosevelt seems in a long line of photographs of ex-Commissioners, like those in a family album, to be only one of the pictures of the dead. And the living around them do not seem young. Not only were there elderly clerks about, but Harry B. Mitchell, of Montana, Democratic president of the Commission, who had been in office for twelve years and no longer listed his age in *Who's Who*, was old enough to have a son in the United States Senate. Born sometime in Scotland, he was a practicing printer in 1887. Mrs. Benton McMillin, his Democratic colleague who arrived in office with him in 1933, had presided as First Lady in the Governor's Mansion of Tennessee in 1899.

I had come to see Arthur Flemming, the young Republican member, who, by virtue of the condition of his arteries and his muscles, apparently runs the Commisson for the Democrats. Mr. Flemming does the talking for the Commission before Congressional committees. He gets around town, from agency to agency, from the Capitol to the White House. He has come up fast. When he was appointed to the Commission, in 1939, having been a Washington newspaperman and a Washington professor, he was only thirty-four. Only one younger Commissioner had ever been appointed. That was Theodore Roosevelt. Mr. Flemming likes to remember that. Indeed, in a Washington where most men dream and the rest have sharp tongues, some have suggested that he lingers overlong upon the similar beginnings in Washington of the two youngest Civil Service Commissioners.

Theodore Roosevelt's job may have involved more reluctant politicians less ready to accept notions of merit when they had deserving Democrats or deserving Republicans who wanted jobs. There were only about 120,000 jobs in the Federal service in the whole country when Roosevelt came to town, and only a part of them were subject to his guardianship. There are more than twice as many as that around Arthur Flemming, in the District of Columbia area alone. The old converted mansions in the old elegant neighborhoods between Connecticut and Massachusetts Avenues are bulging boarding houses full of girls. The beards of the last century are gone. The service has become increasingly feminine since the first statutory recognition of the employment of women (top pay $600 a year) during the manpower shortages of the Civil War. Invention has made Civil Service increasingly technical. Congress and the people have multiplied its tasks. And the more bureaucrats the people and the Congress authorize, the more they complain of the numbers, as if somehow the employees slip in while the people and Congress are not looking. Some of the girls are worth looking at, and some look as if Theodore Roosevelt himself might have hired them when they, incredibly, were young, too.

Flemming was tired, but young tired. He looks like no roaring Roosevelt. In his blue serge and dark tie, with his dark hair graying above his pleasant face, he is almost the picture of the better bureaucrat, industrious, informative, energetic. The statistics are at his hand. He is friendly and persuasive about presenting them. As head of the war recruitment program of a technical government in a technical war, he had in one year directed the placement of 2,700,000 people on the public payroll. Congress authorizes the employment, Civil Service merely finds the people—generally only little people. The big jobs are filled above it without its initiation even when it has to give its approval. Finding people was not always easy. Now the job was reducing jobs. Getting rid of people is not always easy, either. Flemming was leading in that program, too, as the active agent of his older and presumably more weary colleagues. He had been all day on The Hill discussing the Administration's proposals for pay raises for government employees. He talked about it.

Like every other American at that hour, government employees wanted more money; and the Administration was prepared to give it to them. But it was not entirely simple. The workers at the bottom got the most sympathy, as they and their friends have the most votes, though comparatively they were getting the highest wages.

"In one Georgia town," Flemming said, "we had some complaint because the janitor of the Post Office was making more money than the cashier of the bank."

Except for some hourly workers and a few district attorneys, Federal pay is uniform in rich States and poor ones. And everywhere the big mass of bureaucracy is in the lower brackets of Federal wages which have usually been higher than similar private pay around them. More than two-thirds of those on the payroll when the war ended received less than $2,300 a year.

"Or you can put it," said Flemming, "that eighty-eight per cent are getting $3,640 or less."

It seems strange that sympathy should be most justified above that point or that, at least, the problem of the government in buying an efficient public service should begin there. The management of the mass begins above the eighty-eight per cent. The best technicians in the Republic of the machine age are there. And at the top, for their direction, there were only 247 men in the executive branch of the whole big government in the United States who got over $9,800. Some of the men at the top got their pictures in the papers and could at least hope for public plaudits. But the pay for administrators, superior technicians, and managers outside the government had skyrocketed, while only three per cent of the presumed best in bureaucracy got more than $5,000 a year. Many of them are excellent. Not all of them were sticking around. Losing the best might turn out to be even a greater public ex-

travagance than keeping too many of the dull who generally
do not depart.

In framing his hopes, Mr. Flemming has no great gifts for
striking language. His craft, I presume, is lucidity in personnel
procedures. He had a program:

Better men had to get better pay.

"If you raise their pay," I asked him, "how do you know
you're going to get better people and not merely keep the old
ones—some of whom are pretty old—at more pay?"

"You won't have to raise them," he said. "They're per-
missive raises at the top."

I knew, however, that they would go up, pretty much all
along the line. That might keep some excellent men from leaving. It would not make certain that the dull at the top—and
there are some dull ones there—would be replaced. It is an old
government, and anybody who has ever been in an old business understands that difficulty.

"Pay is not all," he said. "The public servant must be put in
his proper niche in the nation's hall of fame."

Mr. Flemming's notion of a niche sounded a little like post-
humous praise. But even in a city of politicians watching
papers, I was not so sure that praise was what was wanted so
much as order and certainty, clear lines and free responsibility.
Undoubtedly, public servants in America can get a little tired
of public brickbats, though nobody is more sharply critical
of public servants than some of the public servants themselves.
I doubt that criticism from without disturbs the best men as
much as frustration from within. Government is complex at
best. Safeguards surround all action. Records are voluminous.
Jealousies seem implicit in the service. Everybody knows what
everybody else gets—even wives know. Under such circumstances envy can be naked. The power complex seems to go all
the way down from the Cabinet to the sections of bureaus.

Sometimes, despite the almost idiotically precise—and often
actually fictional—job descriptions required by Civil Service,
a man in the government may have less idea where his respon-

sibility ends and begins than he would have in less formal private employment. But the Civil Service not only protects him. It also has elaborate regulations, demanded by the people, imposed by the Congress and made legalistically specific by other careful bureaucrats, which pattern all his employment of assistants. All his activities are supervised not only by officials above him but by the expert young men from the Bureau of the Budget, too. These supervisions represent reforms. They are designed to insure order and uniformity in government, but they also surround initiative with rules which sometimes can grow complex to confusion. Initiative can bring advancement in government as in any other activity. But security lies in obeying the rules which come down from Congress, the President, the department heads and the bureau chiefs. Nobody in government is free of them—most of them may be necessary—but they can bind as well as guard. In a government staffed by people in the millions, safeguards may be more essential than official freedom to act. The bureaucrat at his worst has not only not learned all the rules but has acquired an apathetic docility in the midst of his ignorance. At his best, he acquires the skill—a not impossible one—of working with a combination of vigor and selflessness in a system which has sense in it as well as tradition, although the latter sometimes remain after the sense has departed from them. And often in such a maze, the best men quit.

"There must be a more vigorous weeding out of unsatisfactory public servants."

In his office Flemming swings back, smiling, in his chair.

It can be done. It sometimes is. But under the rule, I know, it sometimes takes more governmental energy to eject the incompetent than to do his work around him. The punctual, industrious dull are almost immovable.

Also, sometimes weeding out seems to be reserved for the lively. A Communist hunt sometimes harasses liberals. It never bothers those without any ideas at all. Also, I remember the case of a young woman whose continuance as an employee was suddenly forbidden by the Civil Service Commission on a finding of complete moral unfitness. Apparently, it had begun to investigate her as a possible radical when it came upon a neighbor—a scientist in the Department of Agriculture—who had looked through the windows of her house and had some tales to tell about the lady, her husband and their friends. Civil Service heard the neighbor's ugly stories about her and, without hearing any witnesses in her defense, ordered that she be dropped. It happened that her own boss did not believe the charges. He challenged them. The case was brought to the attention of members of Congress and officials at the White House. Under pressure, Civil Service rechecked the charges, and withdrew the order. The girl kept her character and her job. So did the other bureaucrat who had told the stories about her. Apparently neither promiscuous adultery nor malicious false witness had been committed. But Civil Service succeeded in the case in convincing a good many indignant bureaucrats who knew the young woman that Civil Service was not merely elderly but a Mrs. Grundy equipped with investigators.

Arthur Flemming is no old woman. The public service he hopes to help build is no mass mediocrity. But neither, I suspect, is Arthur Flemming a Theodore Roosevelt nor a man operating before an American public which has passionate feelings about the Civil Service as it did in the 1880's. Today, if it is concerned at all, it is not generally about the quality of the civil servants but that there are too many of them. The mass in the government gets only a sort of dull mass distrust from other citizens. Except for those who are offered better jobs outside or suddenly inside get exceptional publicity in the newspapers, the public servant is not honored in a niche but lost in a mass. He works in a system which somehow seems to think only as a system, and good public servants, like good private ones, are individuals. No Civil Service rules or examinations yet devised can procure or keep exceptional men.

It was not certain at the time I saw him how much more money Mr. Mitchell, Mrs. McMillin and Mr. Flemming would get under possible pay increases. At any price I would not want Flemming's job. He is going to get very little help, I suspect, in improving bureaucracy from those Americans who curse it. For Civil Service has not only developed elaborate rules within itself; it has also been surrounded by organizations of bureaucrats and others who have a variety of vested interests in it. When I saw Flemming, various veterans' organizations in competition for members were all trying to show their power and vigor in getting and extending, for veterans, Civil Service rights and Civil Service preferences. There are labor unions of Civil Service employees now. Their leaders are intent upon rights and protections, pay and privileges for their members. Late in 1945, they were a little confused themselves. They fought to safeguard seniority in job reductions, though as unions they had drawn to their membership many who felt most precarious, since they had least seniority. There were certain to be problems of race. Negroes were likely to be caught shortest in seniority. But the old bitterness of "last hired and first fired" would probably not be stilled, seniority or not. Congressmen would be telephoning, and even in a Civil Service age Congressmen are not to be disregarded.

I told Flemming good-by and went down the old stone stairs. Two elderly gentlemen in their shirt sleeves were discussing a woman of whom they did not seem to approve.

"She came switching into my office," one of them said, "and I just let her talk. She thinks she's it."

The other laughed. I lit a cigarette and stopped to regard a modern advertising display of Civil Service itself which stood against the wall in the almost subterranean entrance hall of the building. I presume it was prepared by a Civil Service employee in the graphic arts. He had earned his pay.

"Every fifteen seconds of every working day," his elaborate sign said, "an American citizen mails an application for examination to the United States Civil Service Commission."

And there were some of the eager applicants electrically displayed in full color, though the light behind one of them seemed to be out and had not been replaced. The people mailing letters in the illuminated pictures looked as if they would certainly make good employees. Arthur Flemming would not have to worry about any one of them. Any official with half an eye would be happy to have in his office the pretty girl in the freshly ironed yellow dress and the big matching yellow hat. The husky fellow in the new blue-and-gold uniform of a Uniontown, Pennsylvania, Legion Post looked definitely employable. And below them, in more brightly lighted pictures, the jobs and the jobholders whom they wished to join in the government seemed actually romantic. Some of them are.

A brown-burned half-naked young man was surveying a desert for the United States Reclamation Service. An airplane inspector, working in a brand new gray hat, was contemplating an engine for the Civil Aeronautics Authority. Aerial photographers for the Soil Conservation Service stood beside a plane marked with a sword stuck through the ace of spades; the symbolism seemed a little obscure, but the men were clearly contented workers. Two gun-carrying border patrolmen were in the dramatic act of catching some rather pathetic-looking Mexicans who had just slipped across a blue river. There were others, including a solemn lady in the State Department impressing the Great Seal of the United States on some momentous document.

But reality stood close to the drama. The marble corridors running beside the pictures were lined with filing cases. Before them, clerks worked with papers which must have related to some of those people who had sent letters every fifteen seconds. The clerks in the hall looked like the filers of papers in an age which no longer has need for the drawers of water. They seemed even older and less decorative than government filing clerks usually are. No graphics expert in his right mind would have taken their pictures. They gossiped as they filed. Obviously, they had no personal feeling about personnel. People were papers. But the paper filers were sadly human. There was no reflection of the exhilaration of great and exciting government among them as their hands moved automatically before those cases. A fat but grim old Negress moved with her papers as if her feet hurt her.

"I don't care," she said to a pimpled girl. "I can't walk that far."

I had dinner that evening with a bureaucrat on his way out of the government. I found myself arguing that he ought to stay in. A man could find satisfaction in a government career. Some excellent men had. Indeed, I knew that some who had left had soon come back to find satisfactions in effective work which they had underestimated before. I mentioned the sense of accomplishment I had felt among men working in the Tennessee Valley Authority which, along with the F.B.I. and the State Department career service, does its own recruiting. Men in departments all over Washington found the same satisfactions. He was needed. He ought to stay. He grinned at me and counted his children, the cash and his free chance outside to do an interesting job. Then he spoke, defensively maybe, about TVA.

"When the dams are built," he said, "when the job comes down to the routine, they'll be gone, too—the best of them here now."

I hope he is wrong; and not only because TVA has been a concrete and dynamic image of public service—as Civil Service was when Civil Service and Theodore Roosevelt were young together. That was a long time ago, but government has to go on. It goes on after a war ends. It continues after the adventure of developing a river is complete. Government may be too big, but nobody contends that it is too efficient. And in a government which, before war came with the 1940's, had been concerned with the welfare of the masses—and had that problem still—the question, in Washington, had come around to the problem of keeping the competence of the few.

My friend shook his head soberly.

"Yes," he said, "they'll be moving—after a while—those who can; and those who can't will run the country and the world."

XI

The Island and the Irishman

BOTH Democrats and Republicans, apparently, like to meet on islands. They have obvious merits as meeting places. Also, both Mackinac Island in the higher Republican reaches of Lake Huron and Jefferson Island in Democratic Chesapeake Bay are pleasant places. Neither island is very accessible, and both parties can be very exclusive between elections. It takes a lot of people to make power, but only a limited number can be included when the pleasantness of power is being passed around. I thought of that as I stood with a little band of Democrats on Lowe's wharf, which is a twisting causeway of decaying oyster shells on the Eastern Shore of Maryland, and waited for the boat to take us to the gathering on the island.

The Democratic Party off there on the green island with the whitewashed tree trunks around the comfortable clubhouse did not seem simple to me that morning. Democrats do not seem simple to me at any time (or Republicans either). But they did not seem strange to the lady who drove up over the dirty oyster shells in a very sporty roadster. She got out, long-legged in bright slacks. Above her sport clothes her hair looked as if it had just been done by Emile. She strode toward us across the shells. And I had a feeling that we Democrats looked a little drab beside the lady. She obviously had, which is always admirable in a lady, a clear and simple idea of the Democratic Party. It was those men out there on that island, and she wanted to ask it to stop by her summer place on its way home for cocktails.

"She's going to try to crash this party," said the Vice-Chairman.

He knew her well. Twice, he said, at one of the party's big Jackson Day dinners (where loyal Democrats get oratory in exchange for contributions) he had had to change the place cards after she had shifted them so that her guests might appropriate the table reserved for Mrs. Roosevelt. It would have been a neat trick if it had worked.

But the lady approached him as if she had never seen him before in her life but could, still be charming in the misty morning. The Vice-Chairman kept his hat on. She wondered if anyone would take a message to the island for her. She had written it, she smiled in the vague amusement people wear who go beautifully dressed to political conventions and prizefights, on the best stationery she had with her—the inside of a matchbook. She held it out in a stubby-fingered hand which seemed somehow incongruous beside her slim figure and her immaculate hair. The Vice-Chairman took the matchbook but still kept his hat on. He looked a little tough, I thought, as if he were regarding One-eye Connelly the gate crasher, and suddenly there above the oyster shells the lady in slacks looked just a little more gaunt than gay.

A political party in Washington can look like anything from a lady who thinks of a Party as—well, as a party—to the body of politicians who hope they are entrenched in its direction. It can be, and often is, composed of ladies and gentlemen who know what they want. It is, of course, composed, when the party is in power, of its chief officeholders and higher party functionaries. Nobody is it so much as the President is. But it is not even the President's private possession. Strange people come to represent it and to quarrel about it. And those who do not come to Washington do not relinquish their sense of its possession. Indeed, they may feel not only that gate-crashers have got into the party but that stowaways have taken possession of the ship. Even when a party is in power, it is hard to tell whether the party is the government or merely the

principal pressure group—or pressure groups—beside it. It is
the chief machinery, undoubtedly, through which pressure is
applied.

Its office is not on an island. In the American democracy,
under the Democrats, it works where the crowding, the contentious and the contributing can easily find it. Even there it
does not look like a political club. It has been compared to a
brokerage office in which American ideas and interests, vanities and people bid against each other. Actually, in the politics
of the age of the atom, it is the center of the highly technical
business of putting people together for power. Far from the
blue water and the green island, the whitewashed trees and the
Democrats at play, its office is a beautiful room. It may even
be, as Postmaster General and National Democratic Chairman
Robert E. Hannegan thinks, the most beautiful room in Washington. Long before Fascism seemed ugly in world politics,
this room for the foremost American politician was decorated
with an ornate motif of fasces. They remain. There is no good
reason why old dead Mussolini should forever dirty a good
symbol. Pre-Fascist fasces make as good a symbolism for
Hannegan as any other that will be found east or west of
Missouri. Certainly they make good emblems for the national
politician whose job it is to bind the boys together throughout
what he likes to call "the length and breadth" of the land.
Political power seems not only great but neat. And President
Truman smiles benignly from a golden frame.

"I am," Hannegan says, "a plain, ordinary, everyday, one
hundred percent, straight organization Democrat."

He regards himself as a sort of sublimated precinct worker,
remembering their troubles and sharing their jobs. He understands that the one desired destination is election.

"There is only one formula for success," he tells other
Democrats. Those most eager for his formula may be a little
disappointed. "That is hard work—perspiration." But he adds:
"I have always believed in running scared."

He does not look sweaty or scared in his big office. He

looks, indeed, both like a neat-to-shining Irish lawyer and like a good, tough, noncommittal cop with excellent connections at City Hall. There is little about him to suggest the image of the city boss transplanted to the capital, except that in his white flat face there is, perhaps, some of the same impassiveness. That impassiveness may not be Boss but Billikin. He was one once when he played fullback (weight 182) for the St. Louis University Billikins. He was a triple-threat man then working with a team which included McConachie, Ramacciotti, Eggler, Schaeffering, Kigi, Schwartz and O'Toole. Their football records do not indicate whether they were Democrats or Republicans. But all of them were Billikins. And Bob Hannegan, working with an even wider diversity of Americans, still looks like a Billikin.

He works at his job. The day after the excursion to the island a gleaming table was already set in one end of his long office for one of the succession of luncheons he holds for prominent Democrats and prospects for Democratic contributions. He uses the telephone to tell people at great distances that he and the President are thinking about them affectionately. He works on The Hill to persuade wandering Democrats to support the President's nominations and measures. Because he believes it, he has an effective way of saying to Senators that party solidarity is personal self-interest.

He fingered a thick list of yellow slips of paper. On them an efficient secretary had written the names of people who wanted to see him. He shook his long head. Despite his pallor he looked healthy, but he seemed to get a melancholy pleasure out of the pommeling pressure of people. I had a feeling that with good Irish fatalism, he enjoyed it and would die only if the procession diminished.

I did not see the procession. Not even deserving Democrats wait outside the National Chairman's office in the informality of a party clubhouse. The Post Office Department was not decorated in person by the paunchy and the pompous and the pathetic, the slick and flashy and shrewd who gather in lesser political places. Democrats come by appointment only, and not in hungry informality for a basket of groceries or a job or a word to the District Attorney about a boy in jail. But a man may come with a contribution or even to collect an ambassadorship. The scenery and costumes are better, but the actors are the same.

Indeed, as chief actor, Bob Hannegan, who is at least as close to President Truman as Jim Farley ever was to FDR, may be the story of the contemporary politician in the United States. I am not entirely incredulous of the story that he did not want to go into politics. He even paid a man, they say, to do his work for him as precinct chairman. He did not want to become chairman of the St. Louis City Committee, but accepted the job because the Republicans were pushing his father around on the St. Louis police force. Once in, however, he and the first vote-getter he ever managed, Mayor Bernard Francis Dickmann, a dull-seeming realtor, were credited by Democrats with redeeming St. Louis, in 1933, after twenty-six "long and weary" years of Republican control. That redemption was at least assisted by the fact that the year before Roosevelt had taken St. Louis into the Democratic column by better than two to one. At any rate, they not only redeemed it but were also loudly charged by the independent and even the Democratic press with riding high, wide and handsome in it.

Indeed, it has been suggested that after President Truman's old friend, Thomas J. Pendergast, left Kansas City for the penitentiary, they got the idea that they were Missouri. They launched, in 1940, a St. Louis candidate for Governor against mounting rural opposition. However, in the same year they helped a desperate Harry Truman who was running with a big Pendergast load and no Pendergast help. (In 1934, when Truman had won in the State by 40,000 votes, Pendergast gave him 100,000 votes in Jackson County alone to 6,000 votes for his opponents. Only St. Louis saved him, in 1940, when Truman squeaked through to the nomination with a margin of 8,400 votes.) While Roosevelt carried the State by nearly

100,000 votes, the Dickmann-Hannegan candidate for Governor was defeated. Also, after the election, Hannegan was charged in a highly involved Missouri political controversy with trying to steal the office from the elected Republican Governor. His denials were hardly heard in the hubbub. A year later, in 1941, Dickmann and Hannegan were also put out of the over-ornamented St. Louis City Hall.

Then suddenly, in 1942, a grateful Harry Truman, safe in the Senate, announced that Hannegan and only Hannegan was going to be United States Collector of Internal Revenue in St. Louis. Hannegan did not want the job. He was politically down but financially up, and the policeman's son has no predilection for poverty even on the government payroll. He was making more than twice as much money as the Collector's job paid. Unfortunately or fortunately for him, the St. Louis papers let loose at what they called a "disgraceful example of plum-passing" to reward "a party henchman whose record is inextricably linked with the brazen attempt to steal the Governorship of Missouri." Hannegan had to crawl or fight. He fought. And on June 1, 1942, he won the office he did not want. One year and four months later, he was appointed Commissioner of Internal Revenue on the announced ground that in that brief period he had become the best collector in the United States. It was fast work; but he was moving fast. He did not want that job either. Then, three months later he got another job he did not want as National Chairman of the Democratic Party.

Hannegan owed his appointment chiefly to Harry S. Truman, who later insisted that he did not want to be Vice-President. Apparently Missouri is a reluctant State, if no longer an incredulous one. But the month after Hannegan took over and contemplated the dust which had accumulated in the Mayflower Hotel offices of the Democratic National Committee, the press was already pointing the possibilities in the conjunction of Missouri Democrats, the Chairmanship and the Vice-Presidency, Hannegan and Truman. In 1940, Truman seemed almost a political refugee from the Pendergast disaster. In 1941, the papers described Hannegan as a discredited St. Louis politician. All that seems a long time ago, but their problems are not simple and will not soon be.

"Hard work—and perspiration," says Bob. "I have always believed in running scared."

It is a plan which has merit. Elections in the United States are not decided by Democrats and Republicans. There is a substantial politically itinerant percentage of the voters who move from party to party in the voting booths, and from victory to victory. Even a perfectly organized Democratic Party, completely happy and absolutely loyal from the precinct to the Post Office Department, cannot elect a President. Indeed, there is some sort of new natural law in American politics that the smaller the vote the greater the chance of the Republicans. It is clear in the records that the Democrats alone did not elect Franklin Roosevelt in any year he ran, certainly not in 1944.

Indeed, sometimes as the Democrats won and won, it was hard to tell whether the Democratic Party was Roosevelt or the Democrats. Some Democratic politicians who enjoyed the ride never quite cared for the notion that they were just passengers. It is an essence of the craft of the politician that he serves a long apprenticeship in subserviency in order to attain a precarious dignity. The politician puts his emphasis on long loyalty, while nothing is so clear in politics as that new loyalties must be won. The big groups which are ready to move must be watched and served—or at least given the impression that they are served. A Democratic Chairman, if he means to be in an administration that lasts longer than one term, has to be more than a Democrat. He must, indeed, understand the strange political fact that in politics people are more important than politicians. It is a fact, however, which not all politicians understand.

Old Jim Watson, former Republican leader of the Senate and now a legal lingerer in Washington, expressed the feeling of Democratic and Republican Party regulars about over-ready newcomers. He did not like Willkie as the candidate of his party.

"Why?"

"He's a Democrat."

"But he's converted. Don't you believe in conversion and forgiveness?"

"Yes," the old man said, "but it never seemed to me that the day after the prostitute was converted she ought to expect to lead the choir."

Sometimes it is hard to tell what a politician is. Neither Bob Hannegan nor any of the officers of his National Committee ever ran for an office and took personally the love or the licks of the voters. Some Congressmen have made much of the fact that some Cabinet officials have never had the experience which facing voters provides. But even Congressmen and national candidates are content that the Democratic Party be run by technicians who, with a different schooling, pretend, as political scientists do, to a knowledge of politics all the same. One of Bob Hannegan's assistants, until he was given the rank of ambassador, learned his politics in the oil business; another in corporation law; another in hotels and insurance and as a Commissioner of the voteless District of Columbia.

(Maybe there is some sort of triumph of the technician over the artist in the fact that all the campaign managers of recent Republican candidates for the Presidency had been candidates, and successful ones, before they became managers —and unsuccessful ones. Indeed, Dewey was campaign manager for Herbert Brownell long before Brownell was manager for Dewey. Incidentally, that time Brownell was defeated too.)

As National Chairman, however, Hannegan as politician fits a simple formula. The Democratic National Chairman must not only be a politician, he must also be an Irish Catholic. That pleases the Irish who, along with the Negroes, the Southerners and the Jews who have largely composed the Democratic Party, seem proscribed as Presidents. Also, in a country which knows the President must be a politician but prefers in high moments to forget it, he protects the President. Even today the Irishman in politics may be useful, as Lord Bryce reported him to be sixty years ago, as the cat is useful in the kitchen to account for the broken plates and the food which disappears. Also, an Irish chairman may help to assure the loyal support of those basic, Irish-captained companies, the city machines.

Below the chairman, and around him, it is increasingly hard to tell the amateurs from the professionals at a time when such potent amateurs are at work as David Dubinsky, whose supporters are supposed to be primarily concerned with making clothes for ladies, and Sidney Hillman who represents the people who make the clothes for men. Hillman's Political Action Committee of the CIO in the 1944 election was a national enterprise in political amateurism, but effective all the same. There were other less well-known ones. There was Harlow Shapley, the Harvard astronomer, who could talk effective politics in the atomic age in understanding that, since all ages are political, science is not sufficient. Jo Davidson also understood that the art of politics is not to be neglected by the sculptor. There were others. There will be again.

There are whole races which stand watching the record of an administration. There are Jews who hated Hitler more than they loved the Democrats; and Negroes who sometimes loved Roosevelt in spite of many Democrats. There are good men and angry men. It may be more important to please them than the politicians who come most often to call—and to collect. There are also in politics big business men who are not merely intent upon principles but watch parties for investment as they watch stocks. There are the strange people of ideas and emotions once called New Dealers. There is a whole body of Americans who do not stay neatly in precincts but follow jobs and hope to find them. There are the people who used to say, "Why in the hell did Roosevelt do that, but after all he's Roosevelt." And there is the ghost of Roosevelt himself. Neither hate nor adoration seems ready to let him sleep within the hemlock hedges at Hyde Park. There are forces and people, and a National Chairman must put enough of them together. That's his whole job. The election and nothing else is the pay-off.

It is a big job for an Irishman. It is a big job for two Missourians who know or should know from Missouri almost everything there is to know about the organization of politics. They divide the work well. Long ago Truman was chosen by the shrewd Boss of Kansas City as a vote-getter, a candidate, a veteran, a farmer. Hannegan was chosen by a St. Louis vote-getter as a political technician. The difference remains, though Truman has lived in political organization and learned every detail of it since. Hannegan had a chance to learn a good deal about ideas and passions in politics in 1944.

It is important that they come from Missouri. Maybe, as some of their articulate friends have said, they bring politics to the central American simplicity of Missouri after a long confusion in the seaboard idea-importing complexity of New York. That sounds like poetry rather than politics. But the Missouriness of Truman is important, nevertheless. Missouri does sit central in America between the plantations and the prairies. It runs from cotton to cattle and corn. The breweries and factories rise in its cities, but Truman is able to emphasize without straining the good small-town quality of a rural State. Country church suppers can be as much a part of politics as poker games. It is a mere incident in an American procession that Missouri has today 40,000 fewer farmers than it had when Harry Truman began to plow, and not all of them have gone to the White House. It is a State which has seen rural radicalism and tough, tight city political organization which took the cash of the insurance companies to lose it on the horse races. American political realism in Missouri is not restricted to Thomas Hart Benton's lively murals in the marble capitol. It has suffered from politics, and understands politics still.

But maybe the important thing about Missouri is the fact that, far better than Maine, it goes politically as the nation goes. Missouri has cast its vote for every President elected in this century and in each election. Maine has missed five times. As Missouri goes seems the nation's way—or Missouri goes the way of America—and if Truman and Hannegan understand anything about America, that understanding begins in Missouri. Of course, Hannegan has misunderstood in the past and lost the State. Harry Truman once was almost caught in Missouri's anger at his political companions. The President and his Irishman could misunderstand or fail again.

All that tough and crowded future seemed a long way off that day on the island. It was a full year before even Congressmen had to run again. It was three years before the big test of a Democratic Party without Roosevelt on the ticket or the radio. Once in a while even a party may be entitled to a picnic. The future and the people, the polls and the pay-off will be waiting all the same. For one Sunday afternoon it seemed safe to forget them. I remember that we were merry in the captain's cabin of the Sandy Point ferryboat on the way back. Most of us in the cabin were friends of James M. Barnes, amiable ex-Congressman from Illinois and my next door neighbor in the Palace Guard. The party on the island had been given for him as he left the government for the law. There were pictures of Maryland politicians on the walls (all of them Democrats, I think). And a colored maid came and brought us coffee and cakes. It was wet outside, but warm and bright in the room.

And somebody told a story which seemed to the contented and coffee-drinking Democrats on the ferryboat to state the difference between the Democrats and the Republicans—or some of them.

"It's a story in two acts," he said.

Act One: It seemed that Henry Pringle, the biographer, had written some years before a profile of Thomas E. Dewey for *The New Yorker* when Dewey was the swift-rising young District Attorney. Pringle showed the manuscript to Dewey.

The young District Attorney liked the story very much—very much indeed. There was just one sentence, and he wondered—

The sentence in question stated that occasionally on Saturday nights District Attorney Dewey and his wife played poker with friends. Would it be possible to change "poker" to "bridge"?

Act Two: Another gentleman, in Tennessee, had written a biography of Cordell Hull. He also submitted the manuscript. In it he had said that when young Cordell, in 1898, had gone off to free Cuba, he had been a soldier for only a very short time before, playing poker, he had won all the money in his company. He got his manuscript back and on it, in Cordell Hull's own handwriting the word "company" had been stricken out and the word "regiment" written in.

I am not sure it is a perfect party parable. It may be an entirely apocryphal story doing equal injustice to the still young Governor Dewey and the venerable Secretary Hull and their parties together. But we enjoyed it in the cabin. And then we drank our coffee quickly and scrambled toward our cars. The ferryboat was landing. It had begun to rain and ahead of us, across the double line of cars, the road to Washington looked crowded and confused. We moved very slowly beyond the lights into the dark.

XII

You Can't Go Back to Pocatello

THAT May I could not quite see Tommy Corcoran's place in the picture. I am not sure I see it now. But when I stopped to speak to Bernard M. Baruch on the park bench under the horse chestnut tree, they were talking about the possibility of Mr. Baruch taking over the operation of chemical companies formerly dominated by Germans in Latin America. Leo Crowley, who was then Alien Property Custodian as well as Director of the Foreign Economic Administration, and Tommy Corcoran sat like small boys on the bench at right angles to Mr. Baruch's. I sat down beside Baruch. We talked of other things.

"I was just up to the Mayflower to see Carter Glass," Leo Crowley said. "There seemed hardly any of him left in the bed, he's so little."

We talked in the sun. Mr. Baruch was shaking his head about chemicals and Latin America and himself. He was content under the horse chestnut tree, as any old gentleman might be, warming his bones. Washington was a well understood part of his world. He had friends in the Senate who had had his friendship and campaign contributions across the years. His counsel was welcome at the White House. He had become elder statesman as a sort of well advertised professional wise man who had much to give but nothing to ask for himself.

"I've got a dollar more than I will ever need."

Mr. Crowley was then business man who had come into

government. Mr. Corcoran was government man who had departed to go into the private practice of the law. Government was very informal under the horse chestnut tree. But somehow they gave me a fresh sense of the complexity of government. It could be a maze to business men and others who approached government without knowing their way around in it. And it can be made to seem even more complex than it is.

Crowley and Corcoran departed. It was very pleasant in the sun under the tree. Washington looked both serene and simple. Some pigeons muttered at our feet, but moved on. They had no use even for Baruch without crumbs. We talked about men and Washington. It had been harder to get good men in World War II, he thought, than in the war before. Business men were no longer independent fellows; they were managers instead of owners. They surrounded themselves with lawyers and public-relations men. They had become a sort of business bureaucracy. There were a few exceptions.

"The du Ponts," he said, "they're very dull people to talk to, but they get things done."

He got up, and we walked up 16th Street, where he kept an apartment at the Carlton. It was, for the Carlton, a nondescript-looking suite, as if it were both seldom used and seldom swept. A blond country-looking secretary, with long gums and short teeth, let us in. All around us there were the suites the other gentlemen and companies and unions and law firms keep for their Washington working and visiting. The Carlton is elegant, of course, even if, as legend said, West Virginia miners (through John L. Lewis) held the mortgage on it. It is always interesting to look at the Carlton, remembering their houses in the grim mine towns. The Carlton seems a long way from the country which contains them. It does not look like the hostelry of bureaucrats. But I came away from the old man of the bench and his wisdom with the feeling that, off the ground of the government, I was still on the property of bureaucracy. It did not stop where the government ended.

What we used to call The Lobby in the simple, forthright and often oversimplified indignations of the past had become a bureaucracy, too.

It uses, indeed, many of the same people. Others besides Tommy Corcoran moved their operations and their offices a few blocks from the government buildings in which they worked before and up a good many thousand dollars to continue the same sort of activities for private enterprise. The procession from public service to private enterprise is only a business of crossing the street. A man certainly is no less able a lawyer because he has been Attorney General, and he can certainly do as well in Washington where he has worked for the government as in Stamford, Connecticut, where he has lived as a citizen. It is no fault of a practicing ex-official that his father-in-law is Majority Leader of the Senate. And sometimes, indeed, ex-officials survive the administrations of their friends. If, for instance, Ellsworth Alvord had been assistant to the Secretary of the Treasury under Hoover, he had made most of his money as a tax lawyer under Roosevelt. Not everybody practices influence law. Some public-relations counsels even give public-relations advice. I am not sure that George Allen, who came out of the government to represent some of the same fire insurance companies which had enriched and embarrassed Mr. Pendergast, ever sold their policies in Washington. But he can still tell very funny jokes to Presidents and other politicians.

I spoke about officials crossing the street from complex government to bewildered business when I went on from the Carlton to the almost spinsterish respectability of the Cosmos Club. I knew some Lobbyists had had rooms there, too. And Dr. Will Alexander, who would probably admit that he is a lobbyist for racial minorities, told me a story. When he was head of the Farm Security Administration, he had visited a place down in Arkansas where the government had experimented in an entirely cooperative plantation on which the group owned the land and worked together for the common cause. He talked to the chairman of the cooperative, who, in the vocabulary of cooperation, expressed his delight with what they were doing. But Dr. Alexander got him off later behind a cooperative barn.

"What do you really think of it?"

The old Arkansas farmer eyed him thoughtfully.

"I tell you," he said, "I'm better off than I ever was before in my life." He looked around to see that they were alone. "I believe a man could stick around here for five or six years and save enough money to go off and buy himself a little hill farm of his own."

Some others under the government have made the same discovery even in Washington. And I thought about Corcoran on the bench and the talk which grew around him as the lawyer who could get things done in Washington. He is certainly not unique in Washington law practice, but somehow he was one born to be a symbol. Long ago, even before the beginning of the Roosevelt Administration, he had come down from Harvard to be, first, secretary to old Justice Oliver Wendell Holmes, and then, a counsel in Hoover's RFC, to which Jesse Jones and Tommy Corcoran came together. He had been Presidential assistant and driving New Dealer. He had seemed almost the individual Justice Felix Frankfurter was writing about when he wrote a piece for *Fortune*, in 1936, called "The Young Men Go to Washington."

Frankfurter had given me the piece in a collection of his writings one day after we had talked in his paneled office in the gleaming white Supreme Court Building.

"More and more," he said, "the ablest of them—in striking contrast to what was true thirty years ago—are eager for government service. They find satisfaction in work which aims at the public good and which presents problems that challenge the best ability and courage of man."

There are still young lawyers coming to Washington with the attitude Frankfurter impressed upon them long ago. And there are lobbyists who are only the young men grown older.

I am not sure that they represent any lapse in the American spirit. The acceptance of the second best is not a contemporary phenomenon. There is nothing new about that menopause of the spirit after which convictions seem less important than cash. It is not always passed without pain. Besides perfectly happy lobbyists in Washington, there are others who never seem quite gay—or too gay. Many of them are ex-Congressmen. Some of them were left behind by passing administrations. In lobbying, as in other things, intelligence lasts. But prestige can fade even faster than beauty. And sometimes lobbyists put up more front for themselves than for their clients.

Indeed, I suspect that clients are cheated more often than the Republic is. One of the comic aspects of Washington is the bewildered business man who hires a lawyer as a guide to take him to a place to which a policeman could direct him. A nickel phone call may be more effective in making an engagement with an official than a fee to a lawyer who pretends he carries influence. Indeed, often the client pays to prejudice his case in advance by hiring such legal assistance. Effective work is done by some effective men around the government in Washington. There are occasionally "fixers" who can fix, though there may be risk in the business for both the lawyer and the client. But I suspect that more money is wasted in Washington on lobbying fees to phonies in the practice than in almost any other corporate spending in the United States.

Mr. Justice Frankfurter may have been unduly optimistic. At about the same time, Harry Truman was not impressed with the young lawyers who had come down from Cambridge or anywhere else.

"The ordinary government mine-run bureaucratic lawyer," he said, "is no more a match for the amiable gentlemen who represent the great railroads, insurance companies and Wall Street bankers than the ordinary lamb is a match for the butcher."

The important word in the President's statement is not

"butcher" but "amiable." Half of the gaiety of Washington would dry up if expense accounts disappeared. Members of Congress have already loudly admitted their poverty on government pay. (Representative Clifton A. Woodrum, of Virginia, explained as he left Congress to become head of the Fertilizer Lobby's euphemistically named American Plant Food Council at a reported $50,000 a year: "I have seen men come to this body in the heyday of hopeful youth, and stay under the blistering spotlight of public service until those once raven locks were frosted by the passing of many winters, until that agile step had slowed and that eagle eye dimmed.") While the bars and the dining rooms were packed to the doors and parties every afternoon filled all available party suites, there were, as Arthur Flemming had told me, only 247 men in the executive branch who were paid, before taxes, as much as $9,800 a year. There were, of course, the rich who moved in, whose only predatory interest was the pleasure to be had around an exciting government. And lobbyists do not merely reach in easy amiability for the check. They are ready also to help a President or a Cabinet member or a Congressman with any little political difficulties he may be having. All for nothing, they collect funds for campaigns, solve embarrassing situations, and take on in their spare time, which always seems ample, any part-time pieces of public service which may need to be done.

The Lobby's members are still, as the name implies, to be found in the lobbies of Congress. (Ex-Congressmen retain the privileges of the floor.) But the gentlemen of push and persuasion are more dramatically seen at their luncheon tables in the Mayflower and lounging easily in the late afternoons in the Carlton bar. And even these are apt to be the small fry. Bigger men will be talking casually in suites around bowls of ice and their own bottles of better bourbon.

Tommy Corcoran may not be bothering with clients at all. His concerns are often greater or smaller. He may be

planning the Presidential future of Mr. Justice William Douglas or teaching Mr. Justice Hugo Black's child how to play
the accordion. He loomed, nevertheless, as a character in the
Washington drama, at least as big as Baruch. Indeed, he
seemed The Lobby 1946 version. The young man who went
to Washington had become the young man who knew how to
operate the town—or play it like an accordion for such clients
as he cared to take.

The trouble when I knew him was that he never would
stop playing the accordion. But he made a picture when he
played it. He always arrived for dinner grinning and somehow bouncing. He was insistently young beyond forty. His
young, gold-haired, sedately pretty wife helped him make
his picture. It was dramatic. But when, after dinner, the
hostess suggested that Tommy might play a piece on his accordion, those who had been to dinner with him before in
Washington knew that conversation for the evening had
ended. He swung his strap about his shoulder. He swung his
whole thickening triangular figure behind the accordion from
his patent-leather shoes to his gray curly hair. The music was
loud, and it did not stop. And Mrs. Corcoran patted a slender
foot.

The music was as confident as the man. But it always seemed
to me Irish-gay and Irish-sad. Maybe, as everybody was saying sometimes apologetically and often with envy, Tommy
was raking in the cash. He was the success story as the lawyer
with influence in Washington who could get things done. He
was, indeed, so flamboyantly successful that he could ostentatiously omit his name and his office from the telephone book.
He wore mystery as well as power. Yet he looked, playing,
less like a success story than a sort of Washington character
for an F. Scott Fitzgerald study in elegant frustration. He
seemed to me to be making loud, gay, continuous music not
so much for his audience as for himself. I had the feeling that
if he stopped for one minute, playing, running, talking, exer-

cising power and taking in fees, the aging Irish face of the bright young man might begin to sag at the corners of his mouth.

"I happen to know," an official beside me said under the music, "that he got—"

The woman with him smiled with pleasant envy, "It's nice work if you can get it."

I was not sure. I was interested in discovering that others were not sure. I rode home that night with an official who had known him for a long time. I spoke of Corcoran's playing, and in the car along the road he laughed in the darkness.

"I wonder who Tommy is kidding, himself or the United States of America. I think the real sucker is Tommy Corcoran."

I waited for an exposition of that one.

"I suppose he's making, as everybody says, a lot of money. But every time I see him I have the impression that what he's doing is trying to prove for himself and in public that he still has the power. It hurts to be dropped as Tommy was dropped, especially in Washington. And he can't prove he still has power except by fees. He was always an effective fellow, and always flamboyant about it. You've got to remember that he wanted to be Solicitor General of the United States. Now he's only getting rich. For an Irishman, it won't be quite an adequate substitute."

He took out a cigarette, and I pushed in the lighter for him. From the top of a hill we could look down on the city full of lights.

"We couldn't get along in Washington, of course, without lobbyists," he said. "Some of them are honorable, hard-working men. Everybody knows that, though we get indignant at the word—most indignant, I guess, when we're lobbying on the other side. But it is a complex government and people sometimes need competent, informed assistance in proper dealings with it. Also, Congress and the departments have to have the information, the opinion and the assistance which

various interests can give them in shaping the directions of
government. The right of petition hasn't become disreputable
—even if there are some disreputable petitioners. And where
else in the world should people press their interests if not to
their government, where it works?"

"I think you're a little charitable as well as right," I said.
"I've gotten a hunch, working here, that more lobbyists cheat
their clients than corrupt the government."

He laughed and lit his cigarette.

"Of course," he agreed. "The predatory lobbyist can be
both phony and pathetic. I know an ex-Senator who's behind
in his rent."

We stopped at a traffic light.

"I guess a few people like Alvord and Cummings and Joe
Davies have really satisfactory law practices. There are others.
But the thing drops fast. Sometimes the Washington lawyers
around the government and so-called public-relations counsels
—you know—they look like a pretty pathetic lot of people
even while they're signing the checks with a flourish. Licking
boots and kidding their clients, eating at the Mayflower on
fat expense accounts and feeling still sometimes cheap as the
devil."

He opened the window and spat out of it.

"In Washington, there's nothing quite as perishable as
prestige."

The sound of Corcoran's music came back into my head
next day when I had lunch (paying my check that time) with
an old writing friend, Captain Richard L. Neuberger, of Portland, Oregon. We were given a very little table against the
wall in the dining room. It was a good vantage point from
which to see the essential process by which citizens and their
representatives and their government get together over the
problems of both. Sometimes, the lobbyist and the official can
turn out to be the same man. There was big swarthy George
Allen telling a joke, and you could not be sure at the distance
whether he was telling it as chief Washington lobbyist for the

fire insurance companies or as assistant to President Truman and Director of the RFC. I noticed that he laughed heartily at his own joke; which may have solved the problem. The biologists have a word for it: autogamy. But George did not look like a flower fertilizing itself with its own pollen.

I nodded to a public-relations man at the next table. I had known him when he was a reporter, then an information man in a government department. Also, I knew that he had two daughters in college. He had a very pretty woman with him, and a rather dazed-seeming little man who looked as if he might be a division chief in the Department of Agriculture. The woman was talking to him as if he were Van Johnson.

Neuberger had just come back from Alaska and was telling me about the cold up there and the state of his kidneys.

"There's Worth Clark," he said suddenly.

Neuberger regards the State of Idaho as a part of his personal province as a writer.

The ex-Senator joined a party at a table.

"Is he living here now since he was defeated?" I asked. "He probably doesn't know it, but he's a distant cousin of mine."

"Yes," said Dick. "I think he is practicing with Tommy Corcoran."

He drank from a glass of milk.

"You know," he said suddenly, "somebody ought to write an article, 'You Can't Go Back to Pocatello.'"

"Pocatello?"

"That's his home town. It's a big town for Idaho. Oh, I guess twenty thousand people."

"Why can't he go back?"

"It isn't Clark. They just can't. They come down here to the Senate or something. Then they get beat. It isn't easy to go back and practice local law and live local lives."

"It is not only the little towns it's hard to go back to," I said.

And while we watched, big Jim Watson, of Indiana, walked across the room. Nobody noticed him. He had been Republican majority leader of the Senate under Hoover. He was an old man, eighty, I guessed. He had been defeated, too, but he was in Washington still.

"You can't go back to Pocatello," I said.

It would be a good story. You couldn't tell in the big dining room who hadn't gone back but had stayed as bureaucrats on the other side of the street. The lobby and the government were laughing together. The only difference would be which picked up the check. And suddenly the big, wicked lobbyists seemed, above the noise of people eating and talking on expense accounts that auditors far away would approve and the Bureau of Internal Revenue might pass, less wicked than sad.

XIII

Are We Being Followed?

I PUT on my reading glasses and ran my finger down the page:

Natl Apple Dryers Assoc Munsey bg......DIst 7925
Natl Apple Institute Munsey bg......EXecutive 0851
Natl Association for the Advancement of
    Colored People 100 Mass av nw......NAtional 5794
Natl Association Against the Return of
    Prohibition Washington bg..........REpublc 1080
Natl Assn of Air Forces Women
    1702 K nw............................DIst 1882
Natl Assn of Alcoholic Beverage Importers
    Inc Natl Press bg.................MEtrpltn 1617
National Assn of Bedding Manufacturers
    1029 Vt av nw........................DIst 4522

The list of organizations standing guard around the Capitol and the White House runs for thirteen tight columns on yellow paper in the back of the directory of the Chesapeake and Potomac Telephone Company. The big office buildings are packed with them. They occupy old residences from which old occupants have retreated to the suburbs. And some of the least of them are in suburbs themselves where a pressure group may be only a man saving money by doubling up on his house and office telephone. Indeed, the force behind an America intent upon its ends may be no more than a man behind a portable typewriter in the corner of a hall bedroom in a boarding house. But the force may sit opposite the White House, as the United States Chamber of Commerce does, be-

hind columns as high as those the government erects, in a
building designed by the same architect who ostentatiously
housed the Supreme Court. And half a block closer to the
White House, the CIO works in a white stone building of its
own, too. It bought it over the head of the Republican National Committee which, as a mere tenant, had to move.

Jim Carey told me about that. He does not look like a
pressure group. He looks, indeed, more like a dark, curly-
headed college boy than the national secretary of the Congress
of Industrial Organizations. He is no boy at a man's work,
however. His boss, Philip Murray, who speaks as slowly and
as gently as a bishop with a Scotch Presbyterian accent in a
Catholic mouth, would not keep Carey in his job if he were
not effective. Carey is actually a prodigy of pressure. He was
the president of a national union when he was twenty-two. As
Congressmen count, but not labor leaders, he has been in
Washington a long time. He was only twenty-seven when
he became CIO's national secretary in 1938. It was not long
afterward that he discovered, as Washington expanded in
preparation for war, that not the least pressure in Washington
was on office space. It seemed to him that every time he found
offices for Murray and his staff old man Jesse Jones moved
in to take them over for the government that was outgrowing
its big buildings.

"Am I being followed?" Carey asked.

Then he found the building on Jackson Place which is the
preferred location for those organizations and forces which
understand that government in democracy is a matter not
merely of elections but of steady applications of power between them. Carey looked at the building. He was shown all
over it by one of the tenants, a gentleman named McTavish of
the Republican National Committee. He was also shown, as
they moved, piles of anti-New Deal literature and, out a back
window, a government parking lot which the Scotch Republican said might better have been left to private property
paying taxes. Carey, who was a New Dealer—then and now

—looked and listened. He did not comment. But when they ended the tour he said that CIO would buy.

McTavish shook his head.

"That's going to mean we'll have to look for space," he said.

"Why," asked Carey, "you don't think you've got a future, do you?"

He recalled it and laughed. We stood across the street from the white stone building in Lafayette Square, by a strange old urn which must commemorate something out of the past. Every pressure group, whether it is as big as a major political party or as small as the man at the end of a party line in Takoma Park, thinks it has a future. Indeed, the whole business of pressure groups is the American future—or particular pieces of it. And, though the pure in America usually say "pressure groups" with puckered mouths, government in the United States would find it difficult to get along without them.

Carey and I looked along the street. From the United States Chamber of Commerce's noble columns, it runs past the National Grange and the CIO to the Carnegie Endowment for International Peace. As long ago as 1845, when statesmen and diplomats and the merely rich lived along there and job seekers congregated before them in the Square, it was known as the "lobby of the White House." It still is. Old man Baruch did not pick the particular park bench he did merely because it was comfortable. All Washington park benches are of standard design and bolted to the ground in a Republic which has learned to trust nobody. But the one Mr. Baruch picked sits where both he and the pressure groups (or maybe he is a one-man pressure group himself) congregate as the job seekers did long ago.

It may be unfortunate, but, as the political scientists have discovered, the national welfare does not move forward behind any straight line. In elections and between them, it bulges forward where the pressures of people are, and the line straightens only when other groups push to straighten the line or push ahead themselves. It may not be an ideal system for those who like to think of the movement of America as a decorous march under flags. It is the real system all the same, and one which is recognized officially now by a sort of semi-official council of pressures. Indeed, the government has asked the chiefs of the pressure groups to sit on so many governmental committees that many of them now have more government work to do than most government officials.

Today neither the politicians nor the pressure men look like the stream of desperate adventurers which Charles Dickens saw when he looked at Washington. But Mr. Dickens was more vivid than prophetic when he minimized the pressures of a republic upon its capital. Some Americans may still see a symbol in the pig he saw back of his hotel, turning up his stomach to the sun, and grunting "that's comfortable." I think he may still be right about his nineteenth-century notion that few people would live in Washington if they were not obliged to reside there. But his idea that the tides of emigration and speculation were little likely to flow in any time toward it was based upon a gone nineteenth-century notion of the meaning of government. The muddy distances between the buildings which he remembered are filled to overflowing. And the "regardless currents" of a pushing America now nowhere push so hard as in Washington. The West may be filled but now sometimes every man's frontier seems the District of Columbia. The Government of the United States may be getting a little short on arable land for settlement, but it seems to possess more than ever the things Americans are seeking.

Above Jim Carey and the thousands of other employees of pressure in Washington, the chief statesmen of perennial petition in person move with an importance not surpassed by Senators. And one of the best places to see them may be at a meeting of the Advisory Board of the Office of War Mobilization and Reconversion. They sit under an able lawyer, former

Governor O. Max Gardner of North Carolina, who represents the public—and with high public spirit. More recently he has also become the Undersecretary of the Treasury with the unanimous advice and consent of the Senate. There are other public representatives and private individuals, but most of the members come from the big offices of big pressure.

They are no more uniform in appearance than Congressmen are, or clerks. Eric Johnston of the United States Chamber of Commerce and Spokane, Washington, may represent, as some of his admirers have said, the youthful spirit of the West, but big Jim Patton of the Farmers' Union is seven years younger and from the West, too. William Green, president of the American Federation of Labor, is seventy-two, and has been a career man on Labor's payroll since before Patton was born in 1902. Only four Senators are still sitting who were in the Senate when Green took over the presidency of the A.F. of L. in 1924.

Young Johnston moved faster than Green. Indeed, his career may indicate that the way for a young man to get ahead in public affairs is to stay out of public affairs. Johnston tried to come to Congress, and ran a poor third. If he had won, he would still be waiting for seniority. (Also, he was defeated again, carrying only one county, when he ran for the Republican nomination for the Senate in 1940. His successful opponent was beaten by a Democrat.) Instead, as the head of the United States Chamber of Commerce he became such a national figure with so ingratiating a way of pleasing everybody that he could retire at forty-nine to the wealth and wages of the movies. He became not an actor, for which he would be well qualified, but president of the Motion Picture Producers and Distributors of America; which is a pressure group, too. (Incidentally, he succeeded Will Hays, who came up the hard way through politics as the Republican National Chairman and got the job when he was forty-three.)

Besides Patton and Green and Johnston, other chiefs of pressure sit on the important committee advising with regard to the American future. Philip Murray of the CIO is an essential figure at the table, and there is Thomas C. Cashen, of the Railway Labor Executives Association. The representatives of organized agriculture are at the table, too: the Farmers' Union's Patton; Albert Goss, president of the National Grange; and Edward A. O'Neal III, president of the American Farm Bureau Federation. Sometimes Robert Wason of the National Association of Manufacturers may sit on committees with them. And waiting expectantly to be heard, if not to sit on the committees, will be the representatives of plate glass and the Polish-Americans, the Jews and the importers of jute, lumber, sugar, silver; of the San Diego Chamber of Commerce, corn and hogs, butter and oleomargarine, world peace and ornamental iron, disabled veterans and the manufacturers of artificial limbs, Negroes and small-loan companies, bankers and the Oxychloride Cement Association.

They consider themselves as representing constituencies no less important than States and Districts. Indeed, some of them claim constituencies larger than whole batches of States. They think themselves quite as patriotic as Congressmen in representing their constituencies. Also, I am sure that, hard-headed pushers for their interests as they are supposed to be, they are at least as eager in the show of action for their constituents as any Congressmen ever are. And human vanity is not necessarily more rare among the gentlemen of pressure than among the gentlemen of politics.

The truth, of course, is that all of them are in politics. That is what pressure is. From the politics within their groups they push on the politics of America. Not all of them are as openly armed as Phil Murray, with his Political Action Committee. But they are all in politics all the same. Down through the hierarchy from his national office through the State and local Farm Bureaus and the county agents—some of whom local Farm Bureaus helped to pay—Ed O'Neal the Third had an organization ready for tough rural politics which was in existence long before PAC. Chambers of Commerce can be political units like country clubs—and often not much more effective.

The politics of pressure is not simple. Certainly when William Green and Philip Murray sit across one of the government's tables, both representing Labor, they can often seem further apart than even labor and industry are. The contentions of mere Democrats and Republicans can be sedate beside their struggling, even as old Senator McKellar seems sedate beside John L. Lewis. Indeed, the fierce institutional pride of the leaders of CIO and A.F. of L., each in his own organization, exceeds the insistent pride of Senators in the Senate. Farm leader can hate farm leader a good deal more energetically than either hates packers, middlemen or even price controllers. Jim Patton of the Farmers' Union is sure that Edward A. O'Neal III (there is an Edward A. O'Neal IV, too) is a pompous and reactionary representative of big farmers and big farming interests. O'Neal is equally confident that Patton is a young radical upstart with more bright ideas than farmers in his union. Albert Goss is closer to O'Neal than Patton in his thinking, but stronger still for Goss and the Grange.

All the chiefs of important pressure groups are as obviously intent upon getting members—and the support of members—as any politicians are on getting votes. In neither case is the process necessarily evil. It is a pretty poor Congressman who cannot convince himself that the best interests of the Republic depend upon his re-election. Such calm self-confidence in the service of their constituents is not denied to farm or labor leaders or the executive secretaries of the organizations of business and industry. They need it in the electoral processes of organizations, which are generally a good deal less freely democratic than elections are in plain politics. Even Congressman Butler B. Hare, of the Third South Carolina District, who got elected to the 79th Congress by the smallest vote in America (13,105 in a district of 304,379 people) may have won in a democracy which, with poll taxes, "White Primary" et al., is more free than that of most pressure groups.

But pressure is people. The chief reason for the furies against Sidney Hillman's direction of PAC was that it dramatized that. One man in Washington may persuade, but only people out where the voters are can really push. Hillman undertook not only to claim power behind pressure but to prove it. He is a strange man, with a reputation, nurtured by his enemies, as a wild ideological intruder from Lithuania, and an obvious vanity of his own based upon the knowledge that he is in fact a highly practical, though emotional man.

I was surprised at the luncheon table—in New York, not Washington—that he spoke with scant patience of the ineffectiveness of some of those with whose philosophies I am sure he agreed. Also, I was a little surprised at the calmness with which he contemplated the struggle then going on for full production and full employment.

"It is inevitable," he said in the thick accents which he still keeps though he walks, swinging his hat in his hand, in American streets as if he had been born to them, indeed, with more confidence than most men showed on those streets that day. Hillman does not wait for the inevitable. The PAC, which he designed and which he led, is an effective group in Washington because it is not in Washington but out by the doorbells and the ballot boxes on the continent.

In Seattle, not Washington, a little later, I met C. B. Baldwin, who had been Hillman's first assistant in the first 1944 campaign of the Political Action Committee. Baldwin and former Governor Elmer A. Benson, of Minnesota, new head of the National Citizens Political Action Committee, were on a circle of the country at the "grass roots" level about which some conservatives talk a great deal and which Hillman and Baldwin and Benson understand. Baldwin needs more attention from the country, which may have been paying too much attention to Tommy Corcoran. He is out of government, too. Though younger, he understands his way

around in it, I think, at least as well as Corcoran does. But
there is a continuity of purpose to his pushing from the outside
which Corcoran's law practice seems to lack.

"Beanie," as everybody calls him, grins as he goes, and I
suspect that at least some of his grinning in pressure grows
from the remembrance of the pushing around some conservative Democrats gave him while he was Director of the Farm
Security Administration. I do not know the exact directions
of Beanie's liberalism or how far to the left it has taken him.
But in pressure, he seems at least as native as his native Virginia.
His first name is Calvin, and he came to the government in
1933, when he was thirty-one, from the status of a small
business man in small East Radford in western Virginia.

The government must always be remembered as by turns
an immovable mountain which not even atomic bombs could
budge and an aluminum door on ball bearings which would
open if a child touched it. And often, nobody can be sure at
any time which it will be. Phony pressures from imaginary
people may be effective, while the actual pressure of millions
may result in arraying other millions against it. So far as I
know, there is no dependable guide to the balance. But almost
the chief business of government itself, in both the legislative
and executive branches, may often be the effort to evaluate the
forces which are constantly bombarding it.

In many cases I had, indeed, the feeling that the politicians
and officials understand the pressure groups far better than
the pressure groups understand the government. I have seen
big stacks of telegrams disregarded for their obviousness. Also,
I have watched corporate interests, which are sometimes described as "predatory," setting up pressure groups in Washington which obviously could have little other effect than
attracting the lightning to them. Often the poor little bureaucrat and the country Congressman seem shrewd beside the
slick suckers who are assessing themselves as persons, firms
and corporations to maintain pressure groups in the capital.
Many of them might do better if they phoned their Congressmen or even the bureaucrat they wish to push.

No pressure group, so far as I know, is admittedly maintained to put improper pressures on government. Most of them, indeed, are said to be designed for self-defense. A good many even seek their own ends in the name of the welfare of America—or even mankind. It is as difficult to find a predatory pressure group as it used to be to determine an aggressor nation. But sometimes their representatives urge some strange procedures and seek some amazing governmental action. I remember going one day into the office of Harold Boeschenstein, then vice-chairman of WPB, and finding him laughing. Some out-of-town junk dealers had been in to see him about a program they proposed in regard to the disposal of some materials as junk. Their suggestion shocked Boeschenstein and he told them so.

"Well," said one of them, "you can't blame a feller for asking."

Perhaps such asking is a part of the right of petition. And perhaps the American notion is that even an impertinent petition is constitutional. But certainly not all pressure groups are composed of the impertinent or the tough. Hardly any city has so large a proportion of persons devoted to noble causes. Not all of them support secretaries. Some of them represent good sense as well as good will. But with the possible exception of New York—and even the New York ones come down—Washington is above all others the American city of the Committee for the Cause. Also, in New York and Washington, it may be closely related to Society. Indeed, the wise woman, who wants to carry her idleness into Society, does not now try to get into a club—she joins a committee. She can make more progress socially addressing letters than giving parties. And it is sometimes as difficult to distinguish self-interest from disinterest among them as it is among diplomats or Senators. I, for one, would not try to do so.

I remember a very luscious lady in a royal purple suit who came to see me about the necessity for better care for the little children in the war. She had begun as a party politician in the middle of America. She had been very effective as a

National Committeewoman in Washington. Her husband back in the little town seemed further and further away. She not only made money but she married a new husband, an elderly gentleman and a rich one. She was pretty. And she was very effective for her cause, which happened also to be the cause of ladies much more firmly established than herself in the society to which she aspired. I hope that afterward they took her into their clubs, and maybe even asked her to dinner. Congressmen and stock salesmen have not hesitated to use similar techniques to get votes or sell bonds. I do not see why a lady in a purple suit should not do likewise without stirring laughter behind her as her slim legs move down the hall.

I spoke about her, smiling, to a newspaperman who came in as she departed.

"She's going to see Senator Soandso," I said. "Do you suppose he'll see her this afternoon?"

"See her? You know darn well he will. He'll pinch her till she's purpler than that suit."

I laughed. "I'd forgotten about him. I was thinking about Senators in general, and this town so crowded with pressure people."

He took a cigarette off my desk.

"You talk," he said, "as if pressure groups were both unwelcome and sinister forces which plagued the government. Some of them may be sinister, but certainly the plaguing does not all work in one direction. Why, if we didn't have pressure groups the politicians would have to invent them. As a matter of fact, most of them were invented by politicians. Pressure groups are no more anxious to have the power the politicians in office possess than the politicians are anxious to give it to them. You'd be surprised, if you could trace it, how often the hunger for votes runs ahead of the hunger for favors. There are politicians in this town staying awake nights thinking about things for pressure groups that have never yet occurred to the groups themselves."

I thought of that statement many times afterward. Of course, there are politicians in power eager for pressure groups to push them, in order that the group may be behind them. Obviously, such groups would not be in business if there were not response to the pressures they apply. Government is made up of men who know what they want quite as clearly as the agents of organized citizens or interests do. But sometimes what ought to be a nation falls, in its processes of decision, into the pieces of pressure which exceed in diversity the continuing geographical division of the nation in States and districts.

A President has to deal not only with a union of States but with a conglomeration of groups. A President may want the electoral votes both of Bilbo's Mississippi and of those Northern States in which Negroes hold important blocks of votes. A President may need the votes of the farmers and the workers to get the votes of Illinois or Ohio. He may depend upon pressure groups, when he cannot count on his party, to seek the enactment by the Congress of programs he proposes. Whether we like it or not, this nation is a federation of groups as well as a Federation of States. In our love of organization, we have made groups as much the parts of our politics, which is our government, as our States are, and often quite as respectable.

Fortunately, pressure has become a game that any number can play. Indeed, I doubt that there is anybody in this country who is not counted in a pressure group. Most of us belong to several of them. And from the very numbers—and the sometimes careless use of numbers in the descriptions of their power—both the groups and the politicians may be pushed back into the democracy of the people. Perhaps, as President Truman said, the American people themselves in their capacities as disinterested citizens are the greatest pressure group in the world. It is a familiar notion. Fortunately, also, it has been generally a recurrent American fact. But pressure and response to it in Washington are not merely recurrent; they are perpetual.

But sometimes even the greatest and toughest pressures run against stonewall men. I remember a conversation in the days when Fred Vinson was, as Director of Economic Stabilization, standing firm against well-armed efforts to break holes in the defense against inflation. Frank Graham, president of the University of North Carolina and then a member of the War Labor Board, spoke in admiration to Vinson about it. Graham is also, though a little man, a hard man to push around. But he asked Vinson for "the secret of your rugged immobility."

I was interested in Vinson's reply. First, he said modestly that he couldn't admit Graham's charge that he had any such special strength in resistance. He looked thoughtful for a moment. Then he said a significant thing, in his Kentucky mountain drawl.

"You know," he said, "where I come from it was dangerous to be afraid."

It can be dangerous still, and not only for a man but for America as well. I thought about that as I stood in the Square by the big buildings of the pressure groups which so long ago had been called the "lobby of the White House." I know that even Presidents, in strength or weakness, look attentively across the White House lawn and the Square to the men in the private buildings of agriculture and commerce and labor around it, quite as much as men in those buildings look eagerly to power across the Square and the street.

Old, erudite, fastidious, pessimistic Henry Adams used to look out on that Square, too. The house he shared with John Hay is gone now. There is a hotel today, where men from the CIO and the Chamber of Commerce, the Grange and the government drop in for lunch. The scene Adams saw has not greatly changed. Andrew Jackson is still out there, looking both Presidential and precarious on a rearing horse. But when Henry Adams looked at the Square and the government, he turned from his window with the feeling that the tragic thing about the men in the government was that they were "pathetic in their helplessness to do anything with power when it came to them."

Henry Adams is as dead now as his great-grandfather, President John. Today in Washington if anybody has any power, he need not be pathetic about knowing what to do with it. He will find those eager to guide him as thick as the grass around Jackson in the Square. The pigeons fertilize that grass and men have to get over a black iron fence to keep it cut.

XIV

The Press Stands Up

THAT night he was a very gay man in the bar of the National Press Club talking very sour doctrine. He looked the whole length of the dark-paneled room as if he were appraising the American Press and its Washington members with affection but without approval.

"You can write it down as Grogan's law," he said. His name was not Grogan, but Grogan will serve. "It is that publishers follow the leads of their Washington correspondents, rather than the opposite as the radicals make the mistake of assuming in damning the capitalistic press."

He drank his Scotch, the sale of which during the war was monopolistically restricted to Press Club members only.

"The proof of the law," he said nodding amiably at the heads huddled over tables in the long room, "is to be found in Grogan's Theory of Substitution. A Congressman gets here by a one-vote plurality in his district and, by golly, he hasn't been here long before he's thinking of himself as The People. Even clerks get the notion that they're The Government. And it's no time at all before newspapermen, who were running after firewagons before they left Chicago, begin to think of themselves as The Press."

I laughed. I had been on both sides of the business of covering Washington and of the Washington that is covered. I had —and I hope I have—more friends among Washington newspapermen than almost any other group. But there was something to what Correspondent Grogan said over his Scotch.

It would be difficult to find a body of men who more clearly represent Washington than the gentlemen of the press who report it. There are notions, carefully cultivated, that they are in Washington but not of it, and that they stand in scrutiny but also in separation. Actually, of course, they are probably more representative of the good and the bad on the capital scene than any other body of bureaucrats. As they stay in Washington, which most of them hope to do, they are at least as remote from the country as the administrators are.

"This idea that they are The Press accounts for the high incidence of horsetails among Washington correspondents." The man whose name was not Grogan did not use the word "horsetails"; that is the Daniels system of substitution. But he went on. "They rapidly lose sight of the fact that they are merely social security numbers on the books of a capitalized printing corporation back in Des Moines or Kansas City and, as The Press, begin to think that part of their function is to save public servants from themselves."

He smiled and drank.

"As you well know, the reactionaries around President Roosevelt used the so-called Sound Men, the solemn, superior and secure members of the Washington press, to point out to Roosevelt, to their publishers and their countrymen that 'You can't fight two wars at once,' 1940, and 'You can't have recovery and reform, too,' 1938. The Gridiron boys—and, hell, I'm just using them as a group—they get to go to the Better Houses and drink really better bourbon with the Sound Men in government. And they pass the word on to their publishers (who generally aren't too bright); not the other way around."

It was an interesting theory, but a little too elaborate. Even Grogan laughed, but he was serious, too. The press as assembled for potation does not look so impressive or impressed with itself. Indeed, you can see the conventional picture of conventional American newspapermen at the Press Club bar. It is a pleasant place to see this picture and be a part of it. In all Washington, so far as I know, it is the only bar where men are permitted to stand up and drink. I forget whether it has a brass rail across the bottom, but the result is the same. And the whisky is good. The standing up in Washington (where the law requires sitting down) is an unconscious gesture of journalistic independence of the petty regulations of a great capital. The press is free.

But the less romantic and more real portrait of the Washington press can better be seen in Arlington or Chevy Chase—or among the better paid Sound Men on Foxhall Road or in Georgetown. In suburbia, the correspondent (and everybody seems to be a correspondent, from copy boys to Arthur Krock) looks like the bureaucrats who live beside him. He may still spend a higher proportion of his income on potables than either the entomologist who lives on one side of him or the fiscal assistant who lives on the other, but looking at them you cannot easily tell them apart. Their worlds, their lives and their language are apt to be much the same. Even young entomologists do not always talk entomology. Occasionally even newspapermen talk about something besides newspapers and newspapering. But in the war years at least, when government brought in many outsiders, the correspondents seemed to belong to an older, more permanently fixed part of Washington bureaucracy.

They had settled down with more security than had the Congressmen. A good many of them had found ruts to ride in. Many appreciated the handouts as paper work which saved them leg work and head work. A good many of them had been in and out of government as both correspondents and government information men by turns. Sometimes in the newspaper ownership of radio stations and in the war period of paper rationing they served not merely as correspondents for their papers but also as agents closely resembling lobbyists before the Federal Communications Commission and the War Production Board.

In war and in peace some of the more prominent among

them are apt to become statesmen if they do not watch themselves and some other newspaperman does not laugh. The
British Ambassador is often happier to see them than Senators
from Iowa or New York. Some correspondents even wear
spats. Some carry umbrellas and even brief cases. And a great
many of them grow old dozing around the Press Club like old
Interior Department bureau chiefs snoring behind their newspapers in the Cosmos Club four blocks away.

Changing government, indeed, may seem a little too fresh
from the country to old-timers of the bureaucracy of the
press. I remember Homer Joseph Dodge telling a story about
that at the Press Club bar. I do not know when Mr. Dodge
arrived in Washington. He seemed pretty settled when I
was a newcomer to the press gallery, in 1925. I know he was
covering the Treasury Department at least as far back as
William Gibbs McAdoo. He seems as essential to the decorations of the Press Club now as the lacquered front-page mats
of American newspapers in the halls. He is white-haired now
—very white-haired against the dark clothes he wears—with
a young face and a deep voice with which he speaks in calm
courtliness to listeners. He awards them titles as he converses.
And in the early part of the Roosevelt Administration he went,
after some absence, to attend one of Henry Morgenthau's
press conferences. He asked a very pointed question.

As Dodge reported the event, Morgenthau looked at him
with some surprise.

"You must be new here, Mr. Dodge."

"No," said Mr. Dodge in his deep voice. "You are new
here."

It is not merely a joke. Actually there are more newspapermen with long records of seniority and service in Washington
than there are men with equal service records among members
of Congress or among the politically changing top men in
the executive departments. The notions about the bright
young men of the press need considerable revision. Unlike
Congress, in which if you are re-elected often enough you are

bound to become prominent, not all old men among the correspondents attain membership in the Gridiron Club, which is the select and exclusive organization of newspapermen. Annually it makes fun of statesmen, but its members take themselves in their organization very seriously all the year round. However, of the forty-eight active members in that most venerated of American newspaper clubs at least twenty-three have been newspapering in Washington for twenty years or more. In the whole of Congress, which is a much less exclusive organization, only thirty-two Congressmen and Senators have proved so durable—no President, no Cabinet member, no Justice of the United States Supreme Court has been in Washington so long.

Outside the Gridiron Club there are many more gentlemen of seniority who have watched brash new governments, strange new ideas, naïve innovators and wild young notions come and go. The press is perpetual, and so seem many of its members. Harry J. Brown, active member of the Gridiron Club and Washington correspondent of the *Salt Lake Tribune* and the *Spokane Spokesman-Review*, began as a Washington correspondent before three members of President Truman's Cabinet were born. Lewis Gaynor Wood, of *The New York Times*, began his service in the press gallery before Senator K. D. McKellar began to accumulate the longest service and seniority in the Senate. Mark Foote, correspondent for Michigan papers, and Carter Field, of the Bell Syndicate, arrived in Washington about the same time Sam Rayburn did. James L. Wright of the *Buffalo Evening News* came to Washington just a little while after Adolph Sabath arrived from Illinois to begin the service that has made him Dean of the House.

Obviously, not all members of the corps of correspondents can be members of the exclusive Gridiron Club. Some do not even own the tails and white tie which are required at peacetime Gridiron Club dinners. Also, the press corps has been freshened, as Congress and bureaucracy have been, by newcomers and the young. Back in 1925 under prohibition, when

I was a Washington correspondent, the club had no bar for either standers or sitters, and there were only 279 members of the press gallery. When I counted in 1946, there were 695 active members of the press gallery, plus a new radio gallery of 116, a periodical gallery of 102, and 89 accredited photographers. Big government was running ahead, but the American press was not being left so very far behind. There were, in 1946, more newspapermen accredited to cover the Congress than Representatives and Senators put together. And, in such a semi-official bureaucracy, a good many were young, not getting rich nor famous nor members of the Gridiron Club. More, old and young, moved in the constant Washington shifting back and forth from free enterprise to public service and the other way around. It is safe to say that in the government's information services the various departments and agencies employ more people to help newspapermen than there are newspapermen to be helped. Helping them, too, are many public-relations men and publicity agents for private causes and interests, both noble in purpose and predatory in intent. The Gridiron is still the House of Lords of the Fourth Estate.

I made my inquiries of Lewis Wood, who is the club's historian, about the gentlemen with the little gold gridirons on their lapels. As a correspondent of *The New York Times*, he ranks well ahead of Republican Majority Leader Joe Martin in seniority in Washington. He is a forthright customer whom after a Gridiron dinner I remember scolding Heywood Broun, with whom he had worked on the copy desk of a New York paper, for ostentatious display. Broun had come to the dinner not in tails and white tie but in a dandruff-decorated blue serge suit. Born in South Carolina, Wood thinks he is a better Southerner than I am because he knew how to spell "Wesson" in Smith & Wesson. (I put a "t" in it.) You didn't need to carry Smith & Wessons or any other guns when I began reporting in the South. He wrote me an affectionately insulting letter about the club.

"P.S.," he said, putting the P.S. at the top of the letter because there was no room left at the bottom, "founded January 24, 1885, or sixty years ago, the Gridiron Club has had, living and dead, only 253 members in all that time."

That would have been in the last days of Chester A. Arthur. Naturally, in that time its members and even the lesser press in Washington have had time to develop an institutional feeling about the dignity of the press and its powers which is approximated only by Senators toward their own institution. Publishers, indeed, have been impressed by this dignity on their payrolls. They come eagerly when their employees in Washington summon them to Gridiron banquets—or even the less exclusive banquets of the organized press. They seem to be getting something more than copy for their money when they hear their hired help calling Cabinet officers by their first names. It is not strange that afterward they listen to their correspondents' suggestions as to policy with respect.

The dignity of the press is not to be spoken of lightly even by Presidents. It must have seemed slightly impertinent for Franklin Roosevelt to win four times in a row with most of the press (though not always the correspondents) against him. And sometimes Franklin Roosevelt turned the knife in the wound. It was probably inevitable, when the New Dealers came as newcomers to town that some of the press, as represented by its elders in eminence, should, after initial sense of rescue, feel about its brashness as the Congress sometimes did and the Supreme Court. There were more than nine old men in Washington, and some of them could use the typewriter.

If many of the New Dealers are gone now, the debate over the power of the press in government and politics remains. Indeed, under Truman, the chief New Deal debater on the subject who "used to be a newspaperman himself," Harold Ickes remained for a while and then departed with more newspaper attention than the press has ever given any departing Cabinet officer. Now once again he is a part of the press he belabored. As I mentioned earlier, Franklin Roosevelt remembered almost too well that he had been editor of *The Harvard Crimson* in 1904. One of the essentials of the American free press apparently is that everybody from Presidents down knows how it should be run to improve it—and often they are right.

Sometimes in amity, and occasionally in irritation, the debate continued as to whether the press had lost its influence and whether the press was free. The answers are not easy. But sometimes both the press and the President (and particularly such Presidential subordinates as Mr. Ickes) seemed to me as both New Dealers and newspapermen to be inclined to oversimplify both the questions and the answers. Demonstration of the power of the press does not require the demonstration that its readers are its stooges, but neither, I suspect, does the disagreement at election time of the people and the papers prove that the press is merely dumbly predatory in its purpose. And even among the most stubbornly reactionary publishers, there is at least a mustard seed of truth in Grogan's law.

Most publishers wanted to beat Roosevelt. (Item from William Jennings Bryan: More people are bribed by their own money than anybody else's.) Their partisanship never seemed to me surprising. But it has always seemed to me a neat question (despite the confidence about it of some radical commentators) as to whether publishers pushed reluctant correspondents or correspondents pushed publishers.

A good part of the art of news depends upon the drama of controversy. Inevitably the reporter, though he be a Washington correspondent, fosters it. His very seeking for it throws him into a critical position with regard to any administration. I remember that when I first went to Washington to work the news stories grew in a pattern of controversy between my boss, James M. Landis, Director of the Office of Civilian Defense, and Fiorello LaGuardia whom he had succeeded. I happened to be in New York, and found my hotel box stuffed with messages from the Mayor. He had to see me.

"You tell Jim for me," he said, "to stop letting these press fellers try to make a fight between us. I haven't said anything about him, but they'll try to make a fight. They always do."

In his shirt sleeves he looked both round and contentedly wise in his chair.

"Jim doesn't understand them," he said. "I know 'em. You take these fellows that have been shooting at me."

He enumerated some of the publishers above the reporters:

1. "He's an appeaser at heart."
2. "He'd rather win an election than win the war."
3. "His ambition is to be Ambassador to Japan."
4. "He's nuts."

I began to smile at the catalogue.

"And Hearst," said His Honor the Mayor, "is still a son-of-a-bitch."

I laughed. I doubted some of the details of the arraignment. I doubted even that most of the publishers were promoting the Landis-LaGuardia fight, much as they might enjoy it. But as newspaperman I know that the Mayor was not necessarily wrong in his idea that newspapermen quote quarrelers back and forth to each other in public until a difference can grow across front pages to the headlined drama of a feud. It is not distortion. In covering a city hall or a national administration, it may be art—and an art implicit in the craft rather than one craftily plotted by publishers.

There are other items to be remembered, though they seldom are, in the free-press debate. The press gallery is in Washington, and Congressmen and Senators are not the only people there who live between statesmanship and demagoguery. Even if some newspapermen can be a little pompous about it and mistake themselves for the institution, The Press *is* an institution in our government, just as Congress is, the Presidency and the Court, and subject to the same human forces which shape them all. Critics of both politicians and newspapermen seem addicted to the obvious. The notion persists that powers or publishers dictate to them. It is a notion which misses the fact that many politicians and some newspapermen hasten to please before they are pushed.

The really strange idea of the press and its friends is that in Washington The Press is somehow free from those forces which The Press is first to recognize as shaping public servants into bureaucrats and old Congressmen into crotchety and nervous politicians. The gentlemen of the press have been there a long time. In their very numbers is diversity. But in Washington they are at least more petted than most other bureaucrats are. A Krock may seem more important than a Cabinet minister—to Krock and other people as well. Reporters, native to small-town Georgia, eat caviar at the Russian Embassy, beside Congressmen from rural Iowa, and to the same physiological and psychological ends.

With bureaucrats and politicians they live in Rogers Heights, and Arlington, Chevy Chase, Silver Spring, the Shoreham, on P Street and in Bethesda. Even in the city of bureaucracy and politics, an entomologist can keep his eyes on his bugs and a meteorologist may keep his mind on the wind and the stars, but a newspaperman's business is bureaucratic bickering and the political parade. He lives closer to the forces that are supposed to transform Americans into something strange in the capital than almost any people in it. He is presumed, of course, to be immune. He represents the lively, productive back country in a nation which thinks of Washington as the sterile, tax-consuming capital. So do Congressmen. Indeed, in the *Official Register of the United States*, old bureaucrats are listed by the States of their origin, but most of them are caught in Washington all the same.

The stereotype of the newspaperman disappears beside the stereotype of the Washingtonian. There are agricultural chemists who drink more than the newspapermen of legend. Some newspapermen, indeed, do not drink at all. They congregate, as other Washington groups do in other places, in their own National Press Club—though Walter Lippmann and Arthur Krock will generally be found lunching at the more elegant

Metropolitan Club, and Drew Pearson will be paying the check at a table at the Mayflower.

In the press gallery and in the departments, some of the best men seem native to America and not merely operators in Washington. Tom Stokes, after twenty-four years in Washington, still talks and looks like Georgia—the top of his head seems as "marginal" in the production of hair as Georgia's old fields where fine cotton used to grow and grows no more. Raymond P. (Pete) Brandt, of the *St. Louis Post-Dispatch*, walks his dog by the houses of Senators, officeholders and local real-estate operators in Spring Valley, but he still seems to keep his feet on a ground as native as Sedalia, Missouri, where every year his and Truman's neighbors hold their State Fair. Neither Stokes nor Brandt looks like a member of Congress of similar seniority. If Stokes is losing his hair, he keeps his objectivity. Brandt is keeping both his objectivity and his hair. They are only two of many excellent men in the press gallery, as there are also excellent men in other branches and institutions, powers and traditions which bring Americans to Washington.

Newspapermen, of course, are no more united than Senators are. They not only guard and cudgel the government, depending upon their own views and the views of their papers, they can quarrel among themselves about each other and about their bosses. I remember still two AP men complaining in the tiny dining room of the Press Club to which ladies are admitted about the dirty deal they thought Edward Kennedy, the AP man with Eisenhower, had received from the AP after his scoop on European victory was officially denounced as confidence-breaking. I remembered how that premature story had hit the White House when I was serving as Press Secretary to the President. It looked as if AP had the great news beat. AP boasted about it. But official information indicated that Kennedy was guilty of the crime in the newspaperman's code of breaking an agreement into which he had entered with the army and with other newspapermen. Then beyond boasting, came the regrets of Robert McLean as president of the AP for what Kennedy had done. The AP men at the table in the Press Club were still sore about that months later.

"Yeah," one said, "he regretted it, but did you know that before that story came in McLean went up to New York and personally took over in the news rooms? He's a helluva fellow to be regretting. Ed was given the gate and the rap."

(I checked: McLean was not in New York during the entire week surrounding the incident.)

Newspapermen's news is not all in their papers. They gossip (and not merely in syndicated columns) in Washington as Congressmen do, and lobbyists and stenographers. That may be one mark of their acclimatization to the capital. But even in Washington, where somehow after a while all men of all crafts seem to be shaped after the capital's own stock of stereotypes, in the Press Club they seem newspapermen still, talking and grousing as they would be, after turning in their copy, in Kansas City or Boston or Seattle. If Washington has marked them, they keep the protective coloration of newspapermen still, city-hall-tough, State-Capitol-hearty, gregarious, talkative, and deeply but secretly sentimental.

It takes all kinds of men to make a press gallery for the Republic, and some must be as skillful as Senators in handling their constituencies. I went around to see Bascom N. Timmons, of Texas, who has been the press gallery's own perennial candidate for the Democratic Vice-Presidential nomination. Political commentators still regard his speech at Pittsburgh, Pennsylvania, on his way to the convention in 1944, as a classic. As I remember it, he took his text from the Johnstown flood and among other things was prepared, if he were nominated, to promise the Johnstown citizens security from acts of God. Actually it should not have been too great a feat for him. Only two members of the Texas delegation in Congress have been in Washington longer than he has. Even more remarkable, he is Washington correspondent for both Jesse Jones's *Houston Chronicle* and Marshall Field's *Chicago*

Sun. To duplicate that feat, a mere Congressman would have to be politically secure in a district with a free ballot which contained both Tupelo, Mississippi, and Harlem, New York City. But Bascom grins, tall and shy and with a slight, ingratiating stutter. The pursuit of politicians has been his profession, but cats rescued from the late, dark Washington streets have been his avocation.

"Politicians are nearly all alike," he told me. "I never saw two cats who even remotely resembled one another. Politicians are pretty noisy. Cats know the expressive power of silence. The cat is the most mistreated and most neglected animal on earth. Most politicians are treated too well. Cats are natural, and I am afraid some politicians are phonies."

But I was in pursuit of the portrait of the politician, the bureaucrat, and the newspaperman, not the cat. On the walls of his office on the twelfth floor of the National Press Building, Timmons had hung the portraits of his heroes: Robert E. Lee, Grover Cleveland, and John L. Sullivan. The picture of John L. Sullivan, ready for the ring, was from the *Police Gazette* (which, in 1945, had no Washington correspondent) and in it, the Boston Strong Boy held his hands modestly across his breast to hide the nipples. Back of Bascom, the picture suddenly seemed to me to represent the full spirit of the American press in the American capital. It is romantic as Lee, dully honest as Cleveland, and, like the Boston Strong Boy, it does not know its strength.

XV

"The Saloon, the Salon and the Salome"

THEY went in, smelling very nice and dressed in their best, to sit on the little formal gold chairs in the East Room of the White House where long ago, as its first mistress, Abigail Adams had hung out her wash. They sat, wide and purposeful on the spindly chairs, or, purposeful still, with slim crossed legs. Under the huge chandeliers the long room was full of attentive ladies. I remember that I felt very lone and male among them. I counted the few masculine heads among the hats.

I come wide for a gold chair, and those in the White House are obviously designed for formality rather than comfort. Nobody is ever supposed to be comfortable on the first floor of the White House. Also, I am a man with few gifts for patient listening to day-long talk, male or female. But I had been appointed ("assigned" is probably the more honest word) as Presidential observer at this meeting devoted to a polite female push for more representation in the affairs of the government and the world. A better world was in the making, and the better women wanted better jobs. But as far as I could ever discover, then or afterward, the chief result of the meeting was to provide a picture of women in government and in Washington.

It was not a perfect picture. Some of the most essential feminine items were missing. Even some of those who attended (I remember one beautifully dressed wife of a Cabinet officer) seemed more bored than concerned. The ladies were still the women, including Clare Luce (who was not there).

And the women, as Representative Luce (Republican—Connecticut) has indicated to us, do not always think of sex and solidarity as one. But the professional women sat and listened. A good many of them spoke. Mrs. Mary McLeod Bethune seemed both professional woman and professional Negro, and somehow both seemed very much the same. A blond girl reporter and I slipped out and had a cigarette together on one of the benches in the basement on which diplomats may sit at receptions while their ladies are getting or depositing their wraps. She inhaled, I remember, like a police reporter in a city room, but she still looked young and pretty. She shook a yellow head about her sisters upstairs. Women, she suggested, could as women sometimes be pretty hard to bear.

"Even in Washington?"

"Especially in Washington," she said.

Being male and in Washington, I laughed. Then I remembered the monumental arrangement by which Washington recognizes women—an arrangement which seems to have been missed by most of the women themselves. That Freedom on top of the Capitol, whose cap was changed by Jefferson Davis lest liberty be taken too seriously by those still in chains, is, of course, a woman. Down below her in Statuary Hall the pretty secretaries of members of Congress move through the Capitol with their hard heels clicking on the stones. (There may be more reasons than cash why many Congressmen have their wives as their secretaries.) And down below Freedom and the secretaries, straight below them, the monument to early suffrage leaders has been consigned alone to the crypt of the Capitol. Guides, pointing out in the dim light the marble block from which the busts of the leaders emerge, refer to it as "The Three Old Ladies in a Bathtub." In their basement together the ladies look a little lost and grim.

My blond companion that day in the White House basement did not look either lost or grim. As reporter, she was a member of a craft in which in Washington there are ten times more women today than there were when I began reporting there in 1925. There were ten lonely ladies in the press gallery then. Now there are more than a hundred. But the progress has not wholly satisfied all the ladies who are parts of it. I remember the private feminist movement of May Craig, Washington correspondent of Maine newspapers, to get herself admitted to the stag dinner of the White House Correspondents' Association. She was a White House correspondent. The White House correspondents were going to have a dinner. There was no trouble with her feminine logic. Unfortunately, she ran straight into male emotionalism. If May were admitted, wives would not stay home. The whole pattern of the party would be altered. May took her case not only to the officers of the White House Correspondents' Association but to the President of the United States. She did not get in— not that year. But I have watched May in a pert hat standing in the front row of a press conference questioning even a President for her Portland papers. My judgment is that she will ask again.

But my observation was that other Washington newspaper-women, in 1945, were considerably less concerned about joining the men at dinner than they were about the continuation of the press conferences of the wife of the President, to which generally only women are admitted. Eleanor Roosevelt was gone and Bess Truman had arrived. That made a difference for women who make a living covering the affairs of women for women. May Craig wanted to banquet in equality, but the other girls were also anxious to survive in segregation. I think May and the other girls together indicated the position and the hopes of women in Washington better than did the White House meeting of determined ladies on the gold chairs.

With considerably more force than politics, the telephone and the typewriter have made Washington seem a more than ordinarily feminine town. The beauty parlors in it seem at least as numerous as the liquor stores; and the liquor stores do not restrict themselves to a masculine clientele. But the strange thing, a quarter of a century after the Nineteenth Amendment, is the acute scarcity of women important in the government of the nation. Nobody even discusses any more the old suggestion that women would elevate and purify the politics of their country. The pertinent present fact is that the women have not done very well even for themselves. Lady orators and men speaking to the lady politicians sometimes make the part played by the women in government sound more impressive than it is. Once there was a lady Cabinet officer. There were ten women in Congress in 1946. But there were even fewer women in the whole executive branch getting as much as $9,000 a year. The electing people have done better by the sex than the appointing officials. And among women, even more than among men, the politicians and the pensioned have most of the good jobs.

The women still hold the well-paid jobs which have always been regarded as women's jobs in relation to women and children, home economics and the like. (Strangely, perhaps, the Children's Bureau has not only always been largely staffed by women, but by childless and unmarried women. There was a joke around Washington to the effect that virginity was a requirement among employees who dealt with maternity.) An overwhelming percentage of all top jobs filled by women are occupied by ladies who (like males in the top jobs) have been party politicians. But the ladies rewarded seem in general older than the political males, and often duller. Apparently such women have also brought a special female tenacity to the old dictum that few die and none resign.

Even today in the Congress, three of the lady statesmen were first elected as the relicts of dead Congressmen. One of them, Edith Nourse Rogers, of Massachusetts, however, has made a good record in her own right as Republican Representative, and there is no reason to believe that the country would lose if a Republican victory made her Chairman of the Committee on World War Veterans' Legislation in place of John Rankin, of Mississippi. Mary Norton, of New Jersey, has been effective as Chairman of the Labor Committee, even if she is less the product of the era of the new woman than of the machine of old Boss Hague, of Jersey City. Now on The Hill a new type of Congresswoman seems to be emerging. The creators of the type seem less women as women than people as people. No Republican or Democrat either would want Clare Luce, including both her coiffure and her claws, to be less feminine than she is. But Luce, and Helen Douglas, of California, and Emily Douglas, of Illinois, seem not merely women in politics but effective showmen at the polls. It may be a pertinent item that all three of them have been connected with the stage. Yet, all of them were made to seem somehow politically old-fashioned by the event which in 1946 brought Helen Douglas Mankin, as a Southern white woman Democrat, to Congress largely as the result of the voting of Negroes in Georgia.

Undoubtedly the Congresswomen are important. The lady occupants of the fattest jobs are important, too. (Hattie Caraway, of Arkansas, apparently has the distinction not only of being the first woman to be a real Senator but the first lady lame duck to get a quiet but remunerative Federal job.) The really significant women in Washington are seldom seen in the newspapers, but they are effective and essential in the operation of government itself. To use a phrase that the men brought into government from business, they are the "knowhow" women. And not even the men who depend upon them often admit how important their "know-how" is in the operation of government itself.

Nobody would try to count them all. There is Ruth Shipley, who is often regarded as a dragon in pince-nez glasses on guard over the State Department's passports. I do not know when she came into the government, but she has been head of the Passport Division since 1933. Nobody has publicly paid much attention to the big part Marguerite Owen has had in the success of the TVA as its Washington representative. Mary E. Switzer, Assistant to the Administrator of the Federal Security Agency, came to Washington in 1922 when she was twenty-two, and not many people have learned more than she has about government in that time. Bess Goodykoontz, who looks like a schoolteacher, came to Washington as one in 1929, but the impression is pretty general that she possesses a good part of such brains as may be found in the United States Office of Education, where she is Assistant Commissioner. Certainly, one of the heartiest and wisest women in Washington is Katherine Blackburn, chief of the Government Information Service in the Bureau of the Budget. She looks like a big Irish woman. I suppose she is one. I know she has combined humor and courage and intelligence in her Washington career.

There are others. Some of them are rather solemn sisters. Getting ahead in government can be a very serious business for a woman. She has to face a lot of humorless superiority from men who are sometimes merely male. A good many of the ladies near—but not at—the top work in connection with the important but often humorless fields of "welfare." But I can report that some of the best Scotch I drank in Washington and some of the best talk I heard there was high in the Hay-Adams where some philanthropic foundation subsidizes a suite for the gathering of gay people, male and female, who are concerned in the government and around it with the welfare of the people of the United States.

Such women as Blackburn and Switzer and the others are the captains of "know-how" among the women of government in Washington. But I doubt that even they are as important as the greater number of the non-coms of "know-how" who as secretaries and assistants to a great many male officials help not only those gentlemen but the people of the United States. They are not only important; a good many of them are pretty. Even in a democracy and under Civil Service looks do a girl no harm. Nor in this age does a telephone voice. The appearance of his secretary builds the dignity of the official. And, if she happens to have brains, too, half his troubles are over. A remarkable number of them do have brains. Maybe because women do not often get the better jobs, some of the best female brains in Washington are in the secretarial places. A man can be made by his secretary. Certainly, a secretary can save him. (I knew one who had the greatest gifts for the plausible protection of her high official whose "conferences" were apt to be his drunks.) But if secretaries can save, they can destroy, too. And Washington has its share of the stupid sisters whose notion of building up their bosses is to impress his callers with their relative insignificance.

Obviously, of course, there are important women in Washington who are not in government. I suppose Gladys Tillett, woman Vice-Chairman of the Democratic National Committee, is not in government, but my own bet is that she has a better political head than Hannegan, who is. A good deal of government meets at the Sunday suppers of Evalyn Walsh McLean, in Georgetown, where society is always a sort of circus of celebrities. Eleanor ("Sissy") Patterson of the Washington *Times-Herald* is perhaps important to government as an irritant. Red-headed Cornelia Bryce (Mrs. Gifford) Pinchot and erect Daisy (Mrs. J. Borden) Harriman march their causes into government offices all over town.

Also, a woman may have a place in society and on a payroll, as Senator Joe Ball's wife does as his secretary—as Harry Truman's wife did. A woman official may seem a society woman, too. I remember once how Frances Perkins, moving toward her desk through her long anterooms in the Department of Labor, seemed to me to look less like a government official than a lady whose chauffeur had just brought her to her palace. My own opinion is that Frances Perkins was a better Secretary of Labor than she ever seemed to be. She was loyal to her President and devoted to the cause of labor. But sometimes in the Labor Department she seemed almost too much the lady. She sat that day at her desk in her big office twisting her white hands together as if she were putting on her gloves. She made a casual gesture about a great problem.

"Labor," she said, "is fresh as paint."

Both Labor and Society remain. Perhaps the high variety of hospitality is passing. Franklin Roosevelt used to like to report the supposedly more elegant past. In World War I, he said, the tired official looking for recreation in the afternoons could take his choice on Massachusetts Avenue of the house where every kind of drink was served, the residence where artists and writers and intellectuals served high talk about an artistic hostess, and a mansion where the music was soft, so were the sofas, and the ladies were very pretty.

"The saloon, the salon, and the Salome," he described them.

I doubt that they are gone. Society in Washington is a very serious business. So far as I know, no ladies have been fighting lately about their seating at the table. But ladies have been struggling all the same. Even in a democracy society has to make some sort of aristocratic pretensions. It has to have some faith in itself. There are groups working hard at the business of being castes. There are women working hard—and as slaveys—over the parties in some Washington clubs as other women do in hinterland villages in preparing the supper for the Epworth League in the basement of the Methodist Church. It is not necessary to own a palace to have a salon. The most reasonable facsimile of a salon I saw while I was in Washington was in the house on H Street of my friend, Agnes Inglis. She is a gay, intelligent woman, now running a Washington school, who has four adopted sons and, at that point, had no dependable income. But her house was a vital place which attracted all sorts of interesting people. The first floor of the house, I remember, had a bookstore, and we called it "the rookery over the bookery." When Agnes organized her school, Daisy Harriman took over the house as the headquarters for some of her good works. However good the work may be, I am sure the house misses the company and the talk.

The belles have not all disappeared. There are beauties in Washington today, some of them filing questionnaires. And there are glamorous ladies. But even Clare Luce is no more majestic and certainly has no more political influence as political beauty than Kate Chase Sprague had nearly a hundred years ago when Kate Chase was young and had no notion that she could ever be old and poor. There are wits still among the ladies, but somehow American wit as circulated from the pretty women of cocktail parties seems to have gone the way of the wise crack and the smut crack. (A rich, prominent, often-married Washington woman married again, and the contemporary lady wit of Washington sent her a telegram: "Anything new?")

There remains, of course, arrogance combined with elegance. There are ladies—and gentlemen, too—who talk more outrageously about their officials than any members of the official opposition would. Some of them, indeed, talk about the living and the dead as violently as does Eleanor Patterson's *Times-Herald*, which is a paper as shrill as a woman who might still want to scream in a palace. (I remember with respect Alice Longworth's rejection with distaste of some of those who thought they shared an enmity with her. "Some of the comments," Theodore Roosevelt's daughter said, "were noticeably lacking in the Greek quality of Aidos—the quality that deters one from defiling the body of a dead enemy.") Some of the members of the old and established families are old and well-established. And some are more insistently reactionary because they are not. Also, some of the most secure are concerned about conditions in the country and not merely about their own places and comforts in the capital.

One of the beautiful things about Washington itself has somehow been the way it is often shaped to dramatize all its own paradoxes, and a great many of America's as well. I thought of that one night on Meridian Hill when I went to Eugene Meyer's house for dinner. Eugene Meyer is important in this story not because he is rich or because he publishes *The Washington Post* or because he is president of the new World Bank, but because he married Agnes Meyer, who is not a mere publisher's wife but a reporter as well as a lady.

The Meyer house is a mansion that looks like a fortress.

From Crescent Place off 16th Street, you go up a steep drive
to a great door. The place will serve as pattern for palace in
Washington. John Russell Pope, the architect who designed
the National Archives Building, built it for Henry White, the
Ambassador. But the important thing about the house is that
Agnes Meyer had gone from it in her late fifties to look at
humans and their housing and their living in America at war.
The result of her enterprise was a little odd: Beyond the notion that government in Washington does not know what goes
on in the country, she came to the realization that neither the
government nor Washingtonians seem to know what goes on
in Washington either.

In the big house on Crescent Place, Mrs. Meyer seems a
timid-looking woman to have gone into all the back streets of
the defense towns. (*Journey Through Chaos;* Harcourt, Brace
& Co.) But she was a reporter on the old *New York Sun* before she married a banker. As lady and mother of five children,
it seemed natural for her to produce in Washington her book,
*Chinese Painting as Reflected in the Thought and Art of Li-
Lung-Mien.* But I doubt that she was ever merely "cultured."
Both Hoover and Roosevelt appointed her as one of the trus-
tees of the endowment funds of the Library of Congress.
Then, in 1943, she wrote about the British home front, which
was not a very safe front for a lady then. It was natural, perhaps, that she should follow that adventure with a journey to
see what was happening on the home front in America. The
most remarkable thing about that journey was her coming
home.

"In my journeys through the war centers," she said, "I have
visited the worst possible housing. But not in the Negro slums
of Detroit, not even in the Southern cities, have I seen human
beings subjected to such unalleviated wretchedness as in the
alleys of our own city of Washington."

In Washington, I was not sure Agnes Meyer was engaged
in a very hopeful enterprise. Ladies may be more socially sensible who devote themselves to the United Nations or the

musicales at the Sulgrave Club. But there have been other women concerned about the alleys in Washington. Indeed, the first Mrs. Woodrow Wilson, just before she died, helped get Congress to pass a law, in 1914, forbidding the use of the stinking, crowded alley dwellings after 1918. No serious attempt was ever made to enforce the act in the years following. In 1934, when some 10,000 Negroes and 500 whites were living in the flimsy shacks, another law was passed for the purpose of providing other housing and eliminating the inhabited alleys before July 1, 1944. Eleanor Roosevelt, being Eleanor Roosevelt, was naturally interested in that. The alley dwellings are still there, more crowded than ever, but the Alley Dwelling Authority, designed to eliminate them, crept into hiding as a part of the National Capital Housing Authority, in 1943, when the backyard slums were even more bulging than ever.

There is some of what Archibald MacLeish called "the pat and triumphant testimony of coincidence" in the fact that the Meyer house sits almost directly above the turreted redstone atrocity on 16th Street which Washington calls Henderson's Castle. It is a boarding house full of young women now, but in it—and during the years after Congress formally abolished the alley dwellings—were planned probably more palaces for the elegant and the rich than anywhere else in Washington. Mrs. John B. Henderson, who built them for ambassadors and millionaires, is dead now, but her palaces still stand—some of them not far from Mrs. Meyer's alleys. And sometimes, in recent years, the plight of the palaces has almost seemed to be more tragic than Mrs. Meyer's description of the alleys.

Mrs. Meyer is not the only Washington woman who has written a book about conditions in the capital. In 1940, Isabel Anderson, one-time historian-general of the Daughters of the American Revolution, whose own palace is now the national headquarters of the Society of the Cincinnati, published a sad book, too. It was the memoir of her husband, Larz Anderson, rich career diplomat who became Ambassador at forty-six. And there, as of the Hoover Administration, the sad fact was in the book: "Our dinners proved successful. The house was full of flowers—azaleas, orchids, lilies and tulips. We remained, I believe, the only house in Washington, except the embassies, which turned out the servants in full-dress livery, shorts and stockings, buckled shoes and braided coats. Those dinners were swan songs to the old order."

I doubt it. Livery and the meaning of the word "shorts" changes. But nothing is quite as durable as the Old Order unless it is the perennial demand for a new one. In Washington, both the slums and society endure, and often close to each other, side by side, as in Georgetown where the rich whites are moving in to join the poor Negroes—or push them out. Also, there remain articulate ladies not merely to talk to Senators and Ambassadors but to write about Washington, too. I doubt that the fact that there are now more than a hundred women officially reporting the scene will make it different or any more clear. I am not sure that the place of women in government or beside it would be advanced if the women gathered again on the spindly White House chairs or May Craig got to a White House correspondents' banquet. Washington is strange, perhaps, but women can be queer, too. Almost everybody else has forgotten her, I suspect, but I remember as a child in Washington seeing Dr. Mary Walker. She wore both curls and pants—the latter, she said, by special permission of the Congress of the United States. But the pertinent thing I recall about Dr. Mary Walker is that she seemed pathetic to men but comic to women. They laughed. And sometimes they laugh at each other in Washington still, not as other people, but as other women.

My favorite reporter in Washington is a woman. She has not only never been invited to the White House Correspondents' Association banquet; she has never been admitted to the press gallery. As a matter of fact, she never writes at all. She comes.

"My dear!" she says, and her eyes are laughing before she speaks.

She drives up in her disreputable gray Ford, which may often be seen parked with the limousines at embassy receptions, gathering old clothes for the Quakers. She is not a gossip. She is a reporter. She was born a member of an old family in an Eastern city and, as far as I can discover, she is kin to almost everybody who is anybody. She married a gentleman in St. Louis. But she knows Washington best of all. She was a woman with red hair and so beautiful a speaking voice that it ought to be preserved in the National Gallery, which is one of her stopping places, as well as the Quaker Meeting House. Her hair is not red any more, but the voice is still firm and warm.

She listens to laundresses and Senators. She sits, as she always does, a little forward on her chair, with her white gloves in her hands while the old Judge with the pink domed forehead talks of Bigness and Confusion. And somehow she sees him (as she sees all others) not as a figure in history but as a character in the never written novel about Washington—the old philosopher with the ladies around him, snug in his old age against the wet Washington wind. She knows the young, too. She listens to women who think they can sing because their husbands are Congressmen and watches ladies who pass cookies as a part of the effort for world peace. She has a way of remembering, when an eminent citizen calls for an American moral awakening, just what year it was that he ran off with his friend's wife and what her maiden name was.

She was married to a beautiful gentleman, tall, white-haired, reticent. They lived, until he died, in a bushy green place well back from the road just north of Washington. Her old Ford rolled out of the driveway toward Washington every day, but he rarely left the place. For her Washington is sometimes ridiculous, occasionally thrilling, always amusing. She is aware of the alleys, and she has friends in the palaces. As I could never hope to do, she understands both women and Washington—and men. She never expects Washington to be simple. She does not lose interest in it when it is not wise.

Her husband stayed at home. To him, Washington was an unnecessarily noisy city down the road. He gave it a fine, full, blue-eyed disregard. He had been a gentleman in St. Louis before Bob Hannegan was born. Washington seemed almost irrelevant to him. She could go hear the Senators, and listen to diplomats and old Judges at teas. He preferred to stay home with the Doberman pinschers he bred. If you threw one of them a stick he would retrieve it. You couldn't be half as sure as that about the Senate. Also, you could look across his place and, as far as you could tell, the hills were green all the way to Gettysburg.

But life, which is the concern of women, was the other way down the road. Not many women would swap it for the hills.

XVI

Security in Compartments

In Washington it is important to remember that Irishmen are not only politicians, they also continue to be cops. And it takes a lot of policemen in uniforms (military and naval uniforms included) and in plain-clothes (white tie and tails included) to guard the domestic tranquillity and the national security of the United States. The chief of the nation's largest Intelligence service in wartime was William Joseph Donovan. The superintendent of Washington's metropolitan police, whose pay and rank are fixed by Congress, is Colonel Edward J. Kelly, and you won't find a better policeman in the United States. A dark-haired, bright-eyed young man named Michael Reilly was the chief of those who guarded Franklin Roosevelt throughout the war. And when, at 6:30 P.M., on December 26, 1941, the Constitution of the United States left Washington as war refugee in Compartment B, car A-1 (Pullman sleeper "Eastlake"), on the National Limited of the B&O, its armed traveling companions were Secret Service Agents Shannon and Moriarty.

There seems to be always an Irish quality about the investigatory and Intelligence activities of the government of the United States. Not only are many Irishmen attracted to them. Also, even those who are not Irish surround their service with a Celtic romanticism. They get help from outside in a romantic land. The very cloistered pattern of their procedures makes at least as much mystery as those procedures solve. In Washington a whisper is a drama. Silence over secrecy

185

is the basic material of melodrama itself. But nothing is ever quite so dramatic as the seclusion which detectives, from admirals to bulge-hipped bodyguards, throw about themselves. In Washington knowing a secret may add more to a man's prestige than getting a promotion. There, also, a Secretary's curiosity or a Congressional Chairman's campaign for publicity may send investigators scurrying as energetically as if the nation's safety depended upon their errands.

But that night after Christmas when Shannon and Moriarty slept by the Constitution on the B&O, they unconsciously did a good deal to make the mystery clear. The truth is that it takes policemen and professors, clerks, collectors and cataloguers, plus some politicians within and without the secret services, to make the pattern of the Intelligence business. Shannon and Moriarty slept with their guns to guard the Constitution, but they shared its guarding with a slim, sharp-featured, youngish man who was then and afterward as much a stereotype of the Intelligence man and investigator as any G-2 general or Civil Service detective. He is not Irish. His name is Verner W. Clapp, and he is Director of the Acquisitions Department of the Library of Congress. The late E. Phillips Oppenheim and all other writers about spies and detectives would probably disregard him for purposes of drama. But his presence on the B&O that night was important not merely to the Constitution but also to understanding of the secret guardings and searchings of the Republic at home and abroad.

There was the Constitution in Compartment B. Agents Shannon and Moriarty and Librarian Clapp were in the compartments adjoining it. In the government, at least until World War II, the secret agents and the scholars seemed always in separate compartments. Married to an Irish wife, I draw no distinction between intelligence and the Irish. Certainly, the scholars in government were, by their own confessions since, at least as remiss in the items they failed to collect as were the detectives in naval and military uniforms and in civilian clothes.

Guarding a republic or a document may be a good deal more complex business than it sometimes seems to be to small boys who have substituted the G-Man for the cowboy in juvenile American adoration or to big boys and girls, too, who stir in the proximity of romance when General Bill Donovan or J. Edgar Hoover strides through the café. The B&O ride of the Constitution made that clear. The problem of Agents Shannon and Moriarty was fairly simple. They could shoot if necessary anybody who tried to steal the Constitution. But Mr. Clapp's duties were more complex.

"There was little doubt," one of his colleagues wrote in describing that journey of the scholar and the secret agents, "that the Depository at Fort Knox, situated far inland (some thirty miles from Louisville) and with a subterranean vault beneath a massive structure of steel and concrete, was invulnerable even to modern bombing attack. But account had to be taken of a more insidious enemy than bombs. In the subterranean level of the vault some dampness had been noted and, from time to time, certain tiny insects. The ravages of insects could be prevented by proper packing, but humidity and changes in temperature would encourage the growth of mold—which, in silence and darkness, has destroyed more precious parchments than bombs or flame."

Messrs. Shannon and Moriarty were not worrying about mold. In Louisville, they were met by other Secret Service Agents, including one named Cassidy. But Mr. Clapp's concern (he worked with sling-psychrometers and recording hygro-thermographs) not only indicated that danger may grow "in silence and darkness"; he also rode on the trip with the agents and the Constitution on the B&O in demonstration that Intelligence itself in peace and in war may depend less on brave boys with big guns than on the slow collection of facts in a process which makes little more noise than the growth of mold.

Obviously, the policemen are easier to see. And there are plenty of them in Washington. Most of the professors who worked with collected knowledge to provide military interpretations have gone back to such jobs as teaching Oriental languages at the University of Chicago or early Christian architecture at Vassar. But in wartime a professor who dropped into Washington with knowledge about the meteorology of Normandy may have been more useful than the more heroic citizen who parachuted into France.

I am glad to have had the chance to know both the professors and the policemen. Not all professors are perfect. (I have one friend who tells me that he is the only man connected with any college anywhere in America who had absolutely nothing to do with the development of the atomic bomb.) And I like policemen. Most of them look very much the same in Washington or St. Louis. And in Washington I was fortunate enough to see them both as the object of their suspicions and as the official recipient of their investigating aid, which was often excellent. The former is a vivid memory.

Before I arrived in Washington as a wartime bureaucrat in a war agency, my own unofficial home-town spy system had informed me that a gentleman with the credentials of the F.B.I. had been in town talking about me to my friends and neighbors, and maybe to some of my neighbors who were not my friends. But soon after I got to Washington and was working myself to death, I received a peremptory direction from a man accustomed to giving peremptory directions to report to his office at a specific hour that afternoon.

I went. His office was in a small, obscure office building on, I believe, L Street and there was an unmistakable atmosphere about it like the rooms used for interrogations by detectives in city halls. I was ushered in with the same general air of welcome given to suspicious characters by cops in plain-clothes from New Orleans to Chicago. I was placed in a straight chair at a small table. The young man sat opposite me. (Edgar Hoover assured me later he was not one of his men.) He lingered over papers before him in a manner which was like the metaphorical application of the rubber hose. Behind my back, a pretty, smartly dressed girl sat with pencil ready to take down the interrogation. At last and grimly the questions came about organizations of which I was said to be a member, and which, I gathered, were alleged fronts for Communists. I had never heard of the American Society for Peace and Intellectual Freedom. But the next possibly subversive organization I had heard of—the American Committee Against Japanese Aggression. I admitted I had served on its Executive Committee along with Henry L. Stimson, then Secretary of War. The young man noted that but he came coldly to his central question.

"It is reported," he said, "that as editor you've written a number of editorials against the Dies Committee."

(That was before Martin Dies had disappeared from Congress just in advance of a pursuing PAC after one of the most successful Congressional enterprises in history in harassing many innocent people. So far as the record shows, his committee and its investigators never caught a dangerous radical but its chairman got a lot of lecture dates. Dies is gone, but some professional defenders of America for political profit remain.)

I looked at the young man across the table.

"Of course, I did," I said trying to convey to him my feeling that I would have been shocked if he had suggested that I had not.

He shuffled his papers. I could smell the perfume of the secretary behind me.

"Would you care to file a statement explaining your opposition to the Dies Committee?"

"No," I said.

"No?"

"No."

He regarded me for a moment and straightened his papers together.

"That will be all," he said.

So far as I ever heard, it was all. No damning dossier pursued me. My experiences afterward were all on the other side of the interrogation table. Not that I was ever a detective or an agent myself but in the nature of my work in Washington I came into contact with investigators and their directors. (Wait a minute: I was a Secret Service Agent, regularly commissioned and all equipped with credentials, in order that I might get through lines of agents thrown about the President.) There were all kinds of them. I remember walking the long dramatic succession of offices across the east front of the Department of Justice to Edgar Hoover's desk. I used to see General Donovan, of the Office of Strategic Services, when he came with dramatic quietness to the White House. Armed messengers from G-2 and OSS came to my door in the State Department—often bringing documents which could safely have been sent by mail. And in the State Department, I knew Adolf Berle. He was no agent at all but, as a little, brilliant Assistant Secretary of State, gorged with secret and esoteric information, he was my candidate for intellectual hero of a swift-paced novel of high, mysterious international adventure.

Beneath dramatic chiefs there were all kinds of investigators. There are still. In wartime, the distinction between "foreign intelligence" and "domestic investigations" became very fuzzy at the edges. Edgar Hoover's F.B.I. extended its operations to cover the Western Hemisphere, and felt a little mistreated that it was not extended to world-wide proportions. The old-time police and detective services (which, as much fine work in preventing enemy sabotage and espionage indicated, were not policemen merely) felt an understandable impatience with the inpouring amateurs, many of whom wore the uniforms of the services. In the Office of Strategic Services, General Donovan put 12,000 people to work all over the world in an enterprise that was comic and courageous, essential to victory and, in some of its departments and personnel, a boondoggle in wartime at the same time. Some of his bravest agents necessarily hid their valor in secrecy while some of his silliest employees used the same secrecy to insinuate a romantic significance about themselves.

OSS (Oh, So Social—Oh, So Silly), Naval Intelligence and Army's G-2 seemed to have an irresistible attraction for (and often insufficient defenses against) social playboys and some playgirls (most of the latter were not beautiful lady spies but filing clerks). Fortunately, as the results have indicated, all found able men, too. Also, at the same time the manpower shortage forced some investigatory organizations to use pathetic plugs whose activities as investigators in peacetime must have been largely restricted to finding out whether time-payment customers were able to meet the installments on the piano.

The chief differences, I think, in agents and their attitudes rode on that B&O train with the Constitution, the Librarian and the Secret Service men. The United States has never been quite as innocent as it has sometimes pretended to be about spies. Before World War II we had sent out some very zealous naval and military attachés, some of whom, fortunately, had done more than watch military parades and attend embassy teas in full uniform. But when war came and Donovan began to train his men for the wonderful jobs some of them did in dangerous territory, the discovery was suddenly made that what spies got in danger was no more important than information we had collected—or should have collected—before the fighting began. Foreign industrial information which the Department of Commerce had gathered for American salesmen suddenly became precious to American soldiers. There was other such information all about town—and literally all over town. Well-educated spies put on their reading glasses. And the men of the Office of Strategic Services took over a whole floor of the big annex of the Library of Congress. The real job of Verner Clapp, who went with the Constitution to Louisville, was acquiring pieces of information. A lot was there. And, unfortunately, a lot was not. Such scholars, doing spy work, do not generally speak in the cryptic language attributed by novelists to spies.

"We have been driven from complacency to dismay," said

Luther Evans, the Librarian of Congress, "by those inequalities in our map resources which the needs of war have grimly made so plain. The want of European city plans (and we lack many) may well have risked the lives of American soldiers, and the absence of navigation charts may have hazarded the operations of our men at sea. Again, our Chinese library, large as it is, distinguished as it is, has been too largely formed on classic, rather than on contemporary, principles with the result that a conflict in modern Asia has sometimes found us inept or actually impotent. Hereafter, we must discriminate between an impulse to rescue the past and the imperative to control the present."

Such as the resources were, and they were in fact very great, using them required agents who could read—and often in many languages—and understand, and correlate. The process does not sound as exciting as dropping out of a plane with a radio set. But there was more (if not always so immediately valuable) essential military information dug out of collections in safe libraries than was sent back by secret radio from hazardous places. Also, agents went after books and papers as well as news of enemy troop movements. The Library had its own man, Brooklyn-born Manuel Sanchez, buying out bookstores in Lisbon and Madrid and, close behind the army, in Rome. Other military and civilian agents sent back still more—three million pieces a year: maps of French railways, tables of meteorological data from Africa, Italian aircraft photographs, German technical journals, Spanish provincial gazettes, microfilms, phonograph recordings, manuscripts. And the emphasis in the reading of such items was not upon rescuing the classical past, even of the Chinese.

Professors and detectives—and it was sometimes increasingly difficult to tell them apart—did a good job. But professors and detectives, including those with stars on their shoulders and wide stripes on their sleeves, can even in wartime be politicians, too, and as contentious as politicians. The truth of the glorious enterprise of American Intelligence in

World War II cannot be told unless there is recognition of the fact that there was hardly a field in Washington at war in which institutional jealousies were more rampant. Sometimes it was almost as hard for one Intelligence agency to see information held by another as it is ever to get any information from a Russian. Counterespionage could represent the contentions of different sets of local spies and the ambitions of their different bosses. And sometimes investigators in the same organization did not like each other either. The certain fact is that, under the lid of secrecy, magnificent, thorough, heroic work was done and that, under the same lid, every human folly was protected. Fortunately, though not entirely, the folly seemed to diminish in direct proportion to the danger or the importance of the operations and their distance from Washington.

And unfortunately, as America operates, the danger is that efficiency may disappear with peace. The Pearl Harbor investigation disclosed some earlier lapses of intelligence in Intelligence. Also, the principal result of the investigation has been that America is no longer in secret possession (so I hear by the grapevine that often grows most luxuriously out of Intelligence agencies) of any other nation's secret codes. On the tip from the Congressional testimony all of them have been changed.

More serious perhaps than contention, today as in the past, is the almost inescapable tendency to develop a sort of hardentions a sensible man learns to trust nobody. Unfortunately, in ing of the suspicions. Perhaps in the darkness of secret operadealing with nations and people some Intelligence men have made such fixed patterns of their suspicions that it was hard to count on the scientific quality of their conclusions. Obviously, Intelligence which is not based upon objective findings and precision thinking is pretty worthless stuff. But plenty of domestic and international, economic and social emotionalism and prejudice have gone with the facts into the shaping of the findings, in great matters and small, by little agents and also by the brass and the braid.

Comic and romantic as America's domestic and foreign Intelligence services can sometimes be, if I were a crook in America or a sinister nation in the world I would not dismiss them lightly. Of course, human vanity can wear a cloak and a dagger as well as a sports suit. Edgar Hoover may love publicity and grab it as gladly as some of his competitive detectives in the government have suggested he does. But sometimes the same qualities which have won him decorations from the Boys' Clubs, the Boy Scouts and the Camp Fire Girls have built morale within his organization and fear of it among the criminal gentry of the country, who generally are also juvenile in mentality. Also, if sometimes his G-Men's pistols pop and their raids bang with a drama that makes special appeal to the afternoon papers, it is not to be forgotten that a good deal of his work, like that of librarians, has been cataloguing fingerprints, up from 12,000, in 1924, to 100,000,000, in 1946. (Publicity note: the 100,000,000th fingerprint was that of child movie star Margaret O'Brien.) His F.B.I. is more publicized but no more efficient than the Inspection Service of the Post Office Department, the Secret Service, the Intelligence Unit of the Bureau of Internal Revenue and others in the government. Such excellent agencies are sometimes embarrassed by "government investigators" in some other units whose agents are sometimes neither too well disciplined nor too bright.

At late last apparently, all of America's "Federal foreign intelligence activities" are to be unified, after the Washington fashion, under one new organization on top of all the old ones. The time may come, indeed, when the National Intelligence Authority may be a word for the melodrama or the fear of the world. It is too early to be sure. Actually, the NIA is not an independent agency but the appendage of another interdepartmental committee composed of the Secretaries of State, War and Navy plus an additional member appointed by the President. It gets its money not from Congress but from the three departments. It does not supplant the old Intelligence branches of the departments, but it is set up to coordinate them and provide policies for them. It can, however, undertake Intelligence operations of its own.

Maybe the NIA presents for the first time one picture of the American spymaster, who very probably will not like that term. His name is Sidney William Souers. His job is Director of Central Intelligence for the NIA. Spymaster or coordinator, he could certainly qualify as romantic personage. He is a business man who got rich; and, even more remarkable, he was a naval reserve officer who got to be an Admiral in World War II. He is a Democrat from Missouri. He has served in the past as a director of the same Aviation Corporation of which President Truman's good friend, George Allen, is (or was) a director, too. After college, he began selling securities. He has worked since in the grocery business. He has been banker and insurance company president. He is a Deke, also a Methodist. He made money in the new American industry which provides clean linen and takes away dirty linen in a service to doctors, barbers, waiters, etc. He was fifty-four in 1946, and had been a bachelor until the year before. In World War II he became Deputy Director of the Office of Naval Intelligence.

There is a great and sometimes disturbing world around Director Souers.* And around him also, Washington remains and, in Intelligence at least, I doubt that Washington is any less complex than the world. There are facilities in it for the collection of Intelligence about the world hardly to be equaled anywhere else on earth. Also, there are probably more investigators in Washington—or getting their pay from Washington—than in any other city in the world (Moscow possibly excepted). And all of them, though they be admirals or generals, State Department personages or members of the metropolitan police force, are as human in their confidential enterprises as any politicians are in public. There are able men among them. Young Irish Matt Connelly, the President's Secretary, came up, as he says, from "the devious ways of investi-

---

* Admiral Souers became a private citizen again in June 1946, and was succeeded by a regular army man, Lt. Gen. Hoyt S. Vandenberg.

gation." There are other able young men like him still serving as those Congressional investigators known as "Committee Dicks." There are men who guard Congressmen in jobs given them by Congressional patronage. Only lawyers or certified public accountants need apply to be agents of the F.B.I. Some professors, who came down with Donovan, remain after Donovan. Verner Clapp is still collecting information for the Library of Congress in its new purpose, come what new wars will, to be ready with the books and the maps and the charts. Incidentally, with the help of the Secret Service, he brought the Constitution back to Washington on September 19, 1944. There is no mold on it, but the Library's collection of items of Intelligence grows as steadily as mold, and in the day as well as in the dark.

I remember talking, soon after the National Intelligence Authority was created by Presidential order, to a man who had been concerned in the creation of the plan for unity in Foreign Intelligence. He was very hopeful but aware of difficulties. He spoke of the attitude of some of the army and navy Intelligence men toward the plan. Sometimes in the past they had felt that the State Department did not always share its information promptly and properly with the services. Sometimes, I know, other departments felt that military and naval men were slow in sharing, too.

"They have long memories," he said, "and little faith."

I wondered if that was a sort of occupational philosophy of all Intelligence men. They had seemed to me in Washington very often subject to the occupational disease—or delusion —of accepting in their secrecy a romantic evaluation of themselves and their roles. That could be amusing in an age in which some of our best spies are librarians, and a fingerprint file in the Department of Justice may be much more important than the most exciting dramatics in the dark. But there would be nothing funny about Foreign Intelligence shaped in terms of long memories and little faith. It would mean the addition of a pessimistic attitude to a romantic posture among men who in Intelligence rarely retain a sense of humor. On a stage that might make a fine comedy at the expense of pompousness and pretension. But in America we are all caught in the melo-drama: long memories and little faith might be the curtains of the spirit on our windows to the world.

XVII

Byzantine Art

"OH GOOD God," said the Polish Ambassador's wife.

It was a very mild expletive as the lady used it constantly throughout the evening. In the hot garden she was a very comfortable-looking woman in a flowered evening dress. Her husband, the Ambassador, in his linen dinner jacket seemed dry, cold and bald as a hawk. But Arthur Bliss Lane, who had just arrived from Bogota to become our Ambassador to Poland, was a well-fed, well-fleshed, red-faced man, and wet. If he had not been a career diplomat I should have said he was sweating. I knew that I was. I do not belong to international society. I had put my evening clothes away for the war. And in State Department society that night I think I smelled a little of moth balls.

I was pleased to see that Sir Kenneth Lee, one of the constant procession of visiting British dignitaries, wore a business suit. The poundage permitted in airplane baggage seemed to have interrupted temporarily the ancient rule that, though the world totters, the Englishman arrays himself for the evening. Sir Kenneth did not seem to be aware that he was shattering tradition. But the international world around him seemed secure that evening, even if its destinies still hung undecided in the world. Ladies and gentlemen remained. The problems of the world were the colloquialisms of professional cosmopolitans. The talk about nations, in the heat in Georgetown, was like the talk of people in Mississippi about crops. Nations seemed like neighboring plantations, and even prime ministers sounded no greater than time merchants. It was hot in the world. A servant passed a tray of drinks. We took them quietly and drank them. We became less languid. A gay woman leaned forward talking about some friends in Cairo. She had a funny story about the domestic difficulties of a diplomat, then concerned with difficulties in the Middle East.

"Oh good God," said the Ambassador's wife.

The garden was a brick-walled box of rather desperately tended green about an inconsiderable pool. And cocktails, I noted, have the same general effect on the pores of the skin of those who deal in international affairs as they do on men whose governmental concern is with agriculture. The heat hung about the dripping glasses in a wartime which kept even diplomats from getting off to the shore. But the ladies were lovely. Even the comfortable wife of the Polish Ambassador was pictorial. I sat beside a Mrs. Winston, young, a widow or divorcee, who was very pretty indeed. The gentlemen seemed quite content in their world, war or not, heat or not. The Polish Ambassador turned even colder when someone mentioned Russia. His expression looked less like fear than like an aristocratic scorn. But my companion and I noticed that two impertinent dirty small boy faces were peeping over the garden wall from next door, which even above the wall was obviously a cluttered Georgetown back yard and not a decorous Georgetown garden.

Maybe there is some sort of design in the fact that Georgetown is like that. It is not the most ostentatious but certainly as a whole the most fashionable section in Washington. But it is old, and keeps slums as well as establishments. Class distinction is often not wider than a property line. Sometimes the shanties of Negroes lean precariously against the great brick walls of modern millionaires in old houses. On the way, I had stopped for cocktails at a house which an architect had managed to make somehow old and new together, with brick walls and plate glass, bright brass and a vividly painted door. But beside it was an unpainted Negro church with an illiterate sign about its denomination and its services. The preacher and his family lived in the loft. The colored children had stared at us from its high door. But here in the garden the faces above the wall were the dirty faces of white boys looking at us in our elegance before dinner. My tuxedo felt even more strange under their eyes. I looked at one of them and he grinned.

Mrs. Winston was very prettily not amused. She had recently moved to Georgetown. She was not as rich as her friends, I gathered, perhaps not as rich as her own past. She had put her boy in the public schools in Georgetown. The young gentleman, she indicated, was having a pretty tough time of it.

"You can't imagine," she said. But looking at her and her friends and the grinning face above the wall, I think I could. Somehow, I got the feeling that her son was in very much the same position as the Polish Ambassador, and in my hot tuxedo I had a very strange feeling that I was not at all sure whether my sympathies were on the frowning right or the grinning wrong side of the wall.

"He's terrified," she said.

"Oh good God," I heard the Ambassador's wife say. It was the expletive of a woman who was not really very much disturbed.

We went in to dinner at a long refectory table. That was in the hot summer of 1943. On that rationed night our hostess served us two huge rib roasts of beef. I could imagine the young face at the wall turning from grin to greed. There are advantages in international society. Some RAF men had gone back to England and had turned their ration books over to our hostess instead of the Ration Board. The ladies, the Ambassadors, and Daniels ate the beef imperturbably; though I could see, while she ate, a certain Puritan glaze in my wife's Southern eyes. (She waited until she got home, full of beef, to declaim in patriotic indignation about it.) I noticed among the Ambassadors that a well-traveled gentleman across the table was looking, even over his beef, at my pretty dinner companion with a well-bred though predatory gleam in his eye.

From beef we turned to gasoline, lightly. The night before *The Washington Post* had attended, uninvited, one of the big Georgetown parties of Evalyn Walsh McLean, who owns the Hope Diamond and a big house. Its reporters had taken down the numbers of the cars of those with extra gasoline stickers who had attended. The names and numbers had been printed in the paper. The wife of another Ambassador, who had come as a single lady that evening, laughed a little nervously. She had been there, but for some reason she had gone home before the reporters had arrived.

The problem seemed somehow inelegantly nearer than foreign affairs. Arthur Bliss Lane turned to talk about oil in South America. The Polish Ambassador spoke about Russia. The lights gleamed on his bald head. He was strangely, leanly decorative. Someone asked him about the great estates in eastern Poland. Were they so vast? So much had been said about the almost feudal state of the landlords and the almost feudal condition, too, of the people on the land.

He looked like a Caesar on a coin.

"Soviet lies," he said.

And his wife said, "Oh good God."

We had conditions in America, I suggested, that needed reform. We had been troubled about problems of tenancy. And somehow, we moved into the problems of people in America at war. I mentioned the articles of Agnes Meyer, wife of the publisher of *The Washington Post*, about conditions in war-crowded towns—particularly in Washington. In general they seemed to me sound.

"If Mrs. Meyer is going to make any other studies," said Mrs. Winston, "she might take a look at the ladies' room at *The Washington Post*."

And we laughed.

It was a very pleasant party. It was interesting to compare the Polish Ambassador and his bald head with the almost identical general physical appearance of Joseph Davies, who as a rich man able to eat as well as any ambassador, had gone to Russia to come back as the almost professional friend of

Russia. Both had bald Roman heads. Both had been ambassadors. I imagine Davies is richer. Maybe he was useful to indicate that even in diplomacy the rich can sometimes be as un-
predictable as the poor.

We went back into the garden for coffee and brandy. There
were no longer any grinning faces above the wall. The heat
had abated a little. Ambassador Lane, reclining in a garden
chair and talking about old days in Mexico, seemed, though
weighing a little above the average, almost the figure of the
American career diplomat.

Maybe he is. He had been president of the Foreign Service
Association, which is, I suppose, the career diplomat's trade
organization. He had been educated abroad, and then at Yale.
He had entered the Foreign Service when he was twenty-two
and had served all over the world in it, but he had never
worked anywhere in the United States except briefly in the
State Department. For all I know, at his foreign posts he may
have made his friends among workers and farmers, the average
folk of the countries to which he was accredited. But in Washington—and at some other capitals where I have been— diplomats seems to congregate only, or largely, with other diplomats.

Sometimes, indeed, the diplomats of all countries seem,
wherever they are, to be not so much in lands that are strange
but in capitals which are identical, the little, closed, high, elegant worlds of diplomats who do so much of their business
socially that sometimes society seems to be their business.
Indeed, some of them seem as isolated from the general population of the countries to which they go as they are isolated
from the ordinary people of the countries from which they
are sent. Tough as it can sometimes be, the whole business of
diplomacy often looks like the club of a society which holds
its meetings drinking the same cocktails and exchanging the
same gossip in Bogota and Warsaw, London, once in Vienna,
even long ago in Tokyo and Berlin. People do not acquire
broad minds by living narrow lives a long way from home.

But the thing is not so simple as the clichés about it. There are, indeed, in high and numerous places in the Foreign Service of our State Department men who seem to be what one career ambassador called "cookie-pushers" when he undertook to refute the general charge of a cookie-pushing Foreign Service. Some rich young men have risen on the career service's escalator to be rich ambassadors. Only the State Department, dominated by career service men, specifically knows how able or stupid they are. There are some who are not rich. There is at least one career envoy extraordinary and minister plenipotentiary now who entered the service from a job he had supervising students in a school for the deaf. One gave up his job as an athletic instructor to begin the process of becoming an ambassador. Two, at least, were schoolteachers. And one was an automobile salesman. As for the Groton-Harvard, St. Paul's-Princeton, Hotchkiss-Yale tradition, several of the career chiefs of mission never went to any college at all.

But, rich and poor alike, they are all part of the process of a procession from clerkships. Some of them remain clerks. The career way to an ambassadorship is the same way as that to the position of division chief in the Treasury Department. Sometimes, if the State Department seems lost in strange foreign distances, it is actually not so much lost in foreign lands as lost in documents, details, rules and regulations, and a sort of detached sterility in procedures for their own sake. I doubt that we have half as much to fear from cookie-pushers engaged in the elegancies of diplomacy as we have from clerk minds.

"Hell," I remember a man saying. He was a wartime temporary in the State Department talking about the career service men about him. "They haven't got it in 'em to be real reactionaries. Of course, most of them would be if they could. They're just dull men. They are afraid of anything that is new. They're more concerned with rules than with realities. The only trouble is that they don't look like clerks, when they are."

He exaggerated. There are able exceptions. But there is a

certain confused look often seen on the face of the returning American diplomat. It may be because he comes down from representing the United States to being just one man in it. Sometimes they seem strangers at home, which many of them are. I remember Franklin Roosevelt, who depended greatly upon the career service (and who, of course, was Groton and Harvard himself), was occasionally wearily impatient with their lack of understanding of American affairs and American opinion.

"It would be a grand idea," he said, "to make career men come home and serve a term every now and then in the office of the Collector of Internal Revenue in St. Louis."

It might be a dangerous test with the taxes. Also, some career diplomat might get to be chairman of the Democratic National Committee. Bob Hannegan did, and without benefit of service in Bogota. But if Bogota is like Washington, a little knowledge of politics would not do a diplomat any harm.

However, the record of political appointees is spotty, too. Some of our best contemporary diplomacy has been carried on by men who came in from large affairs rather than up the escalator of the career service. Unfortunately, sometimes the test for such outside appointments by both Democrats and Republicans has been less large experience than large campaign contributions. Cash on the political barrelhead may bring in a character who is worse than a clerk.

It was very pleasant in the garden that evening. Indeed, whatever may be their faults, diplomats are apt to make pleasantness a part of their profession. They may sometimes speak loud in the world. They also have cultivated the art of small talk and easy talk. Sometimes, indeed, as I remember from some official conversations with a career man who afterward became a minister plenipotentiary, a diplomat can be interminable. I have wondered since of his services in a country where the whole United States as represented by him must seem a bore. He was not there that night. And in the garden over the highballs the Ambassadors to and from

Poland seemed not dull but dramatic figures in a world which curses the diplomacy upon which it depends.

I worked in an office in the State Department for two years. It was straight across the corridor from the offices of Leo Pasvolsky, Special Assistant to the Secretary of State for International Organization and Security Affairs. He had a table in his office as long as his title, and diplomats used to sit around it. Pasvolsky does not look like the accepted version of a career diplomat. He is not one. He is not Groton and Harvard but the College of the City of New York. He looks, indeed, less like an ambassador than like a small stuffed owl.

There seems to be a growing sensitiveness among American diplomats about looking too elegant in office. You hardly ever see a pair of spats in the corridors of the State Department, though the Negro messengers, who crowded them before the Stettinius reform movement, wore a high percentage of zoot suits. Indeed, there is often an almost pathetic sense of inferiority to be found among Foreign Service officers. They are acutely aware of the national notion that they are apt to be effeminate young men, engaged in esoteric dealings which require an undue proficiency with teacups. Some of them seem to be almost insistently masculine. During the war, their elders were disturbed because draft officials were a little unsympathetic about understanding that the career service was a service similar to the army and navy which should not be disrupted. There was some sense in their protestations. Some young diplomats had served in posts of danger. A good many of them had wanted to resign. Unfortunately, the career chiefs sometimes irritated draft officials because they were intent upon keeping Foreign Service officers while they were willing to let non-service officers with even more diplomatic experience go the way of all inductees.

The distinction between Foreign Service officers and other State Department personnel in the Foreign Service of the United States can sometimes look like a class distinction within the ranks of the State Department. Occasionally it obviously is. The Foreign Service officers, having passed the examinations and survived the personal scrutiny of the State Department examiners, do come to a group feeling about themselves which compares with that of the Annapolis men in the navy. Despite efficiency ratings they also perpetuate a good deal of dull refinement in their ranks.

It was a little funny to see Ed Stettinius undertaking the streamlining for a modern world of a State Department which had been getting along very comfortably with its notions of the conduct of international affairs while he was still a hereditary official of United States Steel. There was a radio campaign in which high officials seemed to undertake in a hearty sort of way to slap America on the back and convince it that the diplomats were just some of the boys. Statistics showed clearly that they did not come as a body from Groton. Not all the Foreign Service men had been to Harvard or Yale or the Jesuits' College for Foreign Service at Georgetown. There were, the facts showed indisputably, ministers and ambassadors who had gone to cow colleges in the Middle West.

Also, Stettinius moved the colored messengers out of the corridors where they sat talking—sometimes obviously conversing with the colored girl messengers about other things than messages. Stettinius painted the old, long gray halls a soft pastel green. He named seven Assistant Secretaries (including only Dean Acheson of the old order who survived them all) and when he went, handsome and white-haired, to the Senate was rewarded by a Washington cynicism which referred to him and them as Snow White and the Seven Dwarfs. But in a new breezy State Department of his planning he called them "the team," and even had old Joseph C. Grew (J. P. Morgan's brother-in-law who entered the Foreign Service after Groton and Harvard, in 1904) saying to the Senate that he wanted to "join this team."

It is no secret that behind the new green paint the old State Department did not greatly change. Some of its staff did excellent work. Ed Stettinius himself, despite some callow-seeming enthusiasm in cheerleading his team, began a much-needed reorganization and did effective work in perfecting the design of the United Nations Organization. But, a great deal of creaking inefficiency continued behind the swinging shutter doors of the old high-ceilinged offices with their old-fashioned and over-elaborate frescoes.

James Francis Byrnes came over, to succeed Stettinius, also planning change. His new Assistant Secretary of State in charge of Departmental and Foreign Service Administration was Frank McCarthy, able and only thirty-three. But almost before he began his work, McCarthy, worn out by his army service, had to resign because of his health. Traditionalism never sickens. The bright new plans began to fray at the edges. The old State Department continued to look as content and well-fed as Arthur Bliss Lane had looked in the Georgetown garden on his way from Bogota to the Government of Poland.

Some American liberal and left-wing critics of the State Department have fostered the romantic concept that it is merely reactionary, dull and well-fed. The fact is that all of those charges are too easily made and too often false. There are actually men with pretty radical ideas in the State Department. Some of them, I know, officially outraged old Winston Churchill during World War II by what must have seemed to him wild notions about a free, non-monarchial Italy. I grew to respect as a very cooperative, hard-headed but never hard-bitten woman, Ruth Shipley, Chief of the Passport Division, who was sometimes made by Liberals to seem (and quite ungallantly) the epitome of the old woman of the State Department.

Sometimes I doubted that the department was so much loaded down with the duller graduates of Harvard as somehow captured in a sort of world system of red tape. Protocol is not always professional foolishness. The supposedly direct and non-stuffy Russians can sometimes be greater sticklers about punctilio than, I am sure, any of Disraeli's ambassadors ever were. It is easy to get a little ill over the society aspects of the business of State, but the biggest Washington party every year is the Soviet blowout on the anniversary of the Revolution. Revolution can look very strange beside the groaning tables of food and the flowing bars in the old house that George M. Pullman's widow built sometime after the bloody Pullman strike in 1894.

Apparently world affairs must still be conducted with a sort of Byzantine politeness and formality in a world in which nations keep the quick prides with which individuals are sometimes able to dispense. Maybe it was symbolic that Dumbarton Oaks, in which world security was planned, is filled with objects of Byzantine art which an Ambassador Extraordinary and Minister Plenipotentiary who had made his money out of Castoria had collected. Men can come out of Harvard or Kansas as well as Castoria and become involved in Byzantine notions of international relationships. And beyond them, about human relationships, too. In America, neither Groton nor Harvard has any monopoly on the production of snobs. A free mind can live behind a broad *a*. It does not make so much difference where American diplomats come from as what happens to them after they begin spending their lives among the formalities of diplomacies in the tight little isolated coteries of people in the same business in all the capitals of the world.

"Oh good God," the wife of the Ambassador said.

In the contemplation of our diplomacy it is not so much a mild ejaculation as a devout prayer. Certainly, I doubt that anything less than divine intervention will ever rescue our State Department from the sense of careful ineptitude which sometimes seems to be almost tangible in the long corridors of the baroque old building. I suspect that the whole recent history of American foreign relations is the story of new Secretaries of State going in determined to enliven the whole process by which America plays its part in a world trying to live together. The miasma in the State Department is contagious. Sometimes newcomers are least immune to it.

One man I know who keeps his sense of humor is the policeman who guards the entrance on Executive Avenue where diplomats enter. His name is Jordan, and he bows to diplomats with the country courtliness his mother taught him long ago in Chowan County, North Carolina. He proffers them the pen with which they write their names in the book.

"I think maybe I'd like to be an ambassador myself," he said to me. "I'm down to my last $100,000."

I went on by him to the elevator that runs diplomats in prompt deference up to the Secretary's office two floors above. I had known the colored woman who operated it since I first came to Washington. Both of us had worked in those days in the Office of Civilian Defense and, as no bombs fell, both of us by diverse ways had reached the greater security of the State Department. On a Monday morning she greeted me with news.

"Oh, Mr. Daniels," she said, "you should have seen Mr. Nelson Rockefeller's dining room furniture."

Even in the State Department, I was a little surprised.

"His dining room furniture?"

"Oh, yes, sir," she said. "They brought it in yesterday and it's beautiful."

I could imagine that Rockefeller dining room furniture could be beautiful; but even as we passed the next floor it did not make sense.

"What's he doing with dining room furniture down here?"

"Oh, he's going to have a private dining room."

That was clear, but there were also, then, five other Assistant Secretaries and Undersecretary Grew.

"Are the others going to have private dining rooms, too?"

She considered that seriously.

"I reckon," she decided, "that if they know he is, they will."

She opened the door on the Secretary's floor. It was logical. In diplomacy everything is a nice balance. National sovereignty and world security both must be understood. The Ambassador's seat at dinner is the place of his people among mankind. Each nation must be treated with equal dignity;

and the representatives of nations, too. Dignity and destiny are sometimes hard to tell apart. And if there was going to be one private dining room, there might have to be seven. I don't know what happened. I never saw the furniture. But I remember that in the elevator, the colored girl and I laughed together, and that Mr. James C. Dunn, Assistant Secretary of State, looked at us a little surprised.

"We have the best Foreign Service in the whole world," Mr. Dunn says.

He has been in it for twenty-five years, and may know. It continues little changed in 1946.

I am not sure that I find that encouraging at this moment on the earth.

XVIII

Homesick House

THE Pentagon seems strangely designed for the age of the atom and the air. I never walked its inner corridors during the war without thinking what a joy it might be to a bombardier to drop a bomb within the six-acre slot of its enclosed court and watch the ensuing result in plans and papers, stenographers and generals, concrete and steel. It was, undoubtedly, in wartime a disloyal notion. It is a perverse idea at any time. But the building which Architect George Edwin Bergstrom of California designed for the army seems almost shaped to be the nest for such bombs as Physicist J. Robert Oppenheimer of California helped the army design for Nagasaki.

It looked—and looks—like an old-fashioned fort magnified to mastodonic proportions in a time in which such forts, like mastodons before them, had reached the era of extinction. But in America the always inevitable disintegration of military bigness never waited for experiments with uranium in Tennessee and New Mexico. Indeed, if history has any continuing meaning in the United States, disintegration of military power is standard after wars. That may be the defensive reason why in wars military men build so big and wide for permanence. The fort on the Potomac, I think, does not stand against military technology but in a sort of uniformed futility against some aspects of the American spirit which are not so confused as independent. Long before either Oppenheimer or Hitler, our notion of the State was our hope for an order within which we can do as we please. And in peace, even the

Pentagon in terms of that spirit has become a sort of homesick house.

In the winter after victory when I went there again, the Pentagon still stared at Washington like a fortress keeping guard over a capital which, across the brown river, seemed designed in park and marble for serenity. My Negro taxi driver had got mixed up in the twisting approaches; but we finally reached the River Entrance, and I stood there for a moment on the wide steps looking back across the Potomac. Nothing was changed. Military power still sat elegantly above grass and lagoons. A Wac private sat waiting for swift movement in a general's car. In a moment he could be off for Russia or the Army and Navy Club. I smiled but I was still impressed. Even in peace the army's citadel looked strong and well-swept.

There seemed no change inside beyond the big doors either. The army was still on guard. Pretty girls still sat at the long oak desks to check all visitors before they passed beyond the police. But there was less scrutiny in their blue eyes. They were almost eager to see me, as if the citizens whom they scrutinized came less frequently than they used to come. There was more movement out than in. Even a receptionist in Washington sometimes wants company, like an officer who sees numbers diminishing under his command. I felt there, suddenly, the big emptying of the big place. The army itself. even in its fortress, was quietly slipping away.

That was not a military secret. General Marshall, himself, before he retired, had stated that the demobilization of the army had begun to look like disintegration. General Marshall did not say so, but homesickness seems still a stronger American force than world domination, maybe even than world security. I went up that morning to say farewell to some members of General Marshall's old staff. On the way I passed a major who told me that in two weeks he would be a reporter again on *The New York Times*. Colonel Merrill Pasco, Secretary of the General Staff, was leaving that day to go back to our joint home town. It began to look as if the civilians in arms were about to leave the army to the army.

I rode up on one of the Pentagon's beautiful escalators and walked down the broad gray-green corridor to the offices of the Chief of Staff. Lieutenant-Colonel Warwick Bradfute Davenport, whose wartime work had involved details in the liaison between the Chief of Staff and the Commander-in-Chief, was still busy in his last days in the army before going back to the practice of law in Richmond. Others in the army's top office were leaving, too. In a few minutes the Chief of Staff was going to decorate the departing Colonel Pasco. Around the desks in the offices and in the halls the waiting witnesses had a look about them like the last day of school, of prizes and farewells, eagerness and sadness, release and dispersal, the parade and the packing.

Colonel Frank McCarthy, also of Richmond, who had been the first civilian-soldier Secretary of the General Staff, at thirty-one, had already gone—first to the State Department to try as Assistant Secretary under Byrnes to introduce more administrative efficiency into foreign affairs, then home on doctor's orders and with Presidential regrets to rest. He was entitled to it. Now the other men were hurrying to their own intent diversity. Democracy was not a big word they had fought for. It was the standard to which they returned. They were capable of discipline. They had accepted it in democracy when democracy needed it. Within both discipline and democracy they had made a demonstration of public service. In the big army of big government, they had handled for high command the great secrets and the tiny trivia which are sometimes almost equally important in war as in government. Maybe it was the details—even more than the heroism—which made the victory.

I remember the first time I saw Frank McCarthy. He was only a major then. And in the White House he was putting a dollar bill into his brief case. It seemed a strange item to be going from the offices of the Commander-in-Chief to the responsibility of the Chief of Staff.

"For lemons," said McCarthy.

He grinned. He looked then, as always, like the sort of

young soldier Richard Harding Davis might have designed for a hero. But it took very little time to discover, as General Marshall did, that the decorative soldier was the intelligent soldier, too.

"Lemons for Biddle," McCarthy said.

I don't think anybody ever turned up a job that was too trivial for McCarthy. Once a week, on the basis of some informal arrangement, he picked up the dollar bill, acquired the lemons and dispatched them to London to His Excellency the elegant Anthony Joseph Drexel Biddle, Jr., who did not want to get the scurvy in besieged and rationed London as Ambassador to a whole flock of sad, heroic and comic governments in exile. McCarthy could handle not only Biddle's lemons but the military agenda for the conferences of the Big Three. It was at Potsdam that Byrnes watched him and wanted him. Maybe if the accumulated fatigue of uninterrupted expenditure of energy and intelligence, tact and discretion had not hit him he might have made even the old State Department seem less lost in its halls and our world. But that might be expecting too much. Even McCarthy is a man, not a miracle.

That day Colonel Davenport and I went in and looked at the desk just outside the Chief of Staff's door where McCarthy had worked during the war. Across this desk in the crucial months of the war, every day and most of the nights, went every letter and paper, message and order for the Chief of Staff. They not only went in briefed for Marshall's easiest understanding, but McCarthy also applied intelligence to them before they went in. Such intelligence is steadily needed. Inept bureaucracy and tangled red tape can sometimes be as thick among soldiers as among civil servants. Every paper to Marshall was followed; every detail was remembered. McCarthy will undoubtedly remember mistakes which were made by himself and the staff of other civilian soldiers around him. None of them had been in the army before 1940; all were gone in 1946. But it was the sort of secretariat that experts in public administration dream about. Maybe in America nothing less than a war can fulfill the dream.

Obviously not all the able in the army are departing. I walked what seemed like a mile—and a mile of emptier Pentagon corridors than I had ever seen before—to a luncheon date with my North Carolina neighbor, Kenneth Royall, who was in process of transition from lawyer as Brigadier General to political official as Undersecretary of War. That day he was not quite sure which he was. He had his clothes ready to become civilian official but as a cagey North Carolinian, he waited until the Senate had acted on his confirmation to change.

He was happy to stay. Getting undersecretaries is not a problem in the army or anywhere else. Kenneth was staying in the army to go up as civilian. Soldiers who stay must expect to go down. In uniform that day, he chose the picture of himself that would go into the newspapers. One was grinning; one was serious. He chose, with my counsel, the serious one. He is a good-looking man, so tall that some North Carolina commentators consider it a political liability that most other North Carolinians, who are as a people not natively reverent, have to look up to him though unwillingly. From his long offices, spread across the river face of the Pentagon, we went down to the Secretary's dining room. In the utilitarian building, it did not seem to be designed for mere utility. There was the mark of the interior decorator on its conservative elegance, like a room in an exclusive city club. But the men who came in to eat their lunch were men whose names had been in the papers as the commanders of armies. The whole room seemed to be full of silver stars.

We ate well. In a disintegrating army I noticed that there was still a major presiding as head waiter. He took our orders and changed the glasses. Somehow he made the talk of disintegration seem a little silly in an army that could still spare a major to change the plates. I had heard talk of the extravagance as well as the dangerous futility of letting American power disappear and dissipate in a world which had not quite attained the certainty of world peace. The army and the President spoke of the necessity for universal military training. The major smiled as if we had tipped him. But he seemed a rather depressing detail to me in an army that can sometimes keep up its pretensions while it desperately watches its powers disappear.

A gay, shrewd Major General (who would soon be back at his regular grade as Lieutenant Colonel) joined us for lunch. He had been at the Capitol during the morning. The Congressmen were speaking the language they were hearing from the country. If the problems of combat had diminished, the problems with the Congress had not. The duties of public relations and Congressional relations seemed to grow with the peace. The General took the future philosophically. He was staying in the army, but it was going to be tough. Already, then, men were being discharged at the rate of nearly 50,000 a day. The pressure for more rapid demobilization was not diminishing. America seemed to be about its traditional business of running home in a hell-bent unraveling of its unparalleled powers. Maybe it was extravagance. Perhaps America could no longer afford such a relaxation. But the relaxation seemed to me nowhere so evident as in the Pentagon Building itself. It was obvious that not only the boys from Stumpy Point and Sioux City wanted to get home and were fostering a parental deluge upon Congressmen. The boys—some of whom were not very young—from the Pentagon were also as eager to head homeward as the noisier grumblers in Europe and the Pacific.

The army began to look as if it were going to be left to the army. And that presented personal as well as national problems. Even the General who was going to stay as a Lieutenant Colonel smiled ruefully about some of his colleagues in Europe who in the midst of heroism had formed the habit of sending officers forward to pick out the best villas. He had seen them sitting at the heads of tables in the baronial dining rooms.

"Fat catting," he called it.

They would be coming back, if they could get them, to little apartments in Arlington or Takoma Park.

"Thank God," he said, "I've still got the same two rooms and bath I had when I was a Lieutenant Colonel to live in when I'm a Lieutenant Colonel again."

But the Pentagon Building seemed permanent, even if it also began to seem empty. At the top of the escalator, I ran into another officer who had become a soldier about the time I had become a bureaucrat. Actually, in uniform, he had become a bureaucrat, too. He was going home. No militarist myself, I said, nevertheless, that I was a little disturbed by the emphasis on escape.

"You've been reading after the Big Brass," he said of his star-wearing superiors. "They make sad music."

It did seem a little sad to me, I admitted. We had fought a magnificent war. We had won a great victory.

"Now," I said, "as far as I can see all we want to do with victory is to drop it. I hear people arguing about our occupation policy in Germany and other things like that, but as far as I can see, the only policy we have anywhere from top to bottom is getting home and to hell with what happens behind us."

He laughed then. "That has always been the American policy, and I'm not sure it is not the best policy if freedom is something not merely to defend but enjoy. But wait until I get my discharge before you quote me. Come on in here, I haven't got anything to do but look at the river and wish I was home."

We went into his office, where I knew he had worked harder than he had ever done in civilian life, and sat down. A Wac in a corner was filing her nails.

"You see," he said, "what we've won is democracy. And this is it. Of course, it isn't the ideal government for the State maybe, though I'm not so sure about that, but it is certainly the happiest government for men."

"Check," I said.

"The generals around here are talking against the wind about this universal military training business. They really haven't any more idea what the next war is going to be like than you have. And they're talking—and getting the President to talk—of universal military training at a time when the people want to get out of the Military, and world statesmen are at least talking about an enduring peace which would make the Military obsolete."

He looked out of the window toward the river.

"I'm not sure what this peace means. I doubt if I am very clear about the meaning of democracy."

He gave a big smile to the Potomac.

"But America means home. And home is what we are after —in a hurry."

"Home," I said, "may not be quite as far away from danger as it used to seem to be. We may need the army for prestige as well as power. I'm not sure that prestige without power is widely recognized any more."

"You sound," he said, and I thought he seemed a little prejudiced, "like a member of the West Point Protective Association."

I had heard about that mythical organization often before. Even some of those officers who were not sympathetic with GI protests against an officers' caste system in the army felt that West Pointers maintained one even among officers. West Pointers passed around, they said, the best assignments among themselves. They made a habit of sitting separate and together at mess. They made no secret of their sense of superiority. The WPPA would have to be exclusive. Before World War II, West Point had about the same number of students as the University of Vermont and graduated about the same number every year. The foundations of the caste certainly did not seem aristocratic. Generally appointments to the Military Academy (as to Annapolis) had been given to boys as political patronage to their voting fathers. General Eisenhower was one of a very few who had received their appointments in their States as a result of competitive examination. He had been poor and without political pull. It would be a better Army, I believe, if all its permanent officers were chosen by competitive examination and not only from boys in Congressional Districts but men in the enlisted ranks. Also, I have always doubted that discipline from above was made more effective by any requirement of servility from below.

On its steps the Pentagon did not look like homesick house. I doubt that anywhere there is a building which so symbolizes the power of a people. It is beautiful, too, and behind the ornate offices on its river side it seems as functional as a battleship. I stood on the steps and looked across the green to the Roaches Run Waterfowl Sanctuary. In the parking space there were cars still waiting for generals, some of whom would soon be lieutenant colonels and as such might have to come by bus. The Pentagon might seem a sort of sanctuary for lieutenant colonels when all the civilians had gone and too many generals remained.

Good men would remain. After World War I the whole regular army hit its low point between the wars with a total of 135,000 men in 1925. Also, the task which regular army officers performed in building the World War II army is indicated by the fact that there were only 14,500 commissioned officers in the regular army as late as September 30, 1941— only a part of them West Pointers. (General Marshall could not get an appointment to West Point and went to the Virginia Military Institute.) It was hard to remember in the Pentagon Building that Brehon Burke Somervell, with four stars on his collar, had been a public relief executive in WPA for five of the last seven years before World War II.

Dwight Eisenhower, who was a major in the First World War, did not get to be a permanent lieutenant colonel until 1936. (He was fifty-five when he succeeded Marshall as Chief of Staff. That was nearly six years younger than Pershing had been when he took the position in demobilization after World

War I. In 1865, when Grant came to approximately the same job, he was only forty-three and had the prestige which took him to the Presidency, but demobilization then was "a shapeless affair.")

Already, as Eisenhower came to the same task, engineer officers were thinking about public works projects. Above men in uniform and with them, the Secretary of War fought for the consolidation of the army and navy from his Pentagon office, like a landlord with space to let. And over on Constitution Avenue the Secretary of the Navy and his admirals resisted like suspicious guests. Armed men were already quarreling at home, and glory began to look a little tarnished in the world.

An American army in victory can seem a little sad. I remembered the lights burning nightlong in the offices all over town in which the army sprawled in the early days of preparation for war, when the Pentagon was only a part of that preparation. They were tired men in uniforms they had not yet learned to wear without self-consciousness. But I have a memory that they were happy men, too, though they were sometimes convinced that they were captured and driven in confusion. They worked hard and most of them loved it. Of course, there were laggards and phonies and pretenders among them. Some were more concerned with winning promotions than with winning the war, but not many. Even ambition had an American purpose in it. Push and patriotism were effectively bound together. Sometimes it seemed that America had to wait for war, not only to get rich but to share the recurrent reality of the American spirit. Details on the downgrade were going to be less dramatic, but not necessarily less American.

I thought of that when I heard that day, entirely by accident, a story which I probably should not know. A general asked one of the bright young men continuing on the Chief of Staff's Secretariat in liaison with the Commander-in-Chief what the White House thought about a certain matter important to the army. The young officer grinned.

"I tell you," he said, "I don't know. Over there today they've all got those jars with some kind of liquid in them and a wire loop that throws bubbles. Everybody was playing with them."

"Oh, yes," said the general. "I've heard about those. Will you please get me one?"

I hope the general got it. At that time it was a new invention, like the atomic bomb. And as a symbol maybe not less significant.

XIX

U.S.S. Pinafore

THE Navy Department looked not only as if the war was
over but somehow as if there had never been a war. The men
and women in uniform who moved in and out of the building
seemed no longer dramatic. A Wave carried three boxes of
Lux and a very red mop. Near the doors a pretty woman,
with a very big baby in her arms, was waiting in attendant
domesticity for some man. A whole group of poorly dressed
Negroes, civilian employees, maybe, trooped toward the doors.
Somehow they gave the lobby of the building, which had
been constructed as a durable temporary in the First World
War, the quality of the entrance of an Alabama courthouse.
A citizen might expect the welfare department to be down the
hall, not the Bureau of Navigation. And three officers, who
stood in line at the bootblack stand, seemed neither impatient
nor imperious. Peace looked a little nondescript.

I know that was not a fair picture of the navy. Somewhere
they had plans for a new building, not so expansive probably
as the army's Pentagon, but I was sure it would be at least as
elegant. It is not hard to be confused about the navy. Its professionals have pushed almost as many cookies as the diplomats, and yet they remain somehow salty and tough. It wears
much more shining gold than the army does. It can seem most
impressive when its situation is most precarious. Its officers
have hardly ever worn dress uniforms to so many functions
as they did back in the days after the First World War when,
in Washington, Mr. Harding and Mr. Hughes were shaping

Naval Disarmament at the same big conference table with the Japs. When it is really strongest it wears dungarees. It keeps a high code of honor; yet after World War I, when it was robbed of Teapot Dome, it was made the center of the nation's ugliest scandal.

The navy can stir both the pride and the irritation of a democratic republic. It is, I think, most welcomed and most hated both in seaports and in Washington. And, in 1946, it seemed almost less designed for national defense than for national demonstration of the whole variety of career men and politicians upon whom as a people, in peace and in war, we depend. The Annapolis tradition was intact. So was the political tradition. Blue-eyed admirals paced corridors like quarterdecks. And, with them, in the biggest offices off the corridors, civilian officials made a picture not merely of the navy but of government.

I went up the stairs in the old Navy Building to James Forrestal's office. As civilian chief, he still somehow looked like the navy, tough and elegant together—tougher, indeed, than most naval officers seem. There is a quiet, animal quality about his apparent physical perfection. He has the carriage which the movies give dramatically to better gangsters, swift, easy with the suggestion of the possibility of violence and the surface of perfectly contained restraint. At fifty-two, he lacks the quality of boyish innocence which even tough admirals sometimes, even when they are arrogant, retain. Certainly, he seemed more than ordinarily vital in that building, tough like an almost lacquered gentleman and shrewd like such a gentleman, too. Beyond his small pastel green anterooms, he seemed young and content, even decorative. He wore the procession from Princeton through Wall Street to Government in his clothes. A bright figured tie hung against his blue shirt. His clothes were tweedy and, as I remember, matched his neat gray hair. He seemed a little strange beside the portraits I had passed coming in, of the pink-cheeked elderly gentlemen who had preceded him as Secretary of the Navy.

He had enjoyed government. He did not think that the admirals had pushed him around. He noted that the criterions of success in government were different, less easily recognized, than they had been in business. In Wall Street you made a lot of money or you didn't. He had, in those years when most people hadn't. He spoke without amusement of some business men who had come down to Washington for war and had assumed that the first prerequisite of success was a publicity man. The picture on the magazine cover could be the end of hope, not the beginning of success. He indicated his own picture on the cover of a magazine and smiled. He did not really seem displeased or disturbed about it. From a background of business he had emerged, I felt, as politician, but not as politician merely.

He talked, as if he were a student, of administration and bureaucracy. I remember he quoted Walter Bagehot *(The English Constitution)* and Lord Bryce *(The American Commonwealth)*. Also he quoted some of the shrewder and sharper-eyed men then working in Washington. The weaknesses in government, he thought, were in staff and the lack of really efficient secretariats to keep things moving in order and intelligence.

He lit his pipe, but he did not seem, as a pipe smoker in Washington, like one of those ex-professors of public administration in the Bureau of the Budget who always discuss government by pipe smoke. Somehow he made bureaucracy less suspect by talking about it, and also tougher and more efficient. He smoked his pipe as if he might have had a dog at his feet or be a well-to-do gentleman at ease in a well-ordered club. None of the drabness of the old Navy Department gets into the Secretary's office. Also, war as dramatics seemed a long way off. He spoke of the necessity for intelligent career public servants—"like the British have"—to keep government moving and unconfused.

He stated the need:

"Men with imagination and a dust pan to follow after top

officials and see that things are done. Imagination and a dust pan and, in this big government, a bicycle, too."

I was surprised suddenly, as it came to me, that he was including naval officers, regular officers, Annapolis men, in his talk about government administration as if, under brass and blue clothes, they were only public servants like statisticians, apiculturists, regional directors, fiscal officers and administrative assistants. It was proper. Of course, they were. But strangely such an idea had not occurred to me when I had seen them on ships and at cocktail parties. Some of them at least moved as if they were, in America, an aristocratic caste remote from politics and even sometimes from democracy. With the army, they seemed in American thinking like two big blocks of autocracy set down in a democratic country which did not want them but did not know how to get along without them. In such a country the officers seemed suspended in the American spectacle, not as the result of patronage appointments by political Congressmen but somehow supported by braid alone. I said so.

He dismissed the old school spirit of Annapolis.

"Prep school stuff," he said.

He called it "adolescence."

He relit his pipe, looking and talking over his match.

"Most of them are getting away from it. You've got to remember that they don't make much money; in peacetime nobody pays any attention to them. Then, when war comes, they're expected to be ready to do everything."

I got a picture of disregarded men marching to the sound of "Anchors Aweigh" in a sort of psychological self-defense.

"Like some Congressmen," I suggested, "who are arrogant in Washington because they have to be subservient to their constituents at home."

"Same sort of thing," he said. "Most of them are good men with only the sort of group feeling about themselves that lawyers and doctors and engineers have. Of course, there are some stupid ones. We had to use some retired fellows who knew themselves that they were not very good, some of them—" With his pipe he indicated the possibility of their arrogance to reserve officers below them. "But most of them are good men who understand that they are agents of the President and that the President is the agent of the people."

He swung in his chair.

"Of course, they are public servants," he said.

I had known some of the disregarded men in peacetime. Some cynics had suggested that in such quiet times nobody paid any attention to them except heiresses. In the good old days when naval officers were only talking with a sound of hopefulness about war with Japan, the navy had spent a good deal of its time around Newport. Even between wars young officers are very presentable at balls. I had seen them dancing at San Diego and Norfolk. I remember the jealousy of the entire male community in Pensacola. Some officers have made good catches even in inland States. But marrying well certainly is not an enterprise restricted to the navy. Without the social position a naval uniform implies, some employees of the Department of Agriculture have made good marriages. But even if they marry, as a good many do, for prettiness rather than property, naval officers somehow are not permitted to seem poor. Indeed, some hard-working women have made naval officers' salaries stretch further in a social world than most civilians would dare believe. Theirs must not only be thrift, but thrift with the right clothes and Scotch and soda on the sideboard, thrift in the right neighborhoods, thrift with dues at the club. They may do the laundry but they have to have the hats.

There are forces that make naval officers tribal, if not a separate and elevated caste. It is not a very large tribe. In 1940, before the navy began to grow for war, there were only 13,000 officers, almost all of whom were Annapolis men. Today there may be 15,000 from Annapolis. They are men who spend their whole lives working with their schoolmates. Also, wardrooms throw men close together at sea, and on shore the navy often makes them neighbors as well as class-mates. On sea and on shore, they are a sternly fixed caste above the enlisted personnel. The navy still goes in for servants as well as seamen. Even the modern navy might seem as strange without mess attendants as without mechanics. Democracy was not bred aboard ships.

The civilians are ashore or outside the navy yard gate. The profession of naval officers itself isolates them. Socially they meet generally only the people outside who go to the same parties or the same clubs. They are generally too far from their legal residences to be actual participants in democracy. And, between wars, politicians can seem stingy as well as distaste-ful. In the same way, in a democracy naval officers in peace can seem not only expensive but arrogant, reactionary in the same way State Department career men are said to be, and occasionally dangerously truculent. One attitude is probably as unjust generally as the other. And both attitudes are apt to reappear quickly after wars.

At luncheon that day, a newspaperman knowing my desti-nation for the afternoon had worried out loud, not about the drab appearance the navy makes in its old building but about fears garrulous naval officers had put into his head. They were, he said, always talking about that coming war with Russia. They had done a good job but they were a little full of them-selves.

"You've got to remember," he said, "that they think of themselves as the elite corps, the aristocracy of our armed forces. They don't want to go back to poor mouth and paper ships. There are some of them that I think would do anything to prevent it."

He repeated with a long significance, "Anything."

Then he said what I had been half expecting:

"Half of them are facists at heart, and, even more than that, talk like facists."

I laughed. In general in Washington when anybody calls a naval officer a facist, it has the same meaning as when a naval officer calls a liberal a communist. They are easy words in a talking capital in which naval officers and imaginative liberals can both be garrulous and careless. But I had come across a few naval officers who were more discouraging in reality than my friend's dark romantic report about all of them. I remembered the old Commodore with the blue veins in his cheeks who had settled down for sociability after a speech. He was not only ready for the Russians. He did not care much for American politicians either. Somebody mentioned that the hopes of the navy for continuing strength might be threatened by stories about strutting waste in the navy which some released reserve officers were bringing home. The man told a specific story brought home by one ex-officer. The Commodore looked sourly at his drink.

"Was he a Gentile?" he asked.

It was easy to dismiss him as individually prejudiced. I knew there had been old puffy sailors with blue-veined faces at tables near the bar in the Army and Navy Club at least since the Spanish-American War—probably before. They did more damage than the reserve officers going home. At home people are not merely ex-reserve officers but men. Their neighbors know them under their uniforms. Also, when a reserve officer comes home condemning Annapolis club fellows, Americans know enough to know that prejudice exists, and also that prejudice can be used as the ever-ready alibi for the personal deficiencies of those who complain. In the navy, it is sometimes both.

(However, I found that some young Annapolis men coming back from tough service in the Pacific had left a good many old school notions there. I remember the handsome young Annapolis boy who came back with nine battle stars, a respect for reserve officers and a new feeling that maybe the best officers of the future might come up by examination through the enlisted ranks instead of Congressional patronage. It was heresy. It seemed healthy, too.)

Naval officers work in feast or famine, extravagant war or

penurious peace. Like all men long maintained for an occasional emergency, they sometimes become, between the emer-
gencies, self-indulgent and lazy. They are too often technicians cut off from public affairs. Of course, there are some
fools among them, as there are also men of almost romantic
patriotism combined with hard, keen understanding of reality.
Those old virtues of conformity and continuity, in the navy
as elsewhere, push some dull men forward. And in the navy,
as elsewhere in the government service and outside it, it is
hard to get rid of them.

The danger in the navy is not facism but dullness. Not
even the old ladies of liberalism, I think, need to worry in the
United States about dangers from the overt arrogance still to
be observed in some coup d'état countries in these melodra-
matic times. The only threat to democracy in the navy is the
same relaxation in the public service which sometimes gets to
soil-conservationists in the Department of Agriculture and
Indian agents in the Department of the Interior.

Those dust pans and bicycles that Forrestal mentioned are
equipment as essential to the operation of the navy as radar
and atomic bombs. But the imagination he mentioned is harder
to come by. Neither he nor any of the philosophers and
puzzlers about public administration in Washington has
evolved any specific plan for supplying it. It is needed not
merely in staff work and in an assisting secretariat around a
Cabinet minister but all the way down in all the jobs, civil and
military.

Of course, there is a caste. It can be silly and in its elder
members both pompous and puffy. But even in uniform it
does not look like an aristocracy maintained at public expense.
Indeed, lean, swift-moving Jim Forrestal seems like a man
with more violence in him than his admirals. Somehow Annapolis preserves a certain boyish quality in most of its tougher
officers. A good many of them are as ready to play as to fight.
They obey and order with equal confidence in a system.
They curse the politicians but remain the technicians of their

political decisions. Politicians not only appoint them. Even as heroes, they are politicians' messengers. In a democracy they should never be more. That makes the quality of the politicians as the people's messengers even more important.

I thought about that in connection with the President's abortive proposal that Edwin W. Pauley, of California, move in as Undersecretary. The nomination had been accompanied by much unofficial speculation that Pauley might later succeed Forrestal as Secretary. It was followed by Harold Ickes's charges and departure. ("Be gentle with Ed" began to sound like 1946's equivalent of "Clear it with Sidney.") Pauley was more stubborn than skillful in his own defense. But Pauley also seemed to me, as I thought about it, perfectly designed— and in the perfect place—to dramatize the combination and the contrast in our government of and between the professional politician and the professional public servant.

Pauley is a big man with big green eyes. Deep-voiced and slow-speaking except when he shouts, he always gives me the impression of insensitive power. He brushes a curtain of long side-locks across his wide bald head. He does not seem as young as his forty-three years. There is about him no sense of the muscular coordination of the fencing master which Forrestal's figure suggests. But his big shoulders seem almost primitively designed for push and movement against any obstacles or men.

"We owe a lot to Ed," a Democratic stalwart said to me.

There is not the least doubt about that. He had not only collected enough money, as Democratic treasurer, to free the party of a $750,000 debt and finance its campaigns. He had also collected with the same directness delegates for Truman. In the code of the politician neither Presidents nor parties are permitted to forget such services rendered.

"A plum for Mr. Pauley," said a liberal Missouri voice. "Mr. Pauley makes no pretensions to being a public servant. He is an occupant of public office for the advancement of private business, on his own testimony. On the other hand, Mr. Pauley has made an outstanding success of private life, and is an eminently well-fitted candidate for it."

That seems true, too. He did not go into politics out of interest in public affairs but to lobby in the California Legislature for his private oil interests. He went from lobbying to electioneering for the same purpose. ("It was cheaper to get a new legislature," he told Ed Harris of the *St. Louis Post-Dispatch*.) He came to national politics as political fund raiser but he did not, as such, relax his interest in the relations of government and oil. While Democratic treasurer (as he reports himself) he "publicly, privately and repeatedly" favored Congressional legislation which, in advance of judicial decision, would divest the United States of title to oil reserves which irascible but vigilant Harold Ickes said are "vital to the security of the nation." In 1946, Pauley had come far fast as politician and money raiser. He had also made himself the perfect final adversary for Harold Ickes as Secretary of the Interior and as self-appointed national conscience, curmudgeon and cocklebur. Ickes to the last was not only vigilantly watching the Republic's resources. As an old gentleman getting ready to leave, he had undoubtedly been looking for a body to walk out over. Pauley had told him, Ickes told us, that he could raise several hundred thousand dollars in political contributions if (quid pro quo) the government would not press its suit to guard its title to the oil lands. Pauley denied it.

Between the conflicting testimony, between the political plum and the political debt, Pauley, nevertheless, seemed against the navy's sealine almost silhouetted to show both the gratitude which politicians always expect and the suspicions which politicians sometimes inspire. In such visibility radar is not required. The word "politician" is often unjustly used. (The strange thing is that the important charge against Pauley was not that he was a politician but that he was a business man still bargaining in politics. His crimes, as charged, were not that he brought politics to government but that he used his political connections for his business purposes.) Obviously, all public officials are in politics. We demonstrate the elasticity of language by remembering that the word may relate to both Lincoln and Pauley. The politician works today, as in the past, in the highest art and the lowest craft.

History will determine Mr. Pauley's place in the process. But, in 1946, he seemed, as described in disagreement by his friends and his critics, almost the contemporary model of the professional politician and the business man who understands that since politics is power, business is politics. Indeed, in the halls outside the top offices of the Navy Department and beside the portraits of old Secretaries I thought suddenly that Pauley may be as much a symbol in life as they seemed in art.

I remembered that the oil lands in which he is most interested privately and politically are those in the tideland along the California coast, where both the derricks and the masts of battleships can be seen together. And that is important because once it seemed perfectly clear that when America had been filled from tide to tide the frontier was finished. Ed Pauley and some other oil men in our times broke that legend by going out into the tide itself. More important maybe, in tough politics afterward, they re-illumined the legend with the memory that many of the pioneers who first grabbed the nation's resources were in politics about those resources from the nation's beginning.

Perhaps we grow more punctilious. The people certainly indicated to their Senators that they did not want Pauley. Also, some Senators, as politicians against him, were ready in political righteousness before any word could have come from the country. Politicians tear no victims apart so violently as they tear into other politicians.

In terms of the patterns provided by students of government from Bagehot to Bryce to Forrestal, Pauley certainly never seemed to me to be the perfect public servant. He is undoubtedly bold, determined, not squeamish. He seems a little strange by the neatness of Forrestal's men with imagination, a dust pan and a bicycle in great government. Pauley always seems to me to move like a bulldozer. But I have the feeling that against the background of the navy he presents in person today the old tough problem in democracy of putting the ruthless push of insensitive individualism behind the accomplishment of the general welfare and the common defense.

I smiled doubtfully at the portraits of the old Secretaries. But suddenly about them and me there was a hurrying of people in the hall. Admirals and ensigns, civil servants (but without dust pans) moved precipitately at the day's end in dispersal to their own very important and very personal concerns. I moved with them. The big lobby of the old building did not look inert, if it still seemed nondescript, when I came down to it again. Sea power was shutting down for the day with a converging surge of navy personnel and their civilian assistants. They were pushing home and all of them seemed like intent suburbanites in a continental land. The sidewalk before the building was packed even more thickly with people, and Constitution Avenue was a wide black lane of cars. A taxicab slowed up before me. It was already nearly filled with home-heading navy, but the driver let me in. An officer, crowded close to the driver, spoke of the strikes in motors and steel.

"They're asking for it," the Commander beside him said. "And, by God, we ought to let 'em have it."

"The politicians are scared of 'em," his companion declared.

But beside me on the back seat a young officer, unconcerned about strikes or politicians, was talking quietly with one of the prettiest girls I had ever seen in Washington; talking about his quarters. He had maid service, supposedly, but the landlady had been spoiled by an English officer who had had the rooms before.

"I need a mess boy," he said.

The girl laughed.

"We had a nice boy on the ship. I wish I had him."

"You talk as if you had everything on the ship," she said demurely.

"Well, there's one thing I'll say for the navy, if you have to go, they put on a very nice war."

They laughed together, and I noticed that in her lap against her dark fur coat, he was holding her hand.

Peace did not look nondescript at all. It extended in a whole prospect of pleasant personal concerns. And not many of them involved the manning of the dust pans or the ships.

XX

Hybrid Corn

In the long living room in his apartment in the Wardman Park Hotel, Henry Wallace played "The Little Drunk Girl" on his phonograph. The voice came from the record gay and young in a combination of Spanish and hiccuping. Without understanding Spanish, it was easy to appreciate the lady's condition; but I wondered what sort of accent an American Vice-President, learning Spanish for a wider American concern, might acquire from a girl singing the accents, not of Castile but of inebriation. Fortunately, there were other records to which he had listened with an Iowan's ear in order to learn to speak to the world.

In railroad stations and airports, when I came Eastward by his Iowa to Washington at Christmastime, I thought of that record and that evening. America, then, did not seem much easier to understand than a girl singing drunken Spanish to so sober an official as Mr. Truman's Secretary of Commerce. It seemed to me that I came homeward with an American nation which had all gone West and was in a body fighting its way East again for Christmas. The soldiers from the Pacific stood in the stations. Civilians from everywhere made queues with them at the ticket windows. They were crowded and sleepy, dirty and harassed, but rich. And astonishingly cheerful.

When Henry Wallace was Secretary of Agriculture and before I became a bureaucrat, I had seen such crowds. They were moving out of the agriculture, which he directed then, into the ranks of labor, who later loved him best. They had

been hungry-poor then. Some of them moved from crop fail-
ures to camp construction. Cotton choppers became carpenters at the end of a jaloppy ride—and took carpenters'
wages grinning about it. That time seemed long ago in the
crowded stations. Now the people had money, and sometimes
they were not able even to buy railroad tickets with it. They
seemed, sleeping on the benches—the fragile girl with her
tousled head in a sergeant's lap; the old woman with her
mouth hung open—like the strange rich poor of a continent
that was in a hurry to get home.

Nothing had changed. America was still an adventure, moving. And the items in the adventure would come up as statistics out of Henry Wallace's Bureau of the Census. They
might also come forth as figures in Henry Wallace's articulateness. Under the clocks in the stations which timed the late
trains, they may have been citizens of the century of the common man which had not been outmoded by the arrival of the
atomic age. Henry Wallace had a plan for jobs and plenty,
which he had printed in a book. The members of the National
Association of Manufacturers, who presumably are included
in Henry Wallace's official concern for Commerce, counted
the possibilities of free production for people in the enterprise
of profit. Wallace's old supporter, Sidney Hillman of the
CIO's Political Action Committee, had ideas about full production, too, and a philosophic conviction that it was inevitable. But on the road to Washington production and plenty
did not then appear quite inevitable, as pickets stood outside
motor plants in the snow. Nothing seemed inevitable but
America moving. And America did not seem quite certain
about its directions.

Being both rich and jostled, America did not seem changed.
In the stations, it was the same America that had slept under
viaducts because it was poor. The people slept in stations because everybody was rich and only the lucky, as before, could
get into the beds. So I went to see Henry Wallace, not because
he seemed something almost weirdly new to Senators, who

loved the past because they did not understand it, but because he was not new at all. In biology and bureaucracy, in technology and the theology which is never quite absent from American politics, he was, in the Government of the United States, a central item of American continuity.

The crowded stations and the benches working as beds seemed a long way from his office. Its outer lobby could be turned into a barracks. His big office is in a huge building. Its thirty-seven acres of floor space (big as a good-sized Iowa cornfield) had been designed when Herbert Hoover was Secretary of Commerce, and commerce in the United States was moving on toward 1929. Hoover, like Wallace, was born in Iowa. Harry Hopkins had been another Iowan as Secretary of Commerce. And his WPA writers in describing the building in the Washington, D. C., WPA Guide had said that it had "the reputation of being the easiest place in Washington in which to get lost." It still may be, but it did not seem a maze to me. The corridor to the Secretary's door runs as straight as a section line beside an Iowa corn farm. But the architects had not left the building looking earthy. Commerce is enclosed in an Italian Renaissance Palazzo.

"The Secretary does not like for us to smoke in the office," his friendly secretary said when I offered her a cigarette.

It was not prohibition to me. The asceticism is personal, not official. There were ashtrays about. Also, afterward in his office I saw the burned butts Americans had left behind after talking with him.

Across the office as big as a tennis court, Wallace came with his tennis-court stride to meet me. We sat, I remember, not by his desk but in a group of chairs in the middle of the room arranged like chairs in a club for the comfortable talking of men together. Beyond his striding, he sat, as I had seen him do before, almost inert-seeming in his chair. A lock of gray-brown hair hung down toward his eye. He was grinning. The grin has disturbed some Senators. It is a little confusing. It is shy and friendly, but nervous, too, like his recurrent laugh.

He grins in what seems almost satirical appraisal of his company and the conversation. It does not surprise me that behind that grin he has sometimes seemed strange in Washington. As Vice-President he had not become a hearty comrade to members of the Senate. He never became a member of the club. Indeed, sometimes the man who could speak a phrase into the language of a continent had little ease swapping small talk with Senators. I know he used to puzzle Harry Truman, who once had some strong convictions about the importance of comradeship in government.

"Well," Mr. Truman said as he succeeded Wallace in the Vice-Presidency, "while Garner was Vice-President there was hardly a day when at least half of the members of the Senate did not see him in his office or talk to him somewhere around the Capitol. In the past four years, I doubt if there are half a dozen Senators all told who have been in the Vice-President's office. You can draw your own conclusions."

Mr. Truman drew his own conclusions. Others have. Wallace is not earthy, though he knows about soils. He sometimes seems humanitarian without heartiness. Sometimes he has even seemed an American without any rooted sense of being related to any lesser part of America than the whole of it. I doubt that he is emotionally an Iowan before he is an American. He has a mind for details but a luminous genius sometimes for generalization. I am not sure that he would be an easy man for a stranger to converse with in a crowded station. But he has seemed more than most officials native to big government, and almost intuitively articulate about its meaning to the masses of men in our times. In Washington often he seemed to me to be almost the symbol both for American eagerness for certainty as to its direction and the continuing confusion which attends its purpose to possess the full possibilities of its powers.

Wallace's significance in government in times concerned with full production is not merely that he has been Agriculture's chief, the CIO's choice, and now is Commerce's Secretary. He has also—and no more significantly—seemed almost the center of the quarreling in bureaucracy as when he fought the conservative Jesse Jones. Nobody remembers that his father, who was buried with honors from the White House when Coolidge was there, also fought across a Cabinet with Secretary of Commerce Herbert Hoover, who had wanted to take the marketing functions away from the Department of Agriculture. The father fought, too, when Albert B. Fall, who later took the black satchel for the navy's oil, tried to take the Forest Service into the Department of Interior, which always seems welcomely capacious.

But more important than his father's fighting in the good tradition of American fighting about and in government was his grandfather's wide concern. This early Henry Wallace (1836–1916) who retired from the ministry of the United Presbyterian Church on account of ill-health at forty-one, and lived for thirty-nine years more, is a remarkably similar grandsire of the Secretary who plays tennis at fifty-eight. Iowans liked the old man's paper because it combined sermons with agricultural advice. Theodore Roosevelt called him as the first Wallace to Federal service in a Rooseveltian hope for better rural life. It did not disturb T. R. or the U. S. that the old gentleman's articulateness ran from *Trusts and How to Deal with Them* to *The Doctrines of the Plymouth Brethren.*

The practical and the spiritual have never been far apart in the American tradition—in government or railroad stations. But it could be a little confusing to a Senator to try to talk in our times to a Vice-President who might turn from corn seed to the conviction that the fuller life, including full production, is a thing of the spirit. A Senator moves easily, generally, from corn to hogs. But he can be disturbed by a grinning Iowan who moves casually from genetics to God.

Maybe the only strange thing in the American democracy is that such a ranging inclusiveness is not strange. Americans who remember proudly that America was settled for religious freedom forget easily that it was also settled by people with strong religious notions which flowed into government. Such a flowing now is not odd in Henry Wallace. Mysticism is at least as old a part of government as political machines. Indeed, as bar association orators sometimes speak of it, the Constitution itself—like the drone bee—sometimes seems related to a virgin birth.

But Henry Wallace is strange. He has only recently begun to talk of the precincts and the ringing of doorbells in them. When most politicians in Washington were studying the precincts, he became, at twenty-five, the first private breeder in America to experiment with the inbreeding of corn. And, incidentally, corn breeding goes back to and includes Cotton Mather, who had some notions, also, about the spirit and the State.

We want, as a practical people, a simple government. But we remain concerned about both the Holy Ghost and the atomic bomb, and sometimes seem to find both of them much simpler than using the machines we do understand to produce and distribute the goods we need. The weird thing about Henry Wallace is that he has dared to face the confusion. His experiments with corn, which incidentally have made him private profits, have somehow been related to the efforts of his grandfather—and most of our grandfathers—to bring the practical and the spiritual together. Sometimes it happens in American life and government. Not often enough.

Every Easter Henry Wallace sent his friends in Washington a little box. It was as neat a package for the season as the sort of boxes brides sometimes send out with squares of wedding cake in them. The symbolism is the same. But Henry Wallace's boxes contained the famous Wallace hybrid corn. I always appreciated the box. I had no earth in Washington in which to plant it, so I passed it on to a planting friend in a haphazard dissemination of the fruits of technology. But the corn is important. I even tried to understand what hybrid corn is and read about it in a big thick book the Department of Agriculture published while Henry Wallace was Secretary of Agriculture.

which more practical theologians in the past sometimes promised their more gullible parishioners. It means not a conventional miracle out of a conventional heaven but something also in the spirit of America. It is not easy to see. Not many people in the crowded stations that winter were thinking in such terms. Not many people in government shared any such mysticism about America. The spirit was something for Sunday.

The American spirit is something to roll out on wheels in a pageant or in the round phrases of a political oration. Then it is something as neat as a white combination of a New England Church and Town Hall. It seems unrelated somehow to men working in genetics or seeking through the mysteries of uranium. Or working in the deeper mysteries of man's capabilities by man's knowledge to man's need.

Wallace's phone rang, and he got up to answer it.

"Sure," he said, "in a couple of minutes."

He sat down again as if he were in the chair forever. The room was like a club—or a Congressional cloakroom—not like a church or a laboratory. He talked about men's jobs and the danger of men not having them. America would have to stay twice as well off as it had been in 1929 not to fall back into something deeper than the Depression. I got up to go, knowing how busy he was. I noticed that he looked like a New England farmer, and I had seen that shy grin before, in Vermont.

At the door we met young Assistant Secretary William A. M. Burden. He is one of those who had come with war to government. He is rich. He had built up the best private library on aviation in the United States, probably in the world. I knew its books went back to the times when men first tried to fly, and all the surprising way forward in terms of speed and range. He had come to Washington under Jesse Jones; he remained under Wallace. Behind his spectacles, I knew he was one of those Americans caught in the enthusiasms of the so-quickly-grown technology of our times. But at that moment at the Secretary's door, he was energetically affable, as a politician might have been.

Maybe I was a politician, too.

"I came to get some wisdom about this government of ours," I told him.

Burden nodded his head with emphasis.

"You came to the right place," he said.

I think Burden is right. I am not sure whether Henry Wallace points our directions or merely states our bewilderment as his own. But there is the spirit of adventure and idealism in his seeking. It may need crossing with something less mystical but lusty, willful, and strong like the pushing people still warrich in the war-crowded railroad stations. I doubt, however, that the genetics of government is as simple a business as the breeding of hybrid corn. Maybe always where spirit and power are put together, after a little they produce not the good but the sterile.

I wondered, as I walked down the long corridor of Commerce toward E Street, what had happened to the little box of seed Wallace had sent me the Easter before. I had sent it to a city woman who had gone to live on a little North Carolina mountain farm. It had been a long time since Easter. There had been war then. I had been working for the still living Roosevelt. Now people like myself were hurrying home to peace and Christmas in the big rich crowds they made in the stations and on the trains. But I smiled remembering that Easter. It had been a double celebration that year, to my children's delight. Just before tragedy and victory, Easter, in 1945, had come on April Fool's Day.

I must write to the mountains and ask what has happened to the corn.

XXI

Frontier on the Potomac

In spring in Washington nobody in his right mind would choose any other place as the capital. Spring can begin before April with masses of forsythia back of the President's offices. Pretty girls out of bureaucracy eat their lunches around Andrew Jackson and his rearing stallion in the park. Mr. Baruch might find his bench pre-empted at midday. But even the oldest politicians and the richest lobbyists walk, feeling half young again, through the Square. The sun and the perky pigeons seem as much a part of the government as the young bare-legged girls on the benches. America seems caught in air like amber.

And in April 1946, Harry Truman had been President of the United States for a whole year. It seemed a very little time. He had grown thicker about the middle and a good deal less certain about the comradeship of Congressmen. He had also grown a year older. Time may not have been completely visible, as his Secretary of Agriculture suggested, even in the clear April sunlight. But it moved.

Government in the United States, indeed, has always seemed to be the passing procession of personages from politics to eternity. The pace, despite the feeling of those who are out and want to get in, is always swift in America. The doctrine that few die and none resign is the impatient faith of those who are pushing and not of those who are passing any fixed moment in power at any given time. History is always in a hurry. It is true that a whole generation grew up from infants to infantrymen while Roosevelt remained in the White House. But it was less than one hundred and fifty years from the departure of George Washington to the arrival of Harry Truman. And in each of those years government was people. It will continue to be. I doubt that the picture they make changes with the individuals, the administrations or the parties. Men may go home or into history. Both the heroes and the harpies depart and both the heroes and the harpies remain. And the government of America remains.

We have not had much time in which to learn to look at it. But we begin. For a long time, we seemed as superstitiously reverent about the past as about the dead. We came slowly to the consciousness that even our heroes had been human—and came to it sometimes with a guilty feeling that we were looking through dead men's keyholes. And perhaps it was because we so honored the past that we have been somehow unwilling to feel that our human officials, living and around us, are history, too. That understanding that they are history may help. Certainly we can understand government best as we see it in our times. The past was not made by strangers. This moment is history, too. The only government we shall ever see is the government which we are. The people may change its cast but, barring such an interruption as would almost be an ending, I doubt that they will or can alter the characters. Those characters are always us.

To our profit probably, we have learned to picture the past in terms of a fixed moment. Mr. Rockefeller spent thousands of dollars re-creating, as of its period, the whole old town of Williamsburg, in Virginia, where Patrick Henry spoke and Jefferson both studied law and danced gaily with a girl named Belinda. Not only millionaires but patriotic ladies understand the art of fixing time in its place. In Washington I used to go occasionally, as every good American should, to Mount Vernon, which is just remote enough to be at the capital but not of it. When I went, it was better swept, I am sure, than it was when Martha had slaves to tend it. It looked as if George and

Martha might have moved out the day before, with a fine sense of responsibility to later tenants. And that day has been fixed, by the Regents of Mount Vernon, for eternity. Actually, of course, it was no more fixed than ours is. But nobody at Mount Vernon now is supposed to remember that in 1842, forty-three years after Washington preceded Truman into the bosom of history, Mount Vernon, on the testimony of an eminent geologist, was a worn-out plantation turned back to the bears and the wolves. The future as well as the past is shut out of the unity of any fixed time. But intelligent audiences understand that they are inescapably parts of it all the same.

Actually perhaps there is no independent present. There are no separate periods in history. Every day is a part of all the days, gone and coming. The meaning of Franklin Roosevelt's time ran far back into the accumulation of protest at home and abroad. That time did not end when Harry Truman hurried to the White House. Not even Harry Truman's time will end when he goes to Heaven or Independence, Missouri. I keep remembering Fred Vinson standing between Roosevelt's bold imperatives for the future and the silver plates on his dining room table commemorating the international debt settlements after World War I. Bold as he seemed, he seemed also straight from the Kentucky of Henry Clay whose name in our history is tagged with fruitless compromise. But Vinson knew that he came not only from a Kentucky but also from a history in which it is sometimes dangerous to be afraid.

Beside him, in Washington, diminutive Jimmie Byrnes was a figure between old fear and new—or at least recurrent—hope. People caught in the silliness of tradition which sometimes succeeds only in making an empty snobbery out of history remember that Byrnes was born on the "wrong side of Broad Street" in old slumbering Charleston. Charleston is where Calhoun sleeps; and Calhoun had been Secretary of State, too. Byrnes's task (a big job for a small man) was unity in the world, while Calhoun had turned his arrogant hand to disunity at home.

Old Harold Ickes had stood in the middle of forces as strong as the hungers which filled the continent and as relentless as those who, still pioneer-strong, wanted to grab what was left. Between them, as self-styled curmudgeon, he had stood as guardian of national resources of a nation which long ago had learned to sing "The Battle Hymn of the Republic" at about the same time it was singing, and with equal lustiness, "Uncle Sam Is Rich Enough To Give Us All A Farm." Beside those forces, there were fools and clowns in government in a tradition which was at least as unbroken as the American succession of solemnity. And, if the past is a dependable stool pigeon, there were crooks beside them, too, not yet apprehended by the cops. A few of them may not even be apprehended by history.

Truman's today is history as we may see it. As it works it is government as we may hope to understand it. Even the change in which it stands is an immutable aspect of America. But it is a change like the eternal recurrence of a river, muddy in change like the Potomac, also like the Potomac with some new order in drainage and wall and formalized lagoons along its edges—only along its edges. I remember Franklin Roosevelt riding out in the rain long after George Washington to see it in disturbing flood.

The truth is that even along its monumented shores Washington has not changed. We are unduly impressed by marble. And sometimes unduly blind, both looking back and looking around us, in contemplation of men. They have not changed. Some comparative newcomers seem to hold the ancient American spirit in firmer hands than some men of older stocks whose hands have softened. We are boasting when we speak in awe of our confusion. The Capitol grew in it. All the teamsters were drunk when Lincoln's soldiers once wanted to hurry supplies to a battle. Our irritations are puny. George Washington had to send 15,000 soldiers to collect the whisky taxes in Pennsylvania.

Washington has not changed. Apparently we learn our history from movie westerns. But the big American pioneer pressure was not on the prairie but on Washington, D. C. The Homestead Act preceded most of the homesteads, and from the same processes that now are shaped by pressures around the Congress and LaFayette Square. Southerners opposed the Homestead Act as an extension of anti-slavery territory. The Know-Nothings objected because Catholic immigrants might monopolize the free lands. Railroad promoters wanted to keep the lands for themselves as a governmental bonus for road building (incidentally, they got some 20,000,000 acres). Advocates of high tariffs feared that the government revenues from land sales would eliminate the need for tariff revenue and thus cause a cut in protective duties. And all of them had representatives in Washington. You could see them any day, as Hawthorne did about the time Julia Ward Howe wrote "The Battle Hymn of the Republic" there, in Willard's Hotel drinking gin slings.

The frontier was Washington and the American frontier is Washington still. It is the frontier today not merely because the continental frontier has now run all the way to Ed Pauley's tideland oil holdings. It is the frontier because it has, as it always had, the things the willful, lusty, seeking Americans want. From the beginning the politicians were always the advance agents of the pioneers. Back in England they had been the courtiers who got the grants for the colonies. There is a notion in the heads of courtiers, lobbyists, pressure groups, promoters, that that system works still. Such men have not departed. And it is not a danger if beside them more and more people are seeking more and more in the same place. The more can be not only merrier but safer for democracy.

But the world's biggest frontier town can be disturbing, too. Old Congressmen and overwhelmed old natives do not keep it from being young and lively. Civil Service gathers the girls of a continent. The veterans (who are not old soldiers yet) have special preference in getting its jobs. Its shaded streets seem almost lined with beauty parlors and liquor stores. More than one accordion player plays for its dancing. If Congress danced long ago at the Congress of Vienna there are members of the American Congress dancing still. Even the President sometimes plays on his piano something livelier than Beethoven's Sonata in C Minor—*Pathétique*. The old capital is a young capital still, and an eager one. And not without reason, it is the center of our drama as well as our destiny. Neither seems certainly always moving toward happy end.

"I wish to Almighty God," old Andrew Johnson said, "that the whole American people could be assembled in one vast amphitheater in Washington, so that the veil that now conceals from their view the many abuses could be drawn aside."

If still not quite practical, the prayer is still pertinent even in the age of the radio and the multiplied press. Government is a spectacle to watch at any time. But we shall need to watch America most anxiously when it ceases to be populated by an insatiable people. Our hungers are our powers. The frontier is not on our land but in our determinations. We shall have reason to worry when Washington is no longer our frontier. But a changeless capital is no justification for a complacent people. This government of ours, gleaming and disturbing, by the Potomac, is the vehicle of our destiny. There we keep— if we keep it anywhere—the ark of our covenant with ourselves.

Contention about it is not disturbing. This nation has survived both the Republicans and the Democrats, and will again. Even confusion can sometimes be only a process in our creativeness. The tug and pull of Left and Right, the eternal American uncertainty between minority rights and majority rule, the struggle of the parts with the whole, which seems simple only when stamped in a Latin phrase on a nickel, have pulled us forward, and strangely together not apart. Our dangers never come from the dynamic, however misguided, but from the insensitive, however slick, and the dull, however virtuous, who have never stirred to the meaning of the American dream. Neither birth nor citizenship assures such stirring. Being an American is being both a man and an emotion together, and not merely a human thing counted by Henry Wallace's Bureau of the Census.

There are plenty of such dullards of democracy in Washington. Some are men who regard government as a mechanism which can hire them or hurt them but of which they are never in spirit a part. There are others whose notion of America is also of a mechanism, one which can be made to work for their own regardless purposes. Of course, some of them are fools. Some are crooks. There are cranks and fanatics among them. Some are merely lawyers who have lost contact with life beyond the law. Many of them are men of conscious dignity. Some are confident that they are leading patriots. But there are among them men who make a harlot of their country and pimps of themselves.

And beside them there are men moving in both humility and responsibility. There is pride about America (and their parts in it) in men as well as in the history books. Some of the roughest and readiest-seeming politicians hold to high codes that are stern if they seem sometimes almost secret. An advertising man may move in government from careless ballyhoo to rigid courage against pressure. A pretty woman in politics, who may seem like "a Vanity Fair Huey Long," may still bring imagination as well as vanity to government. The imagination is often there with the diligence beside the dust pans. The insensitive individualism does sometimes serve the general welfare. In their own hearts, some men and women in Washington do put together both America's spirit and its practical purposes. Neither America nor government lives always in elation or resolution. We do have more to fear than fear itself. Together we have known feast and famine, and have survived them. But sometimes, so the story goes, God writes warning on the wall when men are least afraid. Great destiny, as well as great tragedy, requires pity and fear.

We have reason for courage. Those who believe that the dull and the degraded shape our democracy are generally one or the other themselves. I doubt that any honest man can look at Washington long and believe that. I am sure that any such judgment of Washington would have to include America as well as Washington. The city has grown big out of America and as the clear consequence of America's determinations. It is not more remote from American purposes and production and people than it used to be; the planes now swing above the airport overnight from the Pacific. Its powers are great. But it was a very little capital that gave away the West. And always, it is a great capital which watches, eagerly, fearfully but eternally the country which it rules and by which always it is relentlessly ruled in turn.

Washington looks as we would want America to look in April. Georgetown is sweet with lilac in dooryard and by great brick gate. The State Department surrounds itself with almost arrogant red tulips. The magnolias are safe on the northern side of the Potomac. There are wide water lily pads in the pools between the buildings Harold Ickes had left. The roses bud again in the garden by which Harry Truman walked in late afternoon to become President. And if you listen, as Walt Whitman did, there will almost always be in April a thrush singing against the nation's heart.

It is America.

There was a boy in it whistling and a girl laughed. And because I had walked a long time that warm afternoon I got into a taxicab. America was there, too. There was, I noticed, an American flag pasted on the windshield, and beside it the picture of a girl with crossed legs. There was also a frayed tax stamp from the Government of the United States. Suddenly another taxicab almost crowded us to the curb.

"He acts," my driver said, "like a nigger before Roosevelt died."

The Washington trees arched in budding decorum above our heads. On the sidewalks a government of people poured eagerly from offices into the green afternoon.

It is America, lilac and thrush, hope and hardness, the warm heart and sometimes the blind hate.

And America, God bless us or help us, is what we are.

Index